MAKE HEALTH HAPPEN

Training Yourself to Create Wellness

Erik Peper

Katherine H. Gibney

Catherine F. Holt

KENDALL/HUNT PUBLISHING COMPANY
4050 Westmark Drive   Dubuque, Iowa 52002

Taking charge and actively participating in one's own growth and healing process are the fundamental components for life-long learning and health. The information in this book is for personal growth and prevention of dis-ease. As Pete Egoscue (1998) states in his book Pain Free: *"Health care starts with personal responsibility. Any disclaimer that suggests otherwise does a great disservice."*

We strongly support collaborative consultation with healthcare professionals for additional evaluation of individual healthcare needs.

CONTENTS

PREFACE

This book builds upon the concepts and materials from the book *Creating Wholeness: A Self-Healing Workbook Using Dynamic Relaxation, Images, and Thoughts* by Erik Peper and Catherine F. Holt (1993). It grew out of the practices assigned for self-growth and personal development for the class *Holistic Health: Western Perspectives*, offered by the Institute for Holistic Healing Studies at San Francisco State University; for clients and participants at the Biofeedback and Family Therapy Institute and Work Solutions USA in Berkeley; and for participants in peak performance training programs.

The *Western Perspectives* course is a requirement for a Holistic Health Minor and fulfills a part of the general education requirement for integrated and interdisciplinary learning. The structured experiences complement the cognitive/analytical components of lectures and readings. The program offers pragmatic skills to master stress, to set goals, and to experience a deep change in health and worldview. The development of this program at San Francisco State University was due to the foresight and courage of Dr. George Araki.

The goals of this workbook are to offer experiences to facilitate learning life-long self-care skills to enhance health and self-healing, and to augment personal growth. We hope the reader will experience increased autonomy and gain self-mastery skills through exercises that foster awareness and control. The cascading program is based upon uncovering, allowing, and encouraging our intrinsic drive toward integration, wholeness, and health. Each year, many of our students report that practicing these skills has affected them deeply; their lives are changed immeasurably and they are able to achieve control over the trials and tribulations of living and, in some cases, reverse serious illness. Many report that this was the most useful course they had taken at San Francisco State University and that they significantly improved their well-being. For example, one participant who overcame depression reported: ""I know now that I can recover my sense of joy in life... my mood and energy has enabled me to work more effectively and cut down on procrastination... My schedule is still demanding, but is feeling more invigorating than draining as a result of a good balance between work and play...My **only wish for the project is that I had started sooner: Months and months ago.**"

Individuals seeking to change their personal image of health and wholeness and who desire to live, work, and perform at their optimum will find this book to be a useful guide.

ACKNOWLEDGMENTS

This workbook would not have been possible without the honest and sometimes even painful feedback of the students. We feel privileged to have had the opportunity to read their responses and papers that developed from these practices. We want to thank many students for participating in our exploration. They have been outstanding teachers by sharing the wisdom they acquired through their process of self-healing. Their feedback was of great assistance in the shaping of this workbook. We specifically thank the following people for allowing us to quote from their papers: Cie-jae Allen, Collet Campbell, Lisa Green, Wendy Hussey, Janice Mettler, Gayathri Perera, and Susan Wilson. We thank Sarah Smith Rubio for modeling some concept exercises and we thank Shelah Barr for allowing us to use her self-healing drawings, which we adapted for the cover.

We thank Vicci Tibbetts for her many constructive recommendations and Lesli Fullerton for her careful reading of the early versions of the manuscript and helpful suggestions for the first printing. We also thank Dr. Louisa Howe, Dr. Betsy Stetson, Charles Lynch, Jackie Benson, Denis DiBartolomeo, and Dr. Carol Aronoff for their comments and Albert Weijman for the idea of concept exercises. We thank Michael Schermer for his sharing the story of the 'First Time.'

The fine-tuning of this text was greatly enhanced by Kate Huber's constructive comments, Dr. Hiromi Mutsuura's thorough feedback, Samantha Stormer's creativity, Diana Roberts' encouragement and expert editorial comments, and Christopher Gibney's exacting questions and constructive suggestions. We also thank David Wise for his support and a special thanks to Gary Palmer for his generosity in helping us with graphics. We appreciate the support and patience of close family members who had to put up with us as we increased their stress while we worked on the book. We especially thank our spouses, Karen and Christopher, for their continued support and love while we labored.

This book is dedicated to Eliot and Laura for their curiosity, growth, and imagination.

The selected quotes on pages 1, 43, 61, 129, 135, 175, 193, and 217 are reprinted from *Words to Live By: Inspiration for Every Day*, by Eknath Easwaran.

Chapter 1

INTRODUCTION

There is a point of consciousness within everyone, which has the seed of wholeness. By wholeness I mean the potential to realize integration within oneself, and to actively direct the forces of one's life...

DORA VAN GELDER KUNZ

ᔕ SYSTEMS PERSPECTIVE OF HEALTH

The hipbone's connected to the thighbone, the thighbone's connected to the leg bone...

TRADITIONAL SONG

A human being is part of the whole, called by us "universe," a part limited in time and space. He experiences himself, his thoughts and feelings, as something separate from the rest—a kind of optical delusion of consciousness. This delusion is a kind of prison for us, restricting us to our personal desires and to affection for a few persons nearest to us. Our task must be to free ourselves from this prison by widening our circle of compassion to embrace all living creatures and the whole of nature in its beauty.

ALBERT EINSTEIN

A basic premise of holistic health is a systems perspective in which every part in a system affects and is affected by every other part. We are embedded in and part of the whole. In the words of John Donne, "No man is an island, entire of itself; every man is a piece of the continent, a part of the main." This means that how we care for ourselves (live our lives) affects our structure, and our structure affects how we use ourselves.

Our health is the integration of multiple components that influence and augment each other. The factors that affect our health include, among others: genetics, family and socioeconomic background, diet, exercise, social support, risk taking behaviors, attitude,

and spiritual practices. All these factors affect our present and future health. It is important to remember that these components are not separate. A holistic approach to health
recognizes the interconnectedness of body, mind, spirit, and environment. This systems
view perceives the individual as a powerful creator of his or her own health, able to make
conscious choices about nutrition, exercise, social and career paths, thoughts and images.
In regaining control over our own health, some important tools are: relaxation, diaphragmatic breathing, cognitive stress reduction, and imagery for healing and behavior change.
A major theme linking all these components is the importance of mindfulness; that is, the
integration of your new awareness and skills into everyday life situations.

Regardless how healthy or ill we are, we can be an active participant in our own
growth. Arthur Frank (1991), who had a heart attack at age 39 and cancer the following
year, stated in his book, *At the Will of the Body*, "Illness takes away parts of your life, but
in doing so it gives you the opportunity to choose the life you will lead, as opposed to
living out the one you have simply accumulated over the years." (p. 1)

The focus of this workbook is to help you choose the kind of life you will lead. We
offer some strategies that will help you begin to become an active participant in your
growth/health process. It will cover only a few of the many factors that we believe affect
our health. At best we hope to offer support to "nature's self-directed growth process."
This sense of support for growth is radically different from the more traditional health
care—or, actually, illness care—system.

At times, people have made a reductionistic comparison between our soma (body/
mind structure and process) and a car. If something is wrong with the car, you just fix it
by repairing the carburetor or getting a valve job. If you have heart disease, you get a
plastic heart valve or a venous graft for coronary artery bypass surgery. Continuing this
analogy, your body could be like an underpowered car, with a poor transmission and
worn tires. Yet you can nurture the car for a long time by driving carefully and avoiding
jackrabbit starts and stops, hills and potholes; that is, you would maximize the potential
in the situation.

The preceding analogy is faulty because the human being is NOT a mechanical, non-
regenerative machine. It is a generative process. Depending on how you use yourself,
you may regenerate and grow. Imagine a regenerating and evolving car. If you take good
care of your car, the tires would regenerate and develop more tread. (Similarly thus, we
can develop more muscle and strength.) This growth potential is inherent in our soma.
Within our soma there is an intrinsic drive towards integration and wholeness. We are an
energy flow that can only go forward. We cannot go back to being the same as we were
yesterday, any more than a flowing river can go back to containing yesterday's water.
Not to change is unhealthy and abnormal, since the nature of our being is continuous
change, flux, and growth.

This workbook is designed for use on your own, with a guide or therapist, or as part
of a class. You can also create an informal "relaxation and self-healing group." This
workbook focuses on encouraging and allowing the intrinsic drive toward health. Health
and its concurrent quality of life are multidimensional.

MULTIPLE FACTORS CREATE HEALTH

Health is far more than the absence of illness or symptoms. It goes beyond the condition of the physical body and includes emotional, mental, and spiritual factors. We can no longer separate the emotional state from the physical state, since every thought or feeling leaves its traces on the body. As Elmer and Alyce Green (1977), two well-known pioneers in the field of biofeedback, wrote, "Every change in the physiological state is accompanied by an appropriate change in the mental-emotional state, conscious or unconscious, and every change in the mental-emotional state, conscious or unconscious, is accompanied by an appropriate change in the physiological state."

Often, factors in our lifestyles become interwoven. If you feel depressed, you may think, "What's the point?" when it comes to exercise. If you feel overburdened with work, you may decide there's just no time for fun or relaxation. If you are depriving yourself of sleep, caffeine and sugar seem necessary to get you through the day. If you have chronic pain, you may isolate yourself from people. Such circumstances can make change seem difficult, or even impossible—especially if you see many areas out of balance. The good news about these connections, however, is that: no matter where you start, a positive change in one area often sets off a number of other beneficial changes that flow almost effortlessly. For example, exercise can regulate appetite, improve self-esteem, give you more energy, and even alleviate pain; it may enhance your social support network, too, as you meet others in a yoga class, in a swimming pool, or at the gym.

Since it doesn't really matter where you start, you can choose the step that is the easiest, smallest, and most enjoyable for you. As you achieve success with your modest goal, your motivation level is sure to build. One woman realized that she had gotten into the habit of overeating to comfort herself for the loss of a dance class. For her weight loss program, finding a new dance class turned out to be more important than counting calories. As she began dancing, she stopped feeling deprived and automatically ate less. A woman with daily headaches and work overload had stopped calling friends and socializing. She chose to start smiling at strangers and seeing her friends more often, and the headaches disappeared. The self-healing process has a life of its own.

Although it may not be immediately obvious, for many people a connection with nature can be very healing for the body, mind, and spirit. Even doing something positive for the planet, like recycling, seems to have a beneficial effect. Breathing the pure air in the mountains makes us less inclined to eat junk food.

> I pledge allegiance to the Earth:
> I will honor this body given me by birth.
> The body is my connection with the Mother;
> If I pollute one, then I pollute the other.
> The unity of body and mind
> Brings peace and wisdom to humankind.
>
> CATHY HOLT

This workbook will not give you specific information on what constitutes the best diet, exercise program, and so on. We believe there is plenty of literature about those fitness areas (see recommended readings). Rather, we hope to provide a useful guide to help you overcome your obstacles and begin on your self-designed path to greater well-being.

As a starting point, it is good to be aware of where you are with respect to the larger picture of health-supporting behaviors and environment. Look over the following fourteen health areas to get a sense of where your assets and liabilities are. How might you bring more balance into your life? Where might you like to start?

14 Factors That Promote Health

1. Healthful diet
   - Chiefly whole foods, such as fruits, vegetables, whole grains (high fiber, low fat, low salt, low sugar, low meat consumption—eat low on the food chain—few processed foods or food additives)
   - Three meals a day, including a balanced breakfast
   - Sitting down to eat with no concurrent activities (e.g., driving, working)

2. No smoking

3. No recreational drugs

4. Little or no caffeine
   - Fewer than two cups of caffeinated coffee or black tea daily
   - Less than two cola drinks per day

5. Little or no alcohol
   - Fewer than 4 alcoholic drinks per week
   - Limit intake to one alcoholic drink per event
   - Drink only in company and not alone

6. Appropriate weight
   - Neither obese nor anorexic
   - Comfortable about your weight and self-image

7. Regular exercise
   - Some form of aerobic exercise at least three times a week
   - Stretching or movement (e.g., qi gong, tai chi, yoga)

8. Regular relaxation
   - Quiet time/time alone daily and/or time in nature
   - Time for play or fun at least once a week
   - Limited television or computer games

9. Adequate sleep
   - 7-8 hours of sleep per night

10. Safety habits and reduction of environmental risks/pollutants
    ◆ Car seat belt, airbags, and/or motorcycle helmet
    ◆ Safe, nontoxic living and work environments
    ◆ No personal risky behaviors, such as unprotected sex with new or multiple partners

11. Daily resolution of anger/resentment/fear
    ◆ No "unfinished business"
    ◆ Regular conversations about domestic issues with those with whom you live
    ◆ Ability to express feelings
    ◆ Ability to say no without guilt

12. Positive attitude/spiritual connectedness
    ◆ Liking, accepting, and nurturing yourself
    ◆ Having your work or studies be meaningful
    ◆ Finding purpose in life
    ◆ Perceiving problems as opportunities for growth
    ◆ Drawing strength from spiritual beliefs

13. Humor/creativity
    ◆ Listen and tell joke a day
    ◆ Perceive the humor in challenging moments
    ◆ Participate in playfulness
    ◆ Develop a hobby that gives you joy and allows creative expression

14. Social support system/social capital
    ◆ Network of friends/acquaintances/relatives
    ◆ Giving and receiving hugs and affection regularly (at least four hugs a day!)
    ◆ Having at least one friend to confide in
    ◆ Ability to ask for and give help when needed
    ◆ Being a good listener
    ◆ Feeling content with your level of intimacy and sexual activity

We can always find humor by looking at ourselves. An example of taking life with a bit of humor is the following.

Senility Prayer

God, grant me the senility to forget the people I never liked anyway, the good fortune to run into the ones that I do, and the eyesight to tell the difference.

Now that I'm 'older' (but refuse to grow up), here's what I've discovered:

One—I started out with nothing, and I still have most of it.
Two—I finally got my head together; now my body is falling apart.
Three—Funny, I don't remember being absent minded...
Four—It is easier to get older than it is to get wiser.
Five—I wish the buck stopped here; I sure could use a few.
Six—Kids in the back seat cause accidents.
Seven—Accidents in the back seat cause kids.
Eight—It's hard to make a comeback when you haven't been anywhere.
Nine—The only time the world beats a path to your door is when you're in the bathroom.
Ten—It's not hard to meet expenses...they're everywhere.

SOURCE UNKNOWN

WHO CAN BENEFIT FROM USING THIS WORKBOOK?

Those who are suffering from the effects of excess physical and/or mental stress and tension, who are motivated to help heal themselves, and who have a desire for greater self-awareness, can benefit by using this workbook.

Sometimes it is possible to diminish stressors through prioritizing tasks, resolving conflicts, being more assertive, and so on. Even when you are unable to remove the sources of stress in your life, you can begin to reduce the toll stress takes on your body and to recharge your energy reservoirs by learning and using an effective relaxation technique.

There is increasing evidence that stress and attitude are codetermining factors in many illnesses and conditions, such as heart disease, cancer, arthritis, diabetes, hypertension, ulcers, colitis, asthma, allergies, premature aging, depression, eczema, headaches, back pain, insomnia, menstrual irregularities, infertility, increased susceptibility to infections, immune system disorders, and reduced performance (Justice, 2000; Levy, 1985; McEwen, 1990; Ornish, 1998; Pelletier, 1994). In addition, many people who are in relatively good health still suffer from excess fatigue, anxiety, and muscle tension. Our mental and physical states are inextricably intertwined, so an integrated approach must include strategies for both mental and physical relaxation. Thus, even if you believe your problem areas are strictly psychological or interpersonal in origin, use of physical relaxation exercises can be highly beneficial. And even if you believe your condition has a strictly physical origin, cognitive and psychological approaches may be useful as well.

Other benefits may include improved sleep; enhanced awareness of the body; ability to regenerate one's energies quickly; increased concentration; and improvement in athletics, schoolwork, or any performance task. There may be a decrease in emotional reactivity and a concurrent sense of inner peace and integration. Sometimes the benefits are quite unexpected. For example, one woman with panic attacks, who said she had never relaxed in her life before learning dynamic relaxation, finally learned to lower her shoulders. As a result, she reported, "I had to readjust my bra straps!"

ꙅ HOW TO GET THE MOST OUT OF THIS WORKBOOK

Question: "How many psychologists does it take to change a light bulb?"
Answer: "One, but only if it really wants to change."

This workbook demands active participation. The more you put into it—the more you practice—the more you will gain. Learning awareness, relaxation, stress management, acceptance, and control over thoughts and emotions takes time. It is in the practice and actual experience that change occurs. Although many of our students have reported benefits when they practice only a few times, most report that the process of awareness, change, and growth is similar to developing or learning any new skill. Common comments received are:

◆ "Self-monitoring caused me to look at the way all of the factors come together to make a 'good' or 'bad' day."

◆ "I was successful because I wanted to and had to do it."

◆ "I stuck with it despite all odds."

◆ "A realization that I had the power to make changes in my health that would affect my world forever without any guilt."

◆ "Doing the practices faithfully and giving them the respect and time they required. Instead of just talking about them, I put them to direct use and exploration."

◆ "I made this project a priority, which meant making **ME** a priority, and that was a key factor."

◆ "It gave me the self-confidence that I could actually change my problem."

PRACTICE

Many of you know that it took weeks to master driving a car. Remember when you first learned? It took all your concentration to drive down the street. It seemed almost overwhelming to attend simultaneously to other cars, pedestrians, traffic signs, steering the car, pressing the gas pedal or brake, and also pushing the clutch down and shifting gears. Most of you now drive while talking to someone, playing with the radio, dialing a number on a cell phone, or observing the scenery. In fact, sometimes you now get to your destination without remembering ever driving there. How did you shift from this intense concentration and attention to allowing the driving to be automatic? A major component is PRACTICE. To benefit from this workbook the rule is similar: Through practice you reap the benefits.

We recommend that you first glance through the exercises and then sequentially practice them. Generally, the practices each week build upon those of previous weeks, although to some extent they can be done out of order. Practice each exercise daily for at least one week. It usually takes a few days to get used to the practices; after a while they become more automatic. You may find that it takes longer to master some exercises than others. This is normal. Give yourself more time before going on. In addition, you may integrate some components of the practices into your daily routine so that they slowly become part of you.

INVESTIGATE RESISTANCE

Even though we all know that we benefit by making changes, we may find that we hesitate to start, pause in the middle, or even stop. There is nothing wrong with that; it is a common experience. Resistance to change is natural. Changing requires energy. We may fear the unknown: "What if this relaxation stuff opens up a Pandora's box of those things I don't want to remember or feel?" We may also fear failure: "What if I set out to heal myself and I don't succeed? Then I'll blame myself and feel worse!" We may even think, "I'm barely keeping it together now, and if I change anything, I might fall apart!" or, "My spouse (significant other) won't love me if I change."

Resistance to change usually coexists with a will or desire to change. It is as if there are two personalities battling it out inside us: one that fears and resists change and one that welcomes and seeks it. Ask yourself, "What are the benefits and disadvantages of changing or not changing?" In order to move forward, it is important to acknowledge and accept the part that is fearful, while not giving in to it. Where did that part come from?

BE ACCEPTING

As you begin the process of self-exploration and change, be accepting of yourself. Trust that your patterns were meaningful for you and allowed you to survive at some point in the past. You may want to continue and change, yet at the same time, want to give up and avoid changing for a while. Accept, comfort, and reassure the part of you that is fearful, just as an adult would comfort a frightened child.

Most of us went through some difficult and frightening times as small children, and developed various strategies that allowed us to survive. These strategies may no longer be useful in the present. Often, however, we continue to apply the same strategies even though the situation and the rules have changed as we have matured and grown. As an analogy, consider the training of a baby elephant in a circus. An average rope secured to a small stake in the ground is enough to prevent the little fellow from wandering off; he tests it a few times and learns he is unable to pull it up. Years later, the same flimsy rope and stake are enough to hold the enormous adult elephant, who doesn't bother to test it because he has already learned, as a baby, that it is "stronger" than he is.

Children, too, may learn lasting and self-limiting lessons. For example, all children have learned that parents criticize or scold their behaviors: "You shouldn't do that!" They then learn to criticize themselves and stop the behavior, which earns them love and approval from the parents. However, if they grow up being extremely critical of themselves, they may suffer from anxiety, low self-esteem, and poor self-confidence.

You may decide to explore or change your patterns. However, please welcome and respect them; they are part of you. Many seemingly self-destructive patterns were constructive for you at one time. For example, a lot of people tell themselves that they should exercise yet they somehow do not find the time to do it. How could this be, since everyone knows exercise is good for us? Actually, for many people exercise is *not* just associated with feeling fit, hard work, and muscle pain. It is also associated with failure. Failure is the covert message often received when we participate in sports. Most competitive sports are designed to have one winner. Everyone else fails. Who remembers the silver or bronze medallist in the Olympics? Even in team sports, the glory belongs to the team that won—not to the many players who were defeated and lost. It is not only the culture but also our parents who may fail to reward (or may covertly punish) the non-winner. Because we are sometimes the projections of our parents' dreams, they were disappointed if we didn't win. Hence, it is not surprising that many people with the best of intentions to exercise drop out. Who really wants to re-experience the failure and disappointment so embedded in the past experience of participating in a sport?

Similarly, some people may have difficulty stopping smoking. Again, we believe that stopping is most likely more painful than continuing. How can that be? Isn't smoking bad for you? The answer is yes; however, it may have fulfilled a need even though the person may be unaware of it. For example, lighting a cigarette or taking a puff may give some people a momentary pause before they have to react socially. It gives them time to collect themselves. For others, it may have involved the important process of developing autonomy, which each person needs to develop a sense of self. Smoking can be a statement of autonomy, providing an experience of being in charge and in control: "I am independent of my parents, and there is nothing they can do about it." Hence, if smoking is discontinued, what happens to the sense of self?

GENERAL GUIDELINES

1. Leisurely scan the workbook to get a flavor of the themes. Observe how the practices change and develop over time. Before embarking on the practices, read the introductory chapter in its entirety. Give special attention to the sections entitled **Some Precautions** and **Important Variables to Optimize Relaxation Training**.

2. Guide yourself through (or have another person guide you through) the **Concept Exercises** found in the chapters. These are one-time practices that provide an experiential sense of the concept underlying the practices in each chapter.

3. Read the instructions for each practice in detail. There is a written script that guides you through each relaxation, cognitive change, or imagery practice. We encourage you to adapt the words and sequences in the scripts for yourself. To lead yourself through each script, it will be helpful for you to make your own audiotape.[1] Detailed instructions are given in the section **Making Your Own Tapes**.

4. Each of you is different and unique, and will respond in your individual way. As Collet Campbell, a junior at San Francisco State University, wrote: "...it is a highly individualized process. It requires complete objectivity in observing *when* and *how* we respond. It requires experimentation and allowances for problems/mistakes in order to discover what works in facilitating positive change."

5. Set aside 20-30 minutes a day to do each practice, plus additional time to make tapes.

6. Record your experiences—feelings, struggles, successes, sense of change, and so forth—on the log sheets after your practice. At the end of the week review, integrate, and summarize your experiences. We are often unaware of gradual changes. It is only when recorded and reviewed later that we can become aware of patterns or problems, and changes and growth that we have achieved/allowed. These written records can provide evidence that desired changes are indeed occurring, even though, subjectively, we may feel that we have not progressed.

7. At the end of each major segment of the workbook, look back over the previous weeks' experiences. Summarize your experience to facilitate integration and appreciation of your growth.

8. Be sure to practice the short exercises during the day at home and at work. Integrate those short practices into your life pattern. Just thinking about the practice during the day can be the first step. It may offer a momentary distance from habitual patterns. Just being aware is a significant beginning.

9. If possible, do the exercises together with others in a small group each week. Have family members, friends, or colleagues at work do them with you. Group support is very helpful. In addition, sharing in others' experiences will augment your own experience and growth. Have a different group member lead and guide the members through the practice each week.

10. If others in your life are not participating or even frown upon your practice, let that be their experience. Don't force them to participate with you, and don't allow their disapproval to defeat you. Remember, each of us has the right to his or her own judgments.

11. If you are part of a group or class, share your findings and discuss your successes and challenges. Have a group member lead you through the next practice. At the end of the guided session, share your experiences, so that you can adapt or change the practice to benefit you most. Remember, when you share in a group, respect each

---

1. See Appendix A for information on the source for audiotapes for the practices.

person's experience. In the beginning many people are overly concerned about "doing it right." Do not judge yourself or others. There may be similarities or differences in people's experiences. Give each other support for practicing. When working in a group, remember that:[2]

◆ What is shared in the group is confidential information. Be respectful and do not discuss it outside of the group.

◆ One person speaks at a time.

◆ Each person speaks only for himself or herself.

◆ Everyone is allowed to express her or his own feelings and reactions.

◆ Everyone expresses these feelings respectfully. There is no criticism of other's feelings or reactions.

◆ Share feelings and experiences. For example, ask what were your feelings during the practices and how do you feel now?

◆ Explore the effect of the practices upon the group members' lives. For example, ask how life has changed since doing the practice or how friends and family members have responded.

◆ If a participant had difficulty doing the practices, explore strategies that will help him/her perform the practices successfully during the next week.

12. If you have difficulty, stop for a few days, then start again with the same or a previous exercise. Sometimes you may want to skip a specific practice and come back to it later. Respect your own process. If something does not seem to work for you, attempt it once more and then *do something different*. If you resist doing the practices, you may want to be like a detective. You might choose to do a detailed analysis of the benefits of NOT doing the practice. Ask yourself, "What are the consequences and rewards for not allowing something new to occur?" Sometimes all it takes is to prioritize our tasks and set up rewards (positive reinforcers) for following through.

13. Do not expect instant success and do not beat yourself up if you do not attain what you were seeking. Be patient, allow, and enjoy the process. The skills to be learned may take many weeks or even months to master.

14. Remember that your experiences change. Each time you do a practice you are different; therefore, do not expect the same experience. Progress is not always slow and steady. There may be slumps and setbacks; there may also be big leaps ahead.

15. Enjoy the self-exploration and growth. Do it with an attitude of childlike play, with thoughts such as, "I wonder what I'll experience next." We are not static. Remember, each experience is different because we are continuously changing. It is only in death that change no longer occurs. Hence, offer yourself the richness of exploring the uncharted future.

---

2. Adapted from a handout from the offices of Counseling and Psychological Services, Student Affairs, the Office of Human Relations, Disability Programs and Resource Center, San Francisco State University, 2001.

16. Explore the **Suggested Readings** (Appendix B) for more detailed presentations of the concepts.

SPECIFIC INSTRUCTIONS

Because the practices build upon the previous ones, the mastery of the earlier practices will enhance and deepen the later ones. Notice that each chapter contains one or more practices, which are usually introduced by some background material. Each practice includes specific instructions, such as a guided script, and for each there are worksheets for you to complete: daily logs, weekly questions about your logs, and questions for group discussion and conclusions. We have found that participants increase their benefit if they share their experiences with others who are also doing the exercises.

We recommend that you:

1. Begin by scanning the workbook chapters: **Introduction**, **Dynamic Regeneration**, **Cognitive Balance**, and **Self-Healing Through Imagery and Behavior Change**.

2. Practice the **Concept Exercises** in each section before starting the practice.

3. Record your experiences on the practice **Log Sheet** each day after practice.

4. At the end of the week's practice, review your logs and answer the **Questions**.

5. If you are practicing these exercises with others, meet weekly and complete the **Discussion and Conclusions** worksheet.

6. Develop reminders to practice the mini-exercises during the day. It is through these mini-practices that awareness is fostered.

7. Act on your observations and insights; allow yourself to make mistakes. Mistakes offer us the opportunity to learn.

SOME PRECAUTIONS

Do not alter the use of your medications without consulting your health care provider.

The following persons should proceed carefully and should possibly receive guidance or supervision from a trained professional:

◆ Those who are taking medication such as sleeping pills, antihypertensive medication, tranquilizers, antidepressants, insulin, or thyroid supplement. These individuals should have their medications monitored—and altered if necessary—during training.

◆ Those who have suffered traumatic or consciousness-altering experiences such as automobile accidents, near drowning, rape, psychedelic drugs, and (sometimes) anesthesia. These persons often need support in feeling and discharging emotions associated with these experiences; they may also find relaxation difficult.

◆ Persons with other psychological conditions, such as dealing with death of a loved one, experiencing depersonalization (loss of identity), or "fugue" states (out of body experiences). Emotional support and close monitoring will be necessary.

It is further suggested that if illness is present, you should avoid focusing, during the beginning of training, on the area of concern. For example, an asthmatic may have difficulty focusing on breathing initially and should, thus, delay the breathing practice until the fifth or sixth practice session.

If uncomfortable feelings or experiences occur, in some cases you may need to adapt the practices, skip the section, and/or seek outside psychological/medical support. Frequently, it will be possible to resume the practice after a few days' pause, since we all have an underlying drive toward health and integration.

If you generally block or suppress a need to cry or vomit, be aware that in deeply relaxed states such inhibitions occasionally are loosened, and crying or vomiting may occur. This is normal.

⑤ APPROACHES TO SELF-REGULATION: OVERVIEW

With your eyes closed, imagine a lemon. Notice the deep yellow color, the two stubby ends, the sign "Sunkist" stamped on the side. Place the lemon on a cutting board and cut the lemon in half with your favorite kitchen knife. Notice the pressure in your hand as you cut. Feel the droplets of lemon juice sprinkling against your skin. Put the knife down and take one of the half lemons in your hand. Notice the droplets of lemon juice glistening in the light. Observe the half cut seeds, the outer yellow rind, the pale yellow-white inner rind, the pulpy membranes containing the lemon juice. Now get a glass and squeeze the lemon so that the juice goes in the glass. Notice the tension in your hand and arm. Feel the droplets of lemon juice squirting against your skin. Hear the plopping of the seeds and pulp. Smell the pungent, sharp, tart odor. After having squeezed this half, take the other lemon half and squeeze the juice out of it into the glass...Then put that lemon half down, and take the glass in your hand. Feel the coolness of the glass. Bring the glass to your lips, tilt the glass. Notice the pressure and coolness on the lower lip. Now taste and swallow the lemon juice. Observe the pulp and seeds as you swallow. (Peper and Williams, 1981, pp. 187-188)

As you read those words, perhaps you had a direct experience of salivating, swallowing, and puckering your lips. Observe how images and thoughts produced real physiologic responses in the body! We are equally capable of getting physically upset and distraught over an imagined event or worry that may never really happen. These are both examples of how the mind and body are not at all separate; in fact, any event in the mind is accompanied by a response in the body, and vice versa. We are also very much affected by the environment in which we exist: the family and social environment; the quality of the air, water, and food we take in; our work or school situation; and, of course, our perceptions and feelings about all of these.

RATIONALE FOR LEARNING RELAXATION

The rate of change in our society is constantly increasing, bringing greater pressures in many areas of life. We learn to work harder and to juggle multiple roles (such as career, family and school). These pressures and stressors, including major crises and minor hassles, can lead to a breakdown in health. Indeed, up to 80% of today's health problems in America are considered to be linked to stress. When our health breaks down, we often seem to be at the mercy of an impersonal medical system in which we feel helpless and alienated.

People who are chronically stressed are placing an extra load on their bodies. The body has a limited amount of energy to be used for adaptation and change; conserving and regenerating it through relaxation practices is important for health and well-being. Conversely, when we become sick, we draw on our reserves, and can easily get into "deficit spending." Rebuilding the energy reservoir can take time. Think about what happens in a prolonged drought. A single downpour does little to moisten the parched soil, and may simply run off with little beneficial effect. On the other hand, a slow trickle of rain over a long time will gradually restore the soil's moisture. Similarly, a single vacation in Hawaii may do little to build up the depleted energy reserves drained by prolonged stress and/or illness; while a daily relaxation practice carried out over a few weeks or months may be much more restorative.

The body's alarm state, or "fight / flight or freeze" response, involves dramatic changes when a threat is perceived: the pituitary gland triggers the adrenals to secrete adrenalin, cortisol, and other hormones; heart rate and blood pressure increase; muscles tense in anticipation of running or fighting; blood leaves the skin in order to supply the muscles; digestion stops. This response can be life saving when the threat is physical; in modern life, however, it can be life *threatening*, when it is chronically reactivated without the opportunity to be discharged through vigorous physical activity or deep relaxation. When stress is chronic, the body adapts (temporarily) and channels the strain into one or more organ systems. However, ultimately exhaustion ensues and these systems begin to break down; you become vulnerable to illness (Cannon, 1939; Selye, 1956, 1974).

THE HUMAN FUNCTION CURVE

A very useful model that demonstrates the effects of long-term stress on the body is the *Straw That Breaks the Camel's Back* (Nixon and King, 1997), developed by Dr. Peter Nixon, a British cardiologist. He explored why some people can work for long periods in unhealthful settings while others quickly break down, and why some cardiac patients make remarkable recoveries becoming healthier, happier, and more efficient in living while others keep themselves ill with excessive effort. From clinical observations, as well as from earlier studies of soldiers under stress, he developed the *Human Function Curve* (see Figure 1.1), which illustrates the dynamic interactions of health, injury, and recovery (Nixon, 1989).

This curve illustrates that health is the continuous alternation between expending energy and restoration and growth. This natural alternation can be found in other physiological functions: inhaling and exhaling in breathing, systole and diastole in the heart contraction, and the daily cycle of waking and sleeping. When arousal is low and we are relaxing, the body regenerates (anabolic processes). When arousal is high, as well as when triggering the fight/flight/freeze response, the body cannibalizes itself in order to perform (catabolic processes).

The *Human Function Curve* and the impact of arousal on performance are familiar to many performers, such as athletes, musicians, and lecturers. For example, in sports if our arousal is too low we are "flat," while "we are hyped-up and lose control" when it is too high. These feelings are found similarly in playing music—imagine playing the violin and being so nervous that you are shaking and your hands are sweaty and cold. Or think of giving a speech and being so anxious your voice trembles and you can't remember what to say. Excessive stimulation produces cognitive, emotional, behavioral, and physiological consequences. For example, worrying about your job, conflict with your spouse, or concern about your children may increase your arousal and affect your health and sleep. Chronic worrying may cause insomnia or an increase in blood pressure. Our bodies generally respond to these stimuli by triggering components of the alarm reaction (fight or flight) with breath holding and a shift to rapid chest (thoracic) breathing.

Only when we are at an appropriate arousal level for the situation and have sufficient opportunity to regenerate do we perform well. Every performance has an optimum level of arousal. Not even sleep escapes this rule. If our arousal is too low we go into a coma

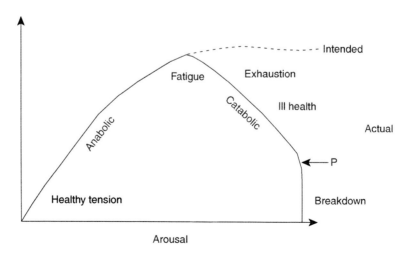

Figure 1.1. The Human Function Curve: A performance-arousal curve used as a model for a systems or biopsychosocial approach to clinical problems. P = point of instability where very little extra arousal is required to produce breakdown (Nixon, 1989).

and die; if our arousal is too high, we experience insomnia. Burnout, breakdown, and illness may occur when we operate at chronic high arousal levels or predominantly at our peak performance without episodic regenerative breaks. This high arousal shifts us into the catabolic state. On the other hand, by shifting to a lower level of arousal, we can move into the anabolic state to promote regeneration and health. This anabolic state is usually induced with relaxation and it implies mental and emotional tranquility. The physiological effects of the anabolic and catabolic processes are shown in Tables 1.1 and 1.2.

The general height of the curve for individual best performance depends upon genetics and how we have used ourselves. Some people are born with a lower curve and quickly go over the top into exhaustion (catabolic state), while others are born with a very high curve and take a long time to go over the top. At the same time, the height is an interactive phenomenon. If individuals take care of themselves and enjoy appropriate development and training, the height of the curve can increase. On the other hand, neglect and self-destructive behavior can reduce it.

This curve can also be seen as a representation of a life-long pattern. Where on this curve do *you* tend to live? In early childhood, we are predominantly on the anabolic side with higher sleep needs and rapid growth. As we get older, we take on more responsibilities. Although we may develop more coping skills, we often do not shed responsibilities. Hence, we may push to increase performance by working longer and harder instead of smarter. We may work later at the office, use caffeine and other stimulants to increase performance, and continue this stressful pattern day after day after day. When working too long in an aroused state, our system gets exhausted and eventually breaks down. Often, the effect of bad habits and habitual destructive catabolic living does not usually

Table 1.1. Hormonal pattern during arousal.	
Catabolic hormones increase	**Anabolic hormones decrease**
Cortisol	Insulin
Epinephrine	Calcitonin
Glucagon	Testoterone
Melatonin	Estrogen
Antidiuretic hormone	Prolactin
Renin	Luteinizing hormone
Angiotensin	Follicle stimulating hormone
Aldosterone	Gondatropin release hormone (GnRH)
Erythropoietin	Prolactin releasing hormone (PRH)
Thyroxine	
Parathormone	

From: Nixon, P.G.F. (1989). Human functions and the heart. In Seedhouse, D. and Cribb, A. (eds). *Changing Ideas in Health Care*. New York: John Wiley & Sons.

Table 1.2. Anabolic and Catabolic States.

Anabolic State
- Increased synthesis of protein, fat, carbohydrate (growth, energy storage)
- Decreased breakdown of protein, fat, carbohydrate (growth, energy storage)
- Increased production of cells for immune system (white blood cells of thymus and bone marrow)
- Increased bone repair and growth
- Increase in sexual processes (cellular, hormonal, and psychological)
- Improved digestion

Catabolic State
- Halt in synthesis of protein, fat, and carbohydrate
- Increased breakdown of protein, free fatty acids, low-density lipoprotein, cholesterol for energy
- Increased production of red blood cells and liver enzymes for energy
- Decreased repair and replacement of bone
- Decreased repair and replacement of cells with normally high turnover (gut, skin, etc.)
- Decreased production of cells for immune system (thymus shrinks, circulating white cells decrease)
- Decreased sexual processes
- Increased blood pressure, cardiac output
- Increased salt and water retention
- Impaired digestion

Adapted from: Nixon, P.G.F. (1989). Human functions and the heart. In Seedhouse, D. and Cribb, A. (eds). *Changing Ideas in Health Care*. New York: John Wiley & Sons.

manifest until we are past middle age. For example, in a long-term study of adults, researchers found that those individuals who exercised in their forties and were not obese have significantly better health in their sixties and seventies as compared to those who did not (Valliant, 2002).

The questions in Table 1.3 can help you ascertain if you are on the downward slope of the *Human Function Curve* (developed by Peter Nixon and Jenny King, 1997).

To improve health and increase the capacity for work/stress, individuals must integrate a model of work hardening into their life pattern. This process is a skill development model in which you learn new skills to cope more effectively and then push yourself to perform for a short period. Periods of stress need to be followed by periods of rest to integrate and regenerate. For example, when beginning to jog, you jog a few blocks and then the next day you walk. Slowly and surely over time you increase the jogging time. Increasing exercise too rapidly and too frequently often results in injuries (perhaps it is

---

Table 1.3. The Human Function Curve Questionnaire.

Am I on The Downslope?
- ◆ Because too much is demanded of me?
- ◆ Because I cannot say 'no' when necessary?
- ◆ Because I am not sufficiently in control? Can't cope?
  - — Too angry, too tense, too upset, too irritable, too indignant?
  - — Too much people-poisoning (caring for too many people and then having nothing left for family members)?
  - — Too many time-pressures?
  - — Too impatient?
- ◆ Because I am not sleeping WELL enough to keep well?
- ◆ Because I am not keeping fit enough to stay well?
- ◆ Because I am not balancing the periods of hard effort with adequate sleep and relaxation?
- ◆ Because I am out of real energy and using sheer will power to keep going?
- ◆ Because I am infallible, indispensable, indestructible, and/or immortal?

The Protesting Body
- ◆ What is it trying to say? Am I listening?
- ◆ Why is it protesting?
- ◆ What makes it protest each time? And why so often?
- ◆ Am I working to make it stronger or am I too upset with myself to succeed?
- ◆ Am I looking for a drug/operation to keep it quiet?

Adapted from Nixon and King, 1997.

nature's way to induce the anabolic state). In these alternating work/rest cycles the system is challenged to perform at a higher level and has enough time to build the structures and skills necessary to perform at this level.

Health consists of working intensely and then balancing it with regeneration. However, it is not easy to quiet the mind of self-blame or the numerous remonstrances, such as *I should, I must, I have to,* and *if only.* Regeneration occurs when both the mind and body are quiet. Sometimes, the answer is to take a vacation. However, a week long vacation may not be sufficient to regenerate after a year of exhaustion and depletion. A more useful strategy is to avoid exhaustion and take multiple breaks to regenerate. During these regenerative breaks, take a walk, relax and, most importantly, allow the mind and emotions to relax. Ask yourself:

- ◆ Where on this *Human Function Curve* am I located?
- ◆ Am I working continuously without rest, leading to burn out?

◆ Am I challenging myself continuously?

◆ What do I do to regenerate?

OBSERVING THE LINK BETWEEN HABITS AND HEALTH

The following two vignettes illustrate Peter Nixon's Human Function Curve and the affects on our health.

Vignette 1: _____

I look up at the clock, it is 2:15 p.m. I have less than three hours to finish writing the report. Can I really summarize all of it in six pages? I am no longer sure. But my boss must have the report—my job is on the line. I have been here since six-thirty this morning. My eyes are blurry. I keep tucking my feet on the chair pedestal to anchor myself in.

Let's focus back on the task... I look up it is 3:25 p.m. I sip some cold coffee to get me through this final stretch.

Where was I? I look to the left to see the monitor and my neck aches. One day, when I have the time, I'll rearrange my desk so that I can look straight ahead. I reach forward and to the side to grab the mouse and feel my arm and hand ache as I continue to edit the text. I bring my hands back to the keyboard and rest my wrists on the wrist pad, lifting my fingers up so I don't press down on the keys. (How do they expect me to have straight wrists using this wrist pad??) I wonder why resting my wrists as I work hasn't helped the pain? I extend my wrists and fingers as I type another correction, telling myself to ignore the pain...I've got to get this done.

"What was that?" I ask myself as I jump at a sound and look over my left shoulder behind me to see if anyone entered my cubicle.... No it was just some noise; not my boss checking how the report is going. I go back to my manuscript...

My shoulders feel tight, especially between my spinal column and right shoulder blade. It seems that the more I reach over my keyboard to use the mouse (my keyboard tray is too narrow for both keyboard and mouse) the more I hurt by the end of the day.

I go back to editing. The letters on the monitor screen compete with the reflection of the overhead fluorescent light; it is like a watermark on paper—my eyes and brain are tired.

Let me finish my third cup of coffee... I already started today tired... My partner was angry that, once again, I had to go in early. Who was going to take Michael and Joan to the school bus stop? I had rushed out before it was resolved...

"Darn, I don't have all the data. I'd better call Martin." As I dial the phone I tuck it between my left shoulder and ear, hurriedly typing away. "Martin, I need the summary findings from last month's business meeting to include in the report. Do you have them?...Great! Can you read the findings while I enter them in the computer? Thanks." So, I rapidly enter the findings as I listen with the phone cradled between my shoulder and ear. Someday, when I have time I'll get a headset.

Well, the report got done. I feel emotionally and physically fried. I wish I had taken time to eat lunch. I have a slight headache and the road signs are hard to read. I keep noticing the slight aching between my shoulder blades. It is just not going away. I guess I need an aspirin—a massage sounds heavenly.

Yet, when I get home I will need to supervise Michael and Joan's homework... Oh, I better get some food for tomorrow's dinner—it is my turn to cook...

Vignette 2: _____

I walk into the office a few minutes early and water my two spider plants and peace lily. I'm glad that I brought them; they cheer up the office. The green reminds me of my summer vacation in Deer Harbor, Maine. I had woken up early, had my yogurt and fruit drink and my favorite coffee. I turn on the laser printer in the small room next door and I walk back to my workstation. Luckily, I can look out and see through the small window on my left the two large Monterey Pines just reaching to the sky.

Here we go again. As I start entering the purchase orders, once again, I silently thank Luciano, my office partner. His creative solution of clamping a wider and deeper wooden plank to the narrow keyboard tray has been a saving grace. Now I can use the mouse without reaching.

Ring, ring,...I put on my headset and lift the receiver from the hook. "Hello, purchasing." "Oh, yes, let me look this up, one moment please." I click on the June 6th icon and open the file. While the computer accesses the file, I drop my hands to my lap and relax my shoulders.

There we are. "Yes, it was ordered from Indol Engineering on June 2nd. I expect that it will be here in another 10 days." ... "If you have any problems just call. Bye."

Back to entering the other purchase orders. I clip the form on the document holder next to the monitor and I enter the data. After each purchase order, I shake my hands and drop them on my lap and for one or two seconds and look out at the Monterey Pines through the window.

After I click the print icon for batch printing of the ten purchase orders, I walk over to the printer, jiggle my shoulders to relax them and pick up the printed forms.

Before I sit down, I check my chair. I pull the lever to slightly raise it to adjust to my higher desk. I roll the chair to my slanted desk and sign the printed forms.

Even though it is the end of the quarter and the purchase orders are piling up, I decide to still take my lunch break. I take a short walk with Mary. Then when I came back, I put my nose to the grindstone, yet every half-hour I get up to move. I have learned that I will not be able to continue unless I nurture and take care of myself while working.

It is four o'clock. I stop data entry, look at the pile of orders still to be processed. I call Margaret, my supervisor. I tell her that I can't finish it by five. She says, "Do you think you could work until seven to finish it?" I look at the stack and answer, "Yes". "Why don't you work till seven and take the time off next week." I agree and for a moment I am already fantasizing staying in bed Friday morning with my partner who is free in the early mornings.

I reach to the phone, dial my number and let my partner know that I will be two hours late. Luckily, I can take time off Friday. Even though I still have two more hours of work I feel alive...

These two vignettes describe different work styles and experiences that impact the health of the individual. The person in the first vignette is much more at risk for developing illness. This individual's dysfunctional work style, poor ergonomic setup, and work and home stress conjointly contribute to injury. The exhaustion and shoulder blade discomfort are NOT just the result of repetitive motions or using the mouse; they are the combined result of all the factors that impact the system. This employee consistently is operating in a catabolic state.

Analyze your day. Ask yourself which vignette sounds most like you. If you are closer to the first, then reorganize your daily life. Your health may depend upon it.

Sometimes it is possible to diminish stressors, through prioritizing tasks, resolving conflicts, being more assertive, and so on. Even when you are unable to remove the sources of stress in your life, you can begin to reduce the toll stress takes on your body and to recharge your energy reservoirs by learning and using an effective relaxation technique.

Moods and Energy Levels

Often, one of the first indications that we have moved into the catabolic state is a shift in mood. Instead of feeling happy, content, and responding to stressors with humor, we begin to feel anxious, irritable, slightly depressed, and quick to react. At this time we often reach for a sweet and begin snacking. Professor Robert Thayer has researched the relationship between moods, energy level, snacking, and exercise. He has shown that we all want to feel good and use self-regulation to feel better. When we are in a bad mood we usually try those things that in the past may have worked to make us feel better or gave us a boost—sugary snack, drink, coffee, cigarettes. These substances will provide only a momentary relief from moods, especially from irritability, and then the cycle of bad moods repeats. On the other hand, if we do some moderate exercise when our mood is low, we begin to feel better immediately.

Thayer's mood model is based upon two axes: calm-tense and energy-tired, as shown in Figure 1.2 (Thayer, 1996, 2001).

The quadrants describe the four different mood dimensions: *Calm-Energy*, *Calm-Tiredness*, *Tense-Energy* and *Tense-Tiredness*. Obviously, there is a large gradient of energy levels and moods. As Thayer points out, our energy level can be affected by exercise and foods. Usually, moderate exercise immediately increases energy—think of those times that you went for a walk when feeling sluggish and, as you walked more rapidly, your energy began to increase. Equally important, exercise can discharge muscle tension generated by the flight/flight/freeze reaction and, thereby, reduce some of the tension; it can help us shift to a more optimistic mood.

Foods equally affect our energy level. Generally, hunger reduces energy and sugar initially increases energy. When individuals use a sugary snack for an energy boost, they commonly find that, after one hour, their energy level has dropped below the pre-snack energy level, their tension level has increased, and they are feeling fatigued. Thayer (1996) describes the major moods and physiological and biological rhythms associated with the four energy quadrants as:

THE SELF-REGULATION OF MOOD

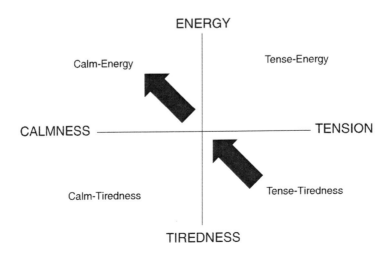

Figure 1.2. Predominant changes in self-regulation of mood (from Thayer, 1996, p. 150)

Calm-Energy (good mood)
- ◆ Cardiovascular system in slight arousal, respiration and heart rate slightly elevated, metabolic rate increased.
- ◆ Time: Midday and after having eaten breakfast with protein and no simple carbohydrates.
- ◆ Feeling in a good mood, peppy and vigorous, confident, sociable, ability to focus on work, and no urgency; just a quiet and relaxed attention.

Calm-Tiredness
- ◆ Cardiovascular system at low level of arousal, respiration and heart rate slightly reduced, metabolic rate decreased.
- ◆ Time: Late evening relaxing, not much active thinking.
- ◆ Feeling in a good mood although less intense than in calm energy; quiet, sleepy or drowsy.

Tense-Energy
- ◆ Cardiovascular system in slight arousal, respiration and heart rate slightly elevated, metabolic rate increased, increase in muscle tension in the jaw, shoulders, neck and back, freeze reaction.
- ◆ Perceived danger or a threat of danger is near.
- ◆ A sense of pressure, time pressure, and urgency (e.g., deadlines). Thoughts are more distracting and scattered.
- ◆ Feelings of energy, pep and vigor with tension and jitteriness (slight anxiety); fast efficient work.

Tense-Tiredness (Bad mood)
- ◆ Exhaustion, poor sleep the night before, more coffee and sweets, and no exercise; fatigue mixed with nervousness.
- ◆ Time: Possibly late in the afternoon. Tendency to eat snacks and drink coffee. Negative thoughts. The future looks bad. At night, tossing and turning while trying to go to sleep.
- ◆ Feelings of exhaustion and negative thoughts keep arising. Insignificant hassles have major impact.

Usually, the bad mood (tense-tired) is more common when we are in the catabolic state and occurs more frequently when our energy is low, generally around 4 p.m. and between 9 and 11 p.m. Consequently, when experiencing a tense-tired mood, ask your self the following questions (from Thayer, 1996):
- ◆ What is the time of day?
- ◆ How much sleep have I gotten recently?
- ◆ When did I eat last (and what kind of food did I consume)?
- ◆ Have I been sedentary for a long period (when did I exercise last)?
- ◆ How good is my general health?

◆ What is my general stress level?

◆ (For women) What time of month is it?

◆ Have I recently been taking psychoactive drugs (including alcohol), or am I avoiding psychoactive drugs (including nicotine and caffeine) on which I have become dependent?

◆ What is my current energy level?

Stress management includes being aware of moods and times of exhaustion and developing skills to master the regenerative process. Observing our harmful patterns and taking positive steps to change them can eliminate disease and negative moods and bring a life-long pattern of health and happiness.

TYPES OF RELAXATION

Deep Relaxation.

Many people believe that relaxation consists of watching TV, socializing with friends, or listening to music. While these may be pleasant, there is a difference between such activities and the ability to achieve deep muscle relaxation, which allows for renewal of vital bodily processes and healing. When the muscles are profoundly relaxed, a rebalancing takes place. Heart rate, blood pressure, breathing, digestion, and metabolism return to a normal state; the immune system's healing abilities are enhanced; repair and restoration takes place.

Relaxation even affects our immune system. Drs. Janice Kiecolt-Glaser and Ronald Glaser at Ohio State University College of Medicine have studied the connection between stress and lowered immunity. When they measured immune functions of medical students during their exam week, they found decreases in the students' T-cell level. After a simple 20-minute guided relaxation session, the students' T-cell counts increased measurably. (Kiecolt-Glaser, McGuire, Robles & Glaser, 2002 (see **Dynamic Relaxation: Practice 2** in Chapter 2).

Breath, which is under both conscious and unconscious control, is a very basic aspect of relaxation. In learning self-regulation of our breathing, we can begin to "switch off" the fight-or-flight response. Slow, deep diaphragmatic breathing is life affirming and restorative. In this breathing pattern, the diameter of the abdomen expands during inhalation and decreases during exhalation. Such a pattern usually occurs when one is at peace and relaxed. It not only brings in more oxygen, enabling clearer thinking, but it lowers the sympathetic nervous system arousal, which is responsible for tight muscles, racing heart, high blood pressure, and feelings of anxiety. Since it is under conscious control, we can always choose to take a few quieting breaths in order to initiate a relaxation process or ease feelings of fear or anger (see **Breathing—The Mind-Body Bridge: Practice 3** in Chapter 2).

Differential Relaxation.

Through this workbook you can learn the skills of differential relaxation, or letting go of muscles not needed for a particular task. For example, while driving, many people unconsciously tense their jaw and shoulder muscles, which are not needed to drive the car effectively. Such wasted muscle effort, known as *dysponesis*, needlessly drains our energy reserves (Whatmore & Kohli, 1974). Systematic practice of dynamic relaxation methods increases your awareness of whether your muscles are tense or relaxed as you go about your daily activities, thus giving you the choice of releasing unnecessary tension. *Awareness gives you choices!* Then you can save that adaptation energy, which would have been wasted on unnecessary muscle tension, for other activities—such as self-healing.

Generalized Relaxation.

When a skill is practiced over and over, in a variety of situations, it becomes automatic; very little conscious awareness is needed to produce the behavior. Also, we can condition certain responses at will. Certain cues in our environment produce automatic responses that can be useful; for example, at a red light or stop sign, we step on the brake almost without thinking about it. Similarly, we can condition ourselves to relax certain muscles, or to breathe slowly and deeply, in response to a cue such as the words *relax*, *calm*, or *serene*. Or we can invoke a relaxing, reassuring image; a small object such as a seashell on the desk or in the pocket can be a reminder of a calmer time (see **Developing A Personal Relaxation Image: Practice 4** in Chapter 2). A cue for relaxation can be anything we choose. With practice we can even train ourselves to let a red light or a ringing telephone become a cue to relax. For example, when the phone rings, you may habitually tighten your shoulders; instead, you now choose to use the phone ringing as a signal to relax your shoulders and breathe, before answering it (see Quic**k and Warm: Practice 5** and **Generalizing Relaxation: Practice 6** in Chapter 2). Systematic practice of relaxation teaches our muscles that tension is no longer the norm; we have the choice of relaxing, and relaxing can become the new habit instead of tension.

Deep Relaxation As A Gateway To The Unconscious.

As restorative as it is all by itself, deep relaxation has still other benefits. When the muscles are quiet, the conscious rational mind also quiets, allowing access to intuition. The highly verbal, analytical, judgmental part of the mind is also sometimes referred to as the left hemisphere, or left-brain. Right-brain is intuitive, visual, and creative, thinks in pictures or images, perceives relationships and wholes, and is more in touch with the emotions.

Most of the time we are not paying attention to the quiet messages from our right-brain because the left-brain is busy censoring them! Deep relaxation can temporarily get the left-brain out of the way and allow right-brain inputs. Thus relaxation can be helpful in interrupting habitual negative thought patterns and in opening the mind to new possibilities. Greater creativity and problem-solving abilities may emerge spontaneously (Green and Green, 1977). Valuable messages about changes we need to make for our greater health and well-being often arise (see **Imagery for Self-healing** in Chapter 4).

COGNITIVE STRESS MANAGEMENT

Our View of the World.

The events in our lives are neither inherently good nor bad, but neutral. It's how we choose to view these events that determines, in large part, how we respond—with helplessness and hopelessness or optimism and humor. If we use language that implies that we're helpless victims, then that view of our world is reinforced; conversely, language that is empowering will strengthen our positive view.

Some of our language use is habitual and outside of our conscious awareness. Our inner dialogue may include not only words, but also pictures, gut feelings, premonitions, and expectations. A person who was abused as a child may have learned a sense of helplessness that extends into adult life, including situations where, in reality, the adult has choices and need not be powerless. The good news is that unrealistic assessments of ourselves and the world (based on past experience) can be revised and changed. Changing language to emphasize our choices and capabilities is a step in that direction. **Changing The Inner Dialogue: Practice 8** in Chapter 3 provides guidelines to assess and change the way we think and view our world.

Our Energy Levels.

A key aspect of coping with stress, as described in the serenity prayer, is to recognize which things we can control and which we can't, and then act appropriately, or let go:

> God grant me the serenity
> To accept the things I cannot change,
> Courage to change the things I can and
> Wisdom to know the difference

Identifying our energy level and the effects of activities and thoughts, and then reducing those activities that are energy drains and increasing those that are energy gains, helps to increase our energy level and promote a more positive attitude (see **Changing Energy Drains and Energy Gains: Practice 9** in Chapter 2).

Interpreting Life's Experiences.

A major cognitive coping process is *reframing*. This is learning to redefine threats as challenges or opportunities and can be very empowering. Look, for example, at the difference between calling a woman "preorgasmic" instead of "frigid." The second term implies a hopeless and negative situation while the first implies a situation that can develop and change and is full of potential.

Reframing threats as opportunities can mean an increased willingness to see even an illness or symptom as meeting a need (which may have been unacknowledged) and can direct us to make a change in our lifestyle. Mental rehearsal, in which we imagine the steps needed for success instead of reliving our failures, is an important tool for overcoming problems and encouraging behavior changes (see **Transforming Failure Into Success: Practice 10** in Chapter 3).

Sometimes developing new solutions or alternative behaviors is challenging. A problem-solving strategy, outlined in **9-Step Problem-Solving** in Chapter 3, can be a helpful guide to brainstorming and resolution.

Another cognitive coping process that encourages self-acceptance and integration is to write about past traumas or practice the optional insight exercises (see **Freeing the Hidden Secrets: Practice 11** in Chapter 3). With this new awareness, we can make changes and find new ways to get our needs met, thus removing the need for the illness or symptom and fulfilling our needs (see **Converting The Advantages Of Illness: Practice 12** in Chapter 3).

SELF-HEALING THOUGH IMAGERY AND BEHAVIOR CHANGE

There is increasing recognition of the power of mental imagery to promote self-healing of diseases. Carl Simonton pioneered this work with cancer patients, and Martin Rossman and David Bresler have reported positive results with people having a wide variety of afflictions, often after little or no progress using traditional allopathic (Western medical) approaches (Rossman, 2000; Simonton, Matthews-Simonton, & Creighton, 1992).

Imagery exercises may take several forms. To begin with, it is useful to practice the previously acquired relaxation skills to allow a free flow of spontaneous imagery. These messages from the right brain may provide valuable insight into the nature of a symptom or illness, as well as offer clues for action steps in the healing process. For example, a man seeking to heal himself of obesity and overeating received images of himself as a child feeling unloved, insecure, and eating to fill the void he felt inside. This led him to the awareness that dieting alone would probably not work; he needed to find ways to obtain nurturance other than by eating.

In imagery practice, first imagine the problem area or area of concern; then imagine the healing process taking place. Finally, imagine yourself whole, healed, filled with energy, and living life without the problem. The emotions evoked by imagery can have powerful, positive effects. Often, it is helpful to make a drawing of each image so that it may be viewed from a different perspective—one that may offer a clearer illustration of the illness and healing process.

Not all imagery is visual in nature. Athletes practice mental imagery using multisensory approaches. For example, a basketball player may imagine the feeling of the ball in his or her hands while dribbling around the court, the sensation in the legs while leaping into the air, the sound of the ball smoothly landing in the net, and so forth. The more senses you can bring to bear, the more successful (and fun!) your practice is likely to be. A number of research studies have demonstrated that imagined practice improves performance and accuracy. For example, the 2002 Super Bowl between the New England Patriots and the St. Louis Rams ended with a game-winning field goal by the Patriots in the last seconds. When interviewed after the game and asked about being nervous, Adam Vinatieri, the Patriots' kicker, said, "No, I kicked that ball a hundred times last night."

Mental rehearsal may have a wide variety of applications for changing behavior, as well as for healing. Worrying is an example of negative mental rehearsal; an image, a word, a feeling is in the background of your mind over a period of time. Think back to a time when you experienced the loss of a love or another depressing event; did you go through the day with the thoughts of your loss running in the back of your mind? Without conscious thought, that underlying awareness colored your daily experiences.

With positive mental rehearsal, successful imagers develop a background awareness of their healing image that is ever present. An important step in successful imagery practice is finding ways to associate imagery with various daily routines. Just as we learn to take mini-breaks for relaxation throughout the day, triggered by cues, so too can we learn to do mini-practices of imagery cued to everyday events such as face-washing, drinking a glass of water, walking, urinating, and so forth. For example, a woman with acne created a face-washing ritual that involved visualizing caves with bits of green scum in them (like an enlarged photo of facial pores harboring bacteria); she visualized the ocean washing through these caves and removing all the scum as she washed her face with warm water several times daily.

Behavior change often follows naturally from exploring imagery. For example, a person seeking to heal a condition of low energy and depression may receive an image of herself hiking or dancing. It will be very important to act upon the insights gained from imagery (in this case to make specific plans to hike or dance) as soon as possible. Helpful guidelines for developing and succeeding in imagery are included in **Imagery Exploration: Practice 13** and **Imagery for Self-Healing: Practice 15** in Chapter 4.

Self-Healing Project

Undertaking behavior change with a sense of excitement, challenge, and support (rather than thinking, "I should," "I ought to," or "I can't") is much more likely when you follow a well-planned strategy. Such a strategy will incorporate setting achievable goals and objectives, choosing positive self-talk, collecting data on your present behavior, manipulating the cues in your environment, rewarding yourself, arranging social support, using mental rehearsal for troubleshooting, keeping records of your progress, and making adaptations as you go. Finally, **Carrying Out and Adapting Your Strategy: Practice 16** in Chapter 4 provides step-by-step guidance for implementing a 4-week healing plan.

ᔐ Logging Your Energy Level, Moods, and Responses to Stress: Practice 1

When you take time to give attention to yourself, you may be surprised to find out things you do not know about yourself, and especially surprised when you find what you thought you knew was not quite right at all.

Student

Before beginning the journey of self-change through dynamic relaxation, images and thoughts, take some time to observe your energy level, mood and patterns of responding to stress. This is a way of taking your bearings and discovering what your *baseline* is, the starting point from which you will measure your progress.

We are all confronted with many stressors in our busy and hectic lives. There are minor and major hassles that occur day after day and add up to a large stress load; there are stressful life events and changes, both positive and negative, which force us to adapt. There are job and interpersonal and home stressors. How aware are you of both the stressors and your responses to them? Our responses to stress include our physical and emotional reactions, what we say to ourselves, and what we do. These responses may be more damaging to us than we realize. They have been learned over time and are often habitual. If these habits are not helpful to us, they can also be unlearned.

Use the **Log Sheet: Energy Level, Moods, & Responses To Stress: Practice 1** for at least 2 days; a week is preferable. This will help you develop awareness and build motivation for change. Some participants have found keeping a stress log gave them insight into ways to resolve chronic, predictable stressors; others noted an increased awareness of how negative and critical their thoughts and self-talk were.

A major component of this workbook is to learn new, less destructive patterns for coping with stress. During this self-monitoring, whenever you are aware of a strong emotional reaction *or* whenever you notice some of the indicators of your body's stress response (such as muscle tension, shallow breathing, tight stomach, racing heart), get out your pen or pencil and jot down some notes. What were the events/situations, the associated emotions, your thoughts, your energy and tension levels, your snacking and exercise behaviors, and your physical response? What did you do (your action)? Describe it on the **Log Sheet: Energy Level, Moods, & Responses to Stress: Practice 1**. At the end of the monitoring period, answer **Questions: Energy Level, Moods, & Responses to Stress: Practice 1**. Then, if you are working in a group, discuss your observations and complete **Group Discussion and Conclusions: Energy Level, Moods, & Responses to Stress: Practice 1**.

Name: _____ Date: _____

Log Sheet: Energy Level, Moods, & Responses To Stress: Practice 1

Whenever you feel stressed, write down: the stressful event/situation, the associated emotions/moods, your thoughts, your energy and tension levels, your snacking and exercise behaviors, and your physical response. Use more pages if you like. (Rate your energy and tension levels from 0=none to 4=very high.)

Stressful event/ situation	Energy level	Tension level	Emotions / mood	Thoughts (self-talk)	Snacking /exercise behaviors	Action	Physical response
Example: *Getting Lost*	*1*	*4+*	*Frustrated and angry*	*I am so stupid! I'll be late*	*Cappuccino took elevator*	*Continued to drive without asking for directions*	*Tight jaw sweaty palms*

Stressful event/ situation	Energy level	Tension level	Emotions / mood	Thoughts (self-talk)	Snacking /exercise behaviors	Action	Physical response

Name: _____ Date: _____

Questions: Energy Level, Moods, & Responses To Stress: Practice 1

1. List the common themes of your stressful events.

2. Were the stressful events/situations you experienced within or outside your control? Were these routine or unexpected?

3. What were your common responses to stressful events?

4. What emotions did the stressors evoke?

5. What physical responses to stress did you notice in your body?

6. Did your body respond similarly or differently to different stressors?

7. What actions did you take to decrease your stress and how did they influence the situations?

8. What were the common conditions under which you experienced low energy/high energy?

9. Was there a relationship between types of snacking and energy/stress levels?

10. What could you do to integrate a short walk or other exercise into your routine instead of a sweet or caffeine snack?

11. How did your thoughts or self-talk affect your mood and situation?

12. What can you now do specifically to reduce your stress?

Name: _____ Date: _____

Group Discussion And Conclusions: Energy Level, Moods, & Responses To Stress:

Practice 1

1. What were the common stressors?

2. What similarities and differences were there in physical, emotional, mental, and behavioral responses to stress?

3. How did gender, stage in the life cycle (e.g., student or parent), and personal responsibilities affect the experience of stress?

4. What affect did snacking or exercise have on the ability to cope with stress?

5. Was there an impact on the response to stressful events that could be attributed to individual health or backgrounds? Explain.

6. List the common thought patterns and self-talk associated with stressors and describe how they affected individual and group experiences to stress.

7. Among group members, what effect did monitoring of stress responses have on the experience of the events?

8. What are the things that group members will now do to reduce their responses to stress?

9. Topics or concerns to be discussed with the instructor:

List your group members:

_____   _____

_____   _____

_____   _____

_____   _____

❧ Important Variables to Optimize Relaxation Training[3]

In order to learn unstressing techniques, you need to optimize the conditions under which you may relax. These conditions involve the reduction of stimuli impinging upon you, both physical/environmental and psychological/internal. You can also adopt behaviors that encourage success.

Physical Variables:

1. Select an environment where the following conditions are met:
   A. Training will not be interrupted. (Unplug the phone, put a note on the outside of the door, inform others that you are going to begin training, etc.) It may be important to explain what you are doing to your family, housemates, or significant others. Enlist their support. With young children, you may need to time your relaxation during their naps. Similarly, it is better to leave the dog or cat outside the room.
   B. Noise is minimal. (Don't begin training next to the TV or recreation room.)
   C. Lighting is subdued, not harsh or glaring;
   D. Temperature is comfortable (a cold room makes it difficult to relax, an overly warm room may induce sleepiness).
   E. Chair, bed, or carpet on which training is done is comfortable and provides good support.

2. Choose the position for training that is most comfortable for you—either lying down or sitting. If you tend to fall asleep very easily or are very tired when doing these practices, you will probably do better in a sitting position.
   A. If lying down, you may want to place a pillow underneath your head so your neck and shoulders are comfortable (see Figure 1.3). Place a pillow underneath your knees so that your lower back is not strained. Be sure that the surface beneath is comfortable (use carpet or foam). Make sure your legs are not crossed and that your toes are pointing outward. Keep your arms at your sides and not touching your trunk.

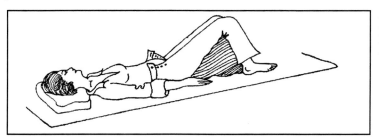

Figure 1.3.
Relaxed position while lying down.

---

3. Adapted from Peper, E. and Williams, E. (1981). *From the Inside Out: A Self-Teaching and Laboratory Manual for Biofeedback*. (New York: Plenum).

B. If sitting, make sure the chair offers sufficient support so that you do not fall over when you relax (see Figure 1.4). Make sure the height of the chair is such that your feet are flat on the floor and that there is not undue pressure on your thighs (if the chair is too high, place a telephone book, pillow, or stool under your feet). Sit with your legs and feet uncrossed and with your thighs relaxed so that your legs are slightly separated. Let your arms rest on the arms of the chair (if present) or rest them gently on your lap. Let your head either hang forward or

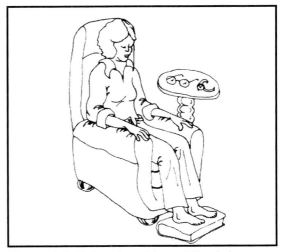

Figure 1.4. Relaxed position while sitting in chair with support for head and arms.

be supported by the back of the chair. Be sure your neck is not strained. A recliner is great.

3. Scan your body and check if there is anything impinging upon and/or constricting it; if so, loosen or remove the constricting or impinging items.

A. Often we become unaware of the constricting nature of our clothing. For example, when you first put on your shoes in the morning, you may feel the shoe enclosing your foot, yet after a few minutes you are unaware of the shoe. When you scan (i.e., feel what is going on inside) your body and attention is brought to your foot, you again become aware of the shoe. During relaxation, we often become aware of the constricting sensation and are distracted from the process of relaxation. Check for such items as shoes, a tight collar, tie, wig, glasses, contact lenses, socks with elastic tops, hair barrette or rubber band, watch, ring, heavy pendant, wallet or keys in pocket, belt, bra, and girdle. If you are working in a group and are uncomfortable about loosening personal items, go through the exercise as best you can, and next time you practice make sure to dress so that these items are not a problem.

B. Items that appear comfortable in our normal posture may physically prevent the process of relaxation. For example, jeans that are tight across the abdomen prevent the letting go and expansion of the abdominal wall. They force thoracic breathing and prevent the more relaxing diaphragmatic breathing. Check for such items as belt, tight pants, panty hose, or tight corset.

C. An item that appears comfortable in our normal posture may demand bracing while we relax. For example, if you are wearing glasses and your head tilts forward during relaxation, you may tend to tighten your neck muscles to prevent your head from nodding and your glasses from falling. Similarly, a woman with a short skirt may hold her knees together and not let her legs relax, and people with dentures may tighten their jaw because of the fear that the dentures may fall out.

D. A physical state may also distract us from relaxing. For example, having a full bladder or being either very hungry or full may make it difficult to relax. Being extremely tired may either cause sleepiness with a wandering mind, or a state of feeling keyed-up. Avoid caffeine for at least two hours prior to relaxation.

PSYCHOLOGICAL VARIABLES

There are certain attitudes of the trainee that encourage relaxation. These include the following:

1. *Passive attention.* This is an attitude of non-striving—of allowing versus forcing or trying—and is characterized by the absence of concern for performance and end result.

2. *Non-judgmental acceptance.* This attitude includes not defining, interpreting, or labeling an experience as good or bad but letting it be and describing it without judgment. It implies not comparing an experience to another but, rather, experiencing each new situation afresh (watch out for words like *because* and *should* and for expressions like *the reason is*). Also, if thoughts and feelings arise, instead of pushing them away, gently accept them and release them.

3. *Mindfulness.* This is an attitude of remaining present, watchful, and aware of what is happening without becoming involved or captured by the images or feelings. Being truly present implies the absence of anticipating, ruminating, or mind-wandering.

BEHAVIORAL VARIABLES

There are a number of strategies that facilitate home practice and generalization of relaxation skills. The following are a few suggestions:

1. Keep log notes. As previously mentioned, these notes concerning your experience, time of day, and mood before and after the practice will provide valuable data to help you choose the best times and settings. Notice situations when it is easy and when it is more difficult for you to practice. This enables you to select those situations that encourage practice. For example, you may find that you practice a relaxation skill with another person more often than by yourself; if so, structure your practice time with a friend or fellow classmate. Also, some participants have reported that looking over their log notes reinspired them.

2. Schedule a regular practice time and associate it with an existing behavior. For example, you may practice after watching the evening news or before dinner. It is preferable not to practice too soon after a large meal. If you tend to fall asleep easily, it is best not to practice late in the evening. It is also best initially not to tie relaxing with going to sleep.

3. Give yourself a reinforcer meaningful to you when you practice. For example, if you practice for a week, treat yourself to a movie or special meal (Thorenson and Mahoney, 1974; Watson and Tharp, 1992).

4. Each day, allot 20 to 30 minutes for the practice. Think of it as a time-out period during which the body and mind are allowed to relax and regenerate.

ꙮ PERSONALIZING YOUR EXPERIENCE

MAKING YOUR OWN TAPES[4]

I was not used to hearing gentle, pleasant, encouraging words from myself.
PARTICIPANT

For each of the relaxation practices there is a script that is designed to be read aloud and taped by the trainee. There are many benefits involved in making your own relaxation tapes. The extra time required can be well worth it. Making your own tapes gives you the ability to tailor a relaxation sequence to your own needs. For example, if you have lower back pain, you might choose to eliminate or change those instructions that might affect your back. If you typically do the practice before starting a work period, you might want to conclude the tape with a suggestion that you are now awake, alert, and mentally focused. If you have trouble relaxing a particular part of your body, you might decide to repeat the tensing and relaxing instructions an extra time for that area. You may want to tape the instructions with your favorite music playing softly in the background. When you make the tape with your personal relaxation imagery, in **Developing a Personal Relaxation Image: Practice 4**, you can provide background sounds such as ocean waves, birds singing, and so forth. If certain words have more pleasant associations for you than those in the scripts, you can substitute them. For example, some people initially respond negatively to the word *relax* because of having been told impatiently, "Would you relax!"

If English is your second language, deep relaxation may be more successful if you translate all the scripts into your native language.

Relaxation is not different from self-acceptance. Listening to your own voice telling you to relax helps you to internalize the instructions and promotes self-acceptance. Many people who began by disliking the sound of their voice on tape ended by enjoying listening to themselves. One woman said that making her own tape, with the appropriate pauses, helped her to learn to listen more in dialogue with other people and to slow down the pace of her hectic life.

---

4. Tapes, pre-recorded with the scripts contained in this book, can be ordered from Work Solutions USA, 2236 Derby Street, Berkeley, CA 94705

Here are some helpful hints for making your tapes:

1. Before making your tape, practice reading the script aloud, if possible to a friend or family member, to get feedback on your pacing. As you make the tape, imagine doing the practice or actually do it (or lead another person through it). This will help your pacing.

2. Make the tape at a time when you're not feeling rushed so that your voice will convey relaxation. Be sure to speak slowly and breathe diaphragmatically throughout. Allow your voice to drop to a slightly lower pitch than you use in everyday speech.

3. Allow plenty of time for the relaxation phase after muscle tensing. A good rule is to allow 7 to 10 seconds for tensing and 15 to 30 seconds for relaxation. Whenever the script indicates ... , pause for a few seconds. Most people tend not to allow enough time for relaxation. Quiet space on the tape is OK.

Like the first pancake, the first attempt at making a tape is not always successful. Think of your first one as an experiment, and if need be, do it over. It will be a good learning experience!

DEVELOPMENT OF A PERSONAL RITUAL FOR RELAXATION

A wonderful fact about the mind is that our responses can be conditioned. Just as we learn to associate certain cues (e.g., a ringing phone or the sight of an angry person) with tension, so too can we learn to associate certain cues with relaxation. As soon as we encounter a relaxation cue, we begin to release tension almost automatically. This can work for you to help deepen your relaxation practices and to allow you to begin relaxing more quickly. The following are some examples of rituals and cues:

◆ Putting on comfortable, loose sweatpants

◆ Getting into your favorite chair

◆ Lighting a candle or stick of incense

◆ Ringing a meditation bell or bowl

◆ Taking three slow, deep breaths

◆ Putting on some quiet, soothing background music

◆ Putting a favorite stuffed animal, blanket, or other comforting item nearby (see Pavlov exercise in **Developing a Personal Relaxation Image: Practice 4** in Chapter 2).

When you are beginning your relaxation practice, it sometimes helps to use a checklist so that important items are not forgotten (see checklist in **Dynamic Relaxation: Practice 2** in Chapter 2).

Why Keep Log Notes?

Writing is an important way of bringing language to our experiences, which helps us to understand, assimilate, and integrate what has happened. Writing brings the amorphous into a concrete form and gives it a sense of containment. It allows us to transport the subtle, evanescent, and easily forgotten inner experience into our everyday consciousness, thus providing the bridge between insight and action. Later, the written words make it possible to look back and reflect upon patterns in our experience that would otherwise not be knowable because so much of our behavior and responses occur automatically.

Another important function of writing is the cultivation of that part of the mind that is the "witness," the part that observes, with calm detachment, everything that we experience. This form of awareness is also developed through meditation. Such awareness can be very valuable in aiding behavior changes. For example, one can simply observe a desire to run away from a frightening stimulus, without giving in to it. Or one can observe, perhaps many times an hour, a desire or craving for, say, alcohol or sugar, again without having to act on it. Thus, we come to know ourselves and to create greater freedom from old habits patterns. Journal keeping is transformative.

Reflection and Integration: Summarizing Your Experiences

Looking over my logs and questions over the last four weeks, I could really notice the improvement. The emotions that were hidden for so long finally came to the surface. I could feel them and accept them for what they were. I was mindful and realized that these are patterns I have repeated for many years. With distance, I could accept and notice movement and change. I finally know that I am growing.
                                                                    Student

Looking back over the previous weeks' experience offers a possibility of integration, acceptance, and growth. We recommend highly that after every major chapter of this workbook, you look back over your comments in the logs and discussion pages. Looking back allows you to organize your experience. As you review the previous weeks' experiences, you may note that significant changes have occurred. These can include increased awareness of more subtle cues of tension; recognition of helpful and destructive life patterns; reduction or disappearance of symptoms, such as tension headaches, migraine, or insomnia; and even an enhanced appreciation of the remarkable self-healing potential intrinsic in each of us.

Instructions for Writing a Summary Paper for Students

After having practiced a series of the exercises, write a summary paper (three to five pages) about your experiences. Write these papers after **Dynamic Relaxation** (Practice 8); **Cognitive Balance** (Practice 12), and **Self-Healing Through Imagery and Behavior Change** (Practice 14). Reflect back over the previous practices by rereading your **Log**

Sheets, Question sheets, and **Discussion and Conclusions** sheets. In these papers address some of the following concerns:

1. What was your experience with the different practices?
2. How did each practice deepen different components of your self?
3. What benefits did you observe as a result?
4. What common patterns underlay your experiences?
5. What difficulties or challenges did you encounter, and how did you cope with them?
6. In what ways were the small group discussions helpful?
7. What have you learned about yourself through the practice of these techniques?
8. If you could do it over again (repeat the practices), what would you do differently?
9. What have you learned that you will apply to the next practice?

Chapter 2

Dynamic Regeneration[1]

The bow too tensely strung is easily broken.

Publilius Syrus

Human beings, once they advance from crawling on all fours to walking on two, no longer need regress to a limping posture once they become older. That is to say, the bodily decrepitude presumed under the myth of aging is not inevitable. It is, by and large, both avoidable and reversible.

Thomas Hanna

ᔥ Introduction to Dynamic Regeneration

First comes awareness of how much we abuse our bodies. Then comes compassion, then behavior change. Compassion and gentleness are healing.

Dynamic regeneration is the ability to, at will, consciously relax, let go of tension, and allow the body's innate healing and rebuilding to occur. It is a balance of the work/rest cycle inherent in nature. Taking time to consciously regenerate helps us to perform at our peak without depleting our vital stores of energy—mental, emotional, physical, and spiritual. The basis of dynamic regeneration can be found in progressive relaxation

Progressive Relaxation

Edmund Jacobson (1970, 1974), a noted physician introduced progressive relaxation, a graded series of muscle tensing and releasing exercises for the learning of profound

---

1. We use the term *Dynamic Regeneration*, which implies restoring, rather than the more common term *Dynamic Relaxation*, which implies just letting go. Many people want to not only to release tension, they also desire to regenerate, which helps them perform at a higher, optimum level. Athletes and business executives use the term *Dynamic Regeneration* in their peak performance practices.

muscular and mental relaxation (Bernstein, Borkovec, Hazlett-Stevens, 2000). Jacobson's premise was that by voluntarily relaxing the muscles we can, in fact, slow down the activity of the sympathetic nervous system, which is responsible for nervous tension, the fight-or-flight response, or the freeze response. When the sympathetic nervous system is quiet, the parasympathetic becomes more dominant, allowing the heart rate and blood pressure to go down, blood vessels to dilate, the internal organs to relax, and restorative body processes to take place. "If you relax your skeletal muscles sufficiently (those over which you have control), the internal muscles tend to relax likewise... Excessive tension...in the visceral muscles depends more or less upon the presence of excessive tension in the skeletal muscles." (Jacobson, 1976, p. 158) Thus, control over processes that we tend to think of as involuntary, such as pulse rate and blood pressure, becomes possible.

Over-fatigued and nervous people lose the natural ability to relax and, in fact, do not know which muscles are tense. With practice, the ability to consciously identify and let go of unnecessary tension can be relearned. The goal at first is to learn how to relax so deeply that even residual tension is gone. When residual tension has been relaxed away, "mental and emotional activity dwindle or disappear for brief periods" (Jacobson, 1976, p. 155). The exercises then progress gradually from the ability to achieve deep relaxation voluntarily while lying down or sitting comfortably to the ability to recognize and eliminate unnecessary muscle tension during everyday activities. Ultimately, relaxation becomes a more habitual state than tension.

Since it was first introduced, many modifications have been made to Jacobson's technique. The original method called for a week of daily practice in relaxing each muscle group (e.g., the right wrist). Our modification of Jacobson's exercises, which we call Dynamic Relaxation,[2] includes larger numbers of muscle groups and incorporates some breathing and visualization techniques as well as the tensing and releasing.

Beginning Your Exploration

In learning dynamic relaxation, it is helpful to have a skilled trainer guide you through the scripts the first time. A trainer may also lead the group discussion, scan log sheets, and observe participants during sessions for unusual physiological or psychological reactions. Another option is for the trainer to use surface electromyography recording and biofeedback to confirm and monitor your ability to relax selected muscle groups. If you are learning these scripts on your own, monitor yourself for unusual reactions and see the section **Some Precautions** in Chapter 1.

The following exercise provides an introductory experience in the basic processes, tensing and releasing muscles, involved in dynamic relaxation. Have someone read the script out loud to you or record it on a tape in your own voice. As you listen, allow your body to respond to the suggestions.

---

2. We borrowed the term dynamic relaxation from Joel Levey's book *The Fine Arts of Relaxation, Concentration and Meditation* (London: Wisdom, 1987).

Choose a comfortable position. Close your eyes. Bend your hand back at the wrist with your fingers pointing upward. Hold this position for 5 to 10 seconds. Check that you are not tightening any other part of your body; check your shoulders and jaw.[3] Are you breathing comfortably? Bring your attention to your forearm. Observe the sensations of tightening. What are they? Mentally describe the sensations in the present tense without judgment. If your attention drifts away, bring it back to your forearm. All at once, completely release the tension that holds your fingers and hand upright. Let gravity pull your hand down; do not actively put it down. Let your hand and arm relax for at least 20 seconds. Relaxing is not doing. Observe the sensations of relaxation (letting go). What are they? How do they differ from those of tightening? If you did not feel any sensations, hold the muscle tight until you feel something, such as pain or discomfort. If you find it difficult to let go, try the exercise after a sauna, hot bath, or a massage.

When you did the exercise, did you notice that you tightened other muscles in addition to the one that you intended to tighten? Did you hold your breath? Did you keep your attention on your arm or did your attention drift (e.g., thoughts such as, *What am I having for lunch? I need to call Anne-Marie,* or *This is silly!*)? If your attention wandered, did you gently bring it back?

The underlying goals of progressive relaxation training are to master the ability to selectively tense and relax muscles, develop awareness of unnecessary muscle tension, and to train the mind to hold gentle passive attention. The effects of relaxation can be experienced when you do the **Concept Exercise: Half Relaxation.** In this exercise, each time you are asked to tense a muscle, avoid tensing other muscles. Tense for about 10 seconds and when you are asked to relax, let go completely and immediately of the all the tension. Allow about 20 seconds for the relaxation while being aware of the changes occurring in the different body areas. If your attentions drifts, just bring it back. In the script, the dots (...) indicate a short pause to allow time to sense the experience. Again, either have someone read aloud or tape record this script for best results.

Concept Exercise: Half-Relaxation

Stand comfortably with your arms hanging at your sides. Gently walk in place and notice how your joints feel. Sense the experience of balance... Then sit comfortably with your hands on your lap and your eyes closed, allowing your body to relax into the chair... Gently bend your right hand upward at the wrist and point your index finger toward the ceiling. Continue to breathe slowly. Allow you left arm, neck, shoulders, and legs to remain relaxed... Let your right hand relax and

---

3. Use surface electromyographic monitoring and feedback to help identify unconscious and unintentional tightening of muscles.

drop to your thigh... Press your right wrist onto your right thigh while your legs, buttocks, neck and shoulders stay relaxed and you continue to breathe... Let go and relax..... While continuing to breathe and keeping your face, neck and shoulders, legs and buttocks relaxed, lift your right hand and arm about 6 inches up from your thigh and make a tight fist. Feel the tension in the muscles of your forearm while your neck and jaw remain relaxed...Let go and relax (allow your right arm and hand to just drop onto your right thigh)... Now roll your right shoulder forward while you continue to breathe. Relax your buttocks, legs, jaw, eyes and neck... Let go and relax... Pull your right shoulder down while continuing to breathe, keeping your left shoulder and arm relaxed and your legs and back relaxed.... Let go and relax... Pull your right shoulder backward while you continue to breathe; keep your back relaxed... Let go and relax... Raise your right shoulder to your right ear while keeping your neck, face, eyes, jaw, legs and feet relaxed... Let go and relax... Be aware of the sensations in your right arm from the shoulder to the fingertips...

Now bring your attention to your right leg and foot. While continuing to breathe and keeping your left leg and foot relaxed, press your right heel down and backward into the floor... Let go and relax... While keeping your right heel on the floor, flex your right ankle and curl your toes toward your right knee. Keep your abdomen, back, neck and shoulders, arms and left leg relaxed... Let go and relax... Rotate your right foot inward so that it points toward the left and notice the pulling in your leg and hip. Continue to breathe and keep your eyes, jaw and the rest of your body relaxed... Let go and relax... Now, rotate your right foot outward so that your toes point to the right, while keeping your left leg, buttocks and the rest of your body relaxed... Let go and relax... Point your right toes down while continuing to breathe and keeping your shoulders, back, and arms relaxed... Let go and relax...

Now lift your right foot a few inches from the floor and draw circles in the air with your foot, rotating it slowly at the ankle. As you do this, keep your left leg, abdomen, neck and shoulders, jaw and eyes relaxed.... As you rotate feel the muscles in your right leg tightening and letting go... Then rotate your foot in the opposite direction while continuing to breathe... Stop rotating and let go and relax (just let your foot drop to the floor)... Notice the sensations in your right leg as it is relaxing...

Now lift your right hand a few inches from your thigh and rotate your hand around the wrist. As you rotate, keep your legs, abdomen, neck and shoulders, jaw and eyes relaxed. Rotate slowly as if your fingers are inscribing a circle... As you rotate, feel the muscles in your right forearm tightening and letting go... Then rotate in the opposite direction while continuing to breathe... Stop rotating and let go and relax (just let your hand drop to your lap)... Notice the sensations in your right arm and hand as they relax...

Imagine that each time you exhale you can allow the exhaled air to flow through your right arm and right leg so that the air flows out of your right hand and right foot... Continue sensing and being aware of your right arm and hand and right leg and foot...

Now compare the sensations between the left and right side of your body (arms and legs). Which side feels heavier, the right or the left? Which side is lighter? Which side feels more alive? Which side feels more streaming? Which shoulder is wider? Which foot feels further away from your hips? Which hand feels warmer? Which fingers and toes have a presence of a pulse? ...

Now gently stand up and with your eyes closed, feel your balance. Are you leaning more to one side or the other? Begin very gently to walk in place... Which joints feel looser, more oiled—the right or the left? Gently sit down.

Note: If you feel unbalanced at this time, quickly tighten your left side of your body and hold... Let go and relax.

Observations: *When people compare the right and left side of their bodies at the end of this exercise, almost all notice a significant difference between the two sides. Most commonly, the right side feels much looser, more relaxed, sometimes heavier, warmer and more alive. At the same time, when they stood up and walked in place, the right-sided joints felt much smoother. Notice the significant positive effects of a short relaxation practice. It is not surprising that, when these skills are practiced over a longer time period, many people report significant improvement in their health, such as reduction in hypertension, improvement in sleep, and less anxiety.*

⑨ Guidelines for Getting Started on Relaxation Exercises

The scripts in this section lead you through the steps for learning dynamic relaxation and diaphragmatic breathing. Each script is to be practiced once each day for a week. You may either memorize these scripts, have a friend guide you through them, or tape record the scripts and play them back during your practice. Tape recording the script and then listening to it tends to lead to the best results. After each daily practice, note your experiences on the appropriate **Log Sheet**, and at the end of each week, review your experiences and answer the **Questions**. Then meet with your group and complete the **Discussion and Conclusions** sheet.

Helpful hints offered by previous participants:

◆ If possible, approach the exercises without expectations—just curiosity.

◆ View the practice time as a reward or "time out for me," not a task.

◆ Don't push yourself to do it "right." Let go of performance issues.

◆ If you are having trouble with a portion of the exercise, modify or omit that part.

◆ At first, try varying the time and place and setting to find what works best for you; try doing it away from home, too. Experiment! After you discover what works well, stay with a standard time and place so that you form a positive habit.

◆ To get into the right mood, begin by recalling a memory of a pleasant experience.

◆ The hardest part may be setting aside 20 to 30 minutes a day for yourself. Remember, you're worth it! You're forming a new, life-enhancing habit. If your mind wanders, visualize each part of the body relaxing as you do the exercises; and be very aware of internal feelings as well. Especially, feel your abdomen expanding and contracting with each breath. If motivation is a problem, give yourself little rewards just for doing the practice each day.

◆ Anticipate possible problems doing relaxation at home or at work. Then develop an alternative plan that you can implement if the problems occur.

◆ If you dislike working with tapes, memorize the script instead. This will be handy in helping you to generalize the skills later.

◆ Create a ritual. Some people light a candle or incense.

◆ To help set the mood, you might want to listen to soft, soothing music (classical or new age); then, later the music will be a conditioned cue for relaxation.

◆ Have a confidant, or buddy, to share your relaxation experiences with. Do it with your roommate or partner. Guide them through it. Be sure to make use of the people in your discussion group. Your input may help someone else and, similarly, you may find solutions and reassurance. Remember, practicing relaxation exercises is a new experience. Be gentle to yourself.

◆ Be aware of and acknowledge which part of your body holds most chronic tension, and spend extra time with that part. Imagine that you are exhaling through tight muscles; as you gently blow, you can see light filtering through the relaxed muscle fibers.

◆ Tailor the end of the script for yourself: If you want a quick energy boost, give yourself some energizing suggestions; if you want to go to sleep soon, give yourself some quieting suggestions.

◆ You can enhance your relaxation by taking a hot bath before, during, or after the practice. Or start out with some gentle stretches or shake out your arms and legs.

◆ Make a note on the scripts of the parts you find helpful. You can use these parts to create your own script later on (see **Creating Your Own Relaxation Script: Practice 7** in Chapter 2).

Optional and highly recommended: Use Surface Electromyography to confirm relaxation of the intended muscles or reveal tightening of unnecessary muscles.

Record the muscle tension and relaxation with surface electromyography (sEMG), which monitors the actual muscle tension. Often, we think that we are relaxed except that, without knowing, we tighten muscles other than those intended. By recording and receiving feedback of the muscle activity, we can learn to feel and then know when our muscles are either relaxed or when they are slightly tense. The sEMG feedback can identify inappropriate muscle tightening (differential relaxation—inhibition of dysponesis) and confirm that the muscles have relaxed (rapid relaxation after minimal tightening). For example, when working at the computer most people are unaware that they tighten their shoulders (upper trapezius and anterior deltoid) as shown in Figure 2.1. They become aware of this unnecessary tension only when shown the sEMG readings and then learn to work without the tension with the aid of the feedback (see Peper and Gibney, 2000, *Healthy Computing with Muscle Biofeedback*).

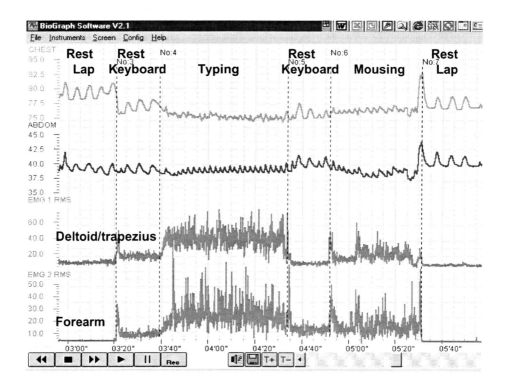

Figure 2.1. Physiological recording of chest and abdomen breathing patterns and muscle tension of the neck and shoulder (Deltoid/trapezius) and forearm during typing and mousing. The subject was completely unaware that, during typing and mousing, his neck and shoulders tightened and his breathing rate increased.

⑨ POSSIBLE PROBLEMS AND SOLUTIONS WHILE PRACTICING RELAXATION

Before commencing the practice, read through the following list of problems that commonly occur during practice and their suggested solutions. If you encounter any of the following problems, refer back to this section.

1. *Muscle cramps.* Stop tightening the muscle when you begin to sense pain or cramping; massage or move the cramped muscle while keeping the rest of your body relaxed.

2. *Laughter or feeling self-conscious.* Practice in private, or just let feelings be and return your attention to practice.

3. *Difficulty maintaining attention.* Describe changing sensations out loud during tension and relaxing; refocus your attention on the sensations.

4. *Ruminating over thoughts.* Write down your thoughts and concerns before you do the practices. By writing them down, you can be reassured that they will not be lost. Or notice the thought and let it go. Schedule a time during the day to review these ruminating thoughts so that you give focused attention to the task. When relaxing, *relax*; when thinking or ruminating, *think* and *contemplate*.

5. *Sleepiness.* Do exercises at different time of day; get enough sleep, and practice while sitting up or for shorter periods of time.

6. *Experience of body parts changing, for example, becoming disassociated or increasing in size.* Allow experience to continue, as this indicates relaxation is occurring; if necessary, open eyes to check out the body part.

7. *Uncomfortable emotion such as anger or sadness arising.* If the emotion is not too threatening, allow yourself to experience it without judgment. This is the body's way of releasing previously unconscious feelings that have been locked into the soma (mind/body awareness and process). Another strategy is to focus upon the breath in order to breathe through the emotion. Sharing the emotions that came up for you with others may also be helpful; often you will discover that you are not alone. If none of the above solutions work for you, you may also want to experiment with a shortened relaxation session; that is, do just half of a script at a given time.

8. *Family members don't understand or accept what you are doing, ridicule you, or bother you during the practice.* Do not keep your relaxation practices a secret from your family, thinking they won't understand. Explain to them, as best you can, what you are doing and why. Invite them to try it with you. Let them know of any positive benefits you are experiencing. Alleviate their fears (if any); some people feel threatened by new behavior in their loved ones and need reassurance that you haven't "gone off the deep end." Share the scientific data on relaxation as one means of stress reduction and health promotion. Also, ask your partner to make sure that your children or pets don't interrupt you. Note: In rare cases, distrust and fear from family

members may interfere with practicing relaxation. If you find this to be so, do them when you are alone, or establish a safe place away from home where you can practice, such as in your car at a quiet park.

9. *Overwhelming emotions, pain, frightening, or excessive reactions.* Stop doing the exercise for a while, then resume with caution. Or seek professional consultation.

✆ DYNAMIC RELAXATION: PRACTICE 2

Hardest Trust

Rumination carries on for precise seconds.
Then a tidal shift,
Mind anticipates for so many more:
A tangled compound worry of cause
to effects to a new cause for each and on.

Then try to trust.
"Let go," the three or four remembered voices
and two or three remembered pairs of hands
tell you all at once, then each in turn.
Let go, you feel then
Trust appears fleetingly of itself,
And then you try it out of itself again.

Rocking back and forth in and out of try,
Out of was, out of will be,
From each to the other, only glimpsing of now.

Trust, again building on itself from step to step,
Moves in and out gently
From back then to someday led by try.
And then, finally,
The balancing point.
Perfect, effortless, for this moment
That does not exist as a moment,
This is present as we don't recognize it—
This is peace.

LESLI FULLERTON

You may complete the dynamic relaxation exercises either lying down or sitting in a chair. If your position inhibits the tightening and letting go of a muscle group or if the directions do not feel quite appropriate or clear, modify the script to make it appropriate for you. Remember the following general points:

1. Each day, allot 20 to 30 minutes for the practice. This time period may be perceived as a "time-out" period during which the body/mind is allowed to relax and regenerate.

2. Keep your attention on the muscle group being tightened and relaxed.

3. Breathe easily and smoothly throughout.

4. Tighten only muscles that you are being directed to tighten, letting the rest of your body stay relaxed.

5. Have a confidant, or buddy, with whom to share and discuss your experiences of dynamic relaxation.

6. Complete your log notes immediately after your practice.

7. Keep a journal to record dreams or other significant insights as they come up.

8. Go over the **Checklist for Relaxation Practice** and set the stage for uninterrupted practice.

Checklist for Relaxation Practice

___ Phone unplugged or turned off (if possible)
___ Pet(s) out of the room
___ Note on door or family/roommate(s) informed
___ Lighting turned low/drapes pulled
___ Temperature adjusted for comfort or sweater or blanket ready, if cool
___ Appropriate pillows for knee and head support
___ Bladder emptied
___ Tape player and pre-recorded tape ready
___ Shoes removed
___ Clothing loosened (especially at neck and waist)
___ Glasses removed
___ Log sheet and pen ready to record before and after notes
___ Clock or watch within view
___ Assume an attitude of passive attention, "Let anything happen that will happen."

Write down your personal ritual steps here. (These are the same behaviors you do each time you begin the relaxation so that they become the conditioned cue for relaxing. See **Development of a Personal Ritual for Relaxation** in Chapter 1):

_____

_____

_____

_____

_____

⑤ DYNAMIC RELAXATION SCRIPT

Begin by doing your personal ritual to initiate the conditioned shift towards relaxation. Remember, the important thing is not to be concerned about doing it "right;" just follow the instructions and observe with a gentle awareness what is going on in your body. Get into a comfortable position. Be sure your belt and pants are loose, your legs are uncrossed, your glasses and watch are off, and your shoulders are loose (gently shake them up and down once or twice if you feel tense). If you wear hard contacts, you may want to remove them. Each time you are asked to tense a muscle, imagine that you are putting all your body tension into that muscle **(tense for about 10 seconds)**. Avoid tensing other muscles while continuing to breathe. When you are asked to relax, let go completely and immediately of all the tension **(relax for 20 seconds)**. Focus your awareness on the sensations in your muscles.

The dots (...) in the script indicate a short pause allowing time to sense the experience.

With your hands on your lap, if sitting, or resting at your sides, if lying down, gently let your eyes close. Then bend your right wrist so that your fingers point up. Bend more and more, tightening the muscles fully... Continue to breathe slowly and deeply from your belly as you bend your wrist. While continuing to breathe, allow your lips to be slightly parted... gently exhale through your mouth, whispering the sound "haaah"... Let the rest of your body stay relaxed... Observe the sensations of tightening. Hold the contraction for about ten seconds... Let go and relax... Observe the contrast in feeling between the bent wrist and the relaxed arm... stay with this relaxation... If your attention wanders to other thoughts, just bring it back to the muscles being relaxed.

Now bend both wrists. Observe the sensations of tightening... keep breathing slowly and diaphragmatically... let the rest of your body stay soft and relaxed... Let go and relax... Observe the sensations and feelings of letting go... If your attention wanders to other things, gently bring it back to the sensations in your arm... and stay with the sensations...

Now bend (flex) your arms by bringing the wrists to your shoulders and hold. At the same time allow your fingers to stay relaxed... observe the sensations of tightening... keep breathing ... slowly... and deeply... Be sure your neck, your jaw, and the rest of your body are soft and relaxed... Let go and relax and let your arms plop to your sides or onto your lap and stay with the sensations of letting go and relaxing....

Straighten your arms and hold them parallel to the floor so that you tense your triceps muscles (the muscles in the back of your upper arms)... let your hands, legs, and jaw stay relaxed. Observe the sensations of tightening ... Let go and relax by allowing your arms to drop to your sides or into your lap... relax all over... Notice the heaviness and warmth spreading down your arms... feel your arms becoming heavier and heavier as you relax more and more...

Frown hard while the rest of your body stays relaxed.... Let go and relax... Then raise your eyebrows. Be sure your tongue, jaw, and neck stay relaxed, soft, and loose... keep breathing slowly and deeply... observe the sensation of tightening... Let go and relax... let your brow be smooth... observe the sensations of relaxation...

Tighten your eyes... tighten the muscles deep in your eyes... tighten the facial muscles around your eyes while your tongue, jaw, back of your neck, and the rest of your body stay relaxed.... Let go and relax your eyes and keep them gently closed... observe the sensations of relaxation....

Clench your jaw and teeth... notice the tension in your jaw while your neck and shoulders and buttocks stay relaxed. Keep breathing slowly and easily.... Let go and relax. Part your lips slightly as you exhale... let the air flow out of your mouth in a soft whispered "hahhhhhhhh"....

Tighten your neck while keeping your face, arms, legs, and abdomen relaxed. Continue to breathe slowly and easily. Feel the tension in your neck... Let go and let your jaw stay relaxed...

Raise your shoulders to your ears... let your face, neck, and the rest of your body stay relaxed... notice the contrast in how your shoulders feel and the rest of your body.... Let go and relax. Let the relaxation deepen and flow into your back, neck, throat, jaw, and face... let it go deeper and deeper... feel the force of gravity pulling on your body...

Take a very deep breath and then hold your breath while your forehead, eyes, jaw, hands, buttocks, legs, and feet stay relaxed. Notice the tension in your abdomen, chest, and shoulders. Allow your shoulders to let go and relax, while still holding your breath... Let go and relax. Exhale and feel the release... Then let the breathing go in and out normally.... Notice that with each exhalation, you feel more and more relaxed... let your chest be loose and soft as you breathe out... (focus only on the exhalation, allow inhalation to occur by itself).

Take another deep breath... hold your breath while you allow your neck and shoulders to be relaxed... Let go and relax and exhale. Feel yourself let go of the tension... let the relaxation spread to your shoulders, neck, back, and arms....

Tighten your stomach as if you were to receive a blow there... make it solid while relaxing your face, jaw, neck, shoulders, arms, and legs... Let go and relax and notice the well-being that accompanies your relaxation...

Suck your stomach in and hold it... Let go and relax and allow your breathing to go easily in... and out. Notice your whole lower abdomen expanding as you inhale... and flattening as you exhale. Allow your whole body to relax as you exhale... Feel the heaviness in your arms and legs...

Now, arch your lower back so there is a space between your back and the chair or floor... feel the tension along your spine and back while your legs and the rest of your body stay relaxed... Let go and relax. Feel your spine and back sinking into the chair or mattress. Feel your whole upper body relaxing and getting heavier...

Tighten your buttocks while your abdomen and the rest of your body stay relaxed... keep breathing slowly and gently... Let go and relax. Feel your buttocks sinking into the chair or mattress...

Press your knees and ankles together and curl your toes while your face, shoulders, abdomen, and arms stay relaxed... Let go and relax. Allow your knees and ankles to separate. Feel the heaviness in your legs, ankles, and feet...

Point your toes downward and stretch them away from you as you continue to breathe while keeping the neck, shoulders, and face relaxed... Let go and relax.... Gently lift your feet slightly from the floor while continuing to breathe.... Let go and relax, allowing your feet and legs to drop down...

Gently attend to the movement in your abdomen... Note how your stomach goes out as you inhale and in as you exhale... Let your attention stay with the movement of your abdomen for a few minutes and if your attention wanders, just gently bring it back to the sensations of movement in your abdomen...

Continue until you feel ready to stop. Then, take a deep breath, slowly sit up, stretch, and gently open your eyes. Observe how you feel and how you perceive your environment. Do you feel quieter, more peaceful and do you notice a difference in brightness, clarity, vividness, aliveness, and depth of vision?

Optional explorations: After a few days of practice, try Dynamic Relaxation before or after an activity, such as meditation, prayer, or exercise; observe its effects. Many people report that, if they practiced Dynamic Relaxation in advance, they felt that they went more deeply into prayer and/or meditation. Alternatively, many report that practice of relaxation after exercise brings a sense of rapid regeneration.

Each day, after you have gone through the script, complete **Log Sheet: Dynamic Relaxation: Practice 2**. If you experience an incongruous response or an "extreme" physical or psychological response, refer to section **Important Variables to Optimize Relaxation Training** in Chapter 1. At the end of the week, answer **Questions: Dynamic Relaxation: Practice 2**. Meet with your group and complete **Group Discussion and Conclusions: Dynamic Relaxation: Practice 2.**

Name: _____ Date: _____

Log Sheet: Dynamic Relaxation: Practice 2

After each practice, describe (a) the practice situation (your mood, the place, your physical position, etc.) and (b) your physical and emotional experiences both during and directly following your practice.

Day 1   a. _____
Date _____   _____
                  _____
                  _____

               b. _____
                  _____
                  _____
                  _____

Day 2   a. _____
Date _____   _____
                  _____
                  _____

               b. _____
                  _____
                  _____
                  _____

Day 3   a. _____
Date _____   _____
                  _____
                  _____

               b. _____
                  _____
                  _____
                  _____

Day 4   a. _____
Date _____   _____
                _____
                _____

             b. _____
                _____
                _____
                _____

Day 5   a. _____
Date _____   _____
                _____
                _____

             b. _____
                _____
                _____
                _____

Day 6   a. _____
Date _____   _____
                _____
                _____

             b. _____
                _____
                _____
                _____

Day 7   a. _____
Date _____   _____
                _____
                _____

             b. _____
                _____
                _____
                _____

Describe the ritual by which you begin the relaxation practice.

_____
_____
_____

Name:_____ Date:_____

Questions: Dynamic Relaxation: Practice 2

1. What benefits occurred as a result of your practice?

_____

_____

_____

2. Did your experiences with Dynamic Relaxation vary during the sessions? If so, how did these differences relate to the conditions under which you practiced? (e.g., It was difficult to maintain attention during practice at the end of the day or I became sleepy.)

_____

_____

_____

3. Did you notice that you held your breath and/or tightened muscles other than the intended muscle during your practice? Which ones? How did your ability to selectively tighten muscles change over the week?

_____

_____

_____

4. What problems/challenges, if any, occurred?

_____

_____

_____

5. How did you solve the problems/challenges?

_____

_____

_____

6. If you could do the practice over, how would you do it differently?

_____

_____

_____

Name: _____ Date: _____

Group Discussion and Conclusions: Dynamic Relaxation: Practice 2

1. What benefits did the group members notice as a result of the practices?

   _____

   _____

   _____

   _____

2. What rituals used by other participants might you adapt for your own use?

   _____

   _____

   _____

   _____

3. What difficulties were encountered and how did the group members solve them?

   _____

   _____

   _____

   _____

4. How did the experiences that occurred during and following Dynamic Relaxation vary among group members? Was there any correlation between these differences and age, gender, medical background, previous experience with relaxation techniques, etc.?

   _____

   _____

   _____

   _____

5. Topics or concerns to discuss with the instructor:

   _____

   _____

   _____

   _____

List your group members:

_____   _____

_____   _____

_____   _____

_____   _____

☸ BREATHING—THE MIND-BODY BRIDGE: PRACTICE 3[4]

Breath is the bridge that connects life to consciousness, which unites your body to your thoughts.

THICH NHAT HANH

Show me how you breathe, and I'll show you how you live...

ANONYMOUS

Consider the following words and expressions: don't breathe a word, don't waste your breath, breathtaking, sigh of relief, breath of fresh air, with bated breath, breathless, long-winded, to breathe life into, the breath of life. Our common vocabulary is imbued with expressions, such as these, that acknowledge that we link our emotions and breathing.

Explore three different breathing patterns and the corresponding emotions in the following **Concept Exercise: Fear, Tenderness and Laughter**.

Concept Exercise: Fear, Tenderness and Laughter[5]

Evoke the feeling of fear. While sitting on the edge of your chair, inhale sharply through your open mouth. Hold most of this breath and begin breathing shallowly and irregularly with your eyes wide open. Tense your body and lean slightly backward, as if trying to avoid an attack. Breathe for one minute in this pattern and observe how you feel. If this feels somewhat familiar as when you work at the computer and/or drive your car, or if you notice a slight increase in your usual discomfort symptoms, then this type of posture may increase your irritation.

Reverse this fearful bearing by breathing with tenderness. Breathe very evenly through your nose while smiling slightly with your eyes open and eyelids relaxed. Tilt your head slightly to one side, keeping your body very relaxed. Take 10 slow breaths in this pattern. Breathe this way—with tenderness—many times during the day.

Energize yourself with laughter. Inhale sharply through your nose and exhale through your mouth in staccato bursts of breath. As you exhale, stretch your lips horizontally drawing the corners of your mouth up and back. At the same time, keep your eyes semi-closed, your body very relaxed, and your head hanging loosely backwards. Repeat this breathing pattern while vocalizing, "Ha, Ha, Ha, Ha, Ha" until you experience a few chuckles.

---

4. Adapted from E. Peper. (1990). *Breathing for Health*, Montreal: Thought Technology.
5. Adapted from the work by Bloch, Lemeignan & Aguilera, 1991.

Observations: Most people quickly experience specific emotions when they breathe in these prescribed patterns. Obviously, some may find it easier to evoke one emotion with breathing than another. It does suggest that breathing is a powerful expressive agent as well as modulator of emotions.

Breathing is an essential process for human life. Breath patterns influence our physiology, our psychological state, and our unconscious. We are, however, most often unaware of our breathing. Breathing is under both conscious and unconscious control, and thus provides a bridge between the two and a way of learning that mind and body are not separate. Breath (*qi, chi, prana*) in many philosophical systems is considered the vital link to energy, awareness, emotions, and transcendence. Reflect on the double meaning of the words *inspire* and *expire*.

Because breathing reflects both your emotional and physical states, quieting your breathing will soothe your emotions and mental processes as well as calm your body. Many performers, including athletes and musicians, use diaphragmatic breathing as an essential part of their training to perform at peak level. Diaphragmatic breathing will affect all areas of your life, some subtle and some very obvious.

The Physiology of Breathing

Breathing is a natural process that occurs without conscious control. Babies and young children usually breathe effortlessly. Most of the movement associated with their breathing occurs primarily in the lower abdominal area: As they exhale, the abdomen goes in slightly; when they inhale the abdomen expands outward and to the sides just like a Buddha statue. Most adults, however, no longer breathe in this healthy pattern. Instead of breathing diaphragmatically, they hold their abdomen rigid ("stand-up straight and hold in your stomach!") or slouch, while using a significant amount of effort to inhale with the scalene and upper trapezius muscles (accessory muscles of breathing).

The major muscle involved in proper breathing is called the diaphragm. This is a dome-shaped muscle located beneath the lungs and above the abdomen. In order to inhale, the diaphragm descends and flattens as the lower ribs widen. This activity displaces (pushes down on) the liquid contents of the abdomen and, thereby, creates a larger space in the chest. As this space is created, the pressure in the atmosphere exceeds the pressure in the chest and air flows in to balance these pressures, as shown in Figure 2.2. To exhale, the diaphragm must relax and be raised (pushed) upward, compressing the air in the chest and allowing the air to flow out. Thus, inhalation requires that the abdominal area relax and expand, while exhalation requires the abdominal area to decrease in diameter. The chest and shoulders should remain relaxed throughout the breathing cycle, although, near the end of the inhalation phase, there is some chest expansion.

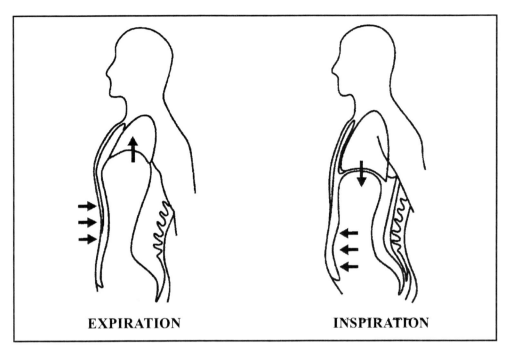

EXPIRATION   **INSPIRATION**

Figure 2.2. Breathing while sitting or standing.

Breathing While Lying Down Versus Sitting Up.

The muscular efforts involved in breathing are different depending on whether you are lying down or sitting up. When you are lying down on your back, gravity acts to push your abdomen in (down). Therefore, when you inhale your diaphragm descends, which pushes your abdomen outward. You may perceive this as effort. Exhaling is effortless because gravity pushes your abdomen down and, thereby, pushes your diaphragm upward into your chest as shown in Figure 2.3. When you are sitting or standing, a slight effort is required to pull the abdomen in so that the diaphragm is pushed back up at end of the exhalation. Inhalation in the vertical position (standing or sitting) is much more effortless, since you just relax the abdominal wall and allow the diaphragm to go down.

DYSFUNCTIONAL (UNHEALTHY) BREATHING PATTERNS

I found that I would really allow myself to get caught up in the feeling of the moment; it was at these times that I would stop breathing and feel my body tense up. I was able, by the end of the practice, to focus in those moments of fear or pain and to breathe them through, instead of keeping them inside myself to fester. I found that this exercise has also helped my self-confidence.

STUDENT

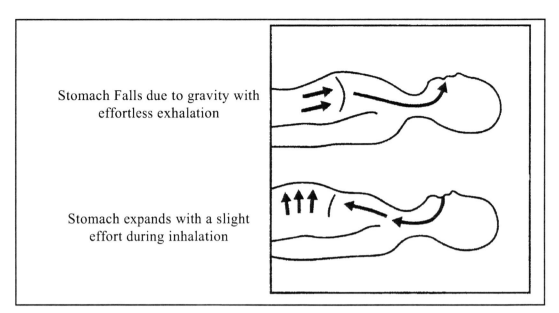

Stomach Falls due to gravity with effortless exhalation

Stomach expands with a slight effort during inhalation

Figure 2.3. Breathing while lying down.

There are two major breath patterns associated with a sense of breathlessness and/or illness: thoracic (chest) breathing and shallow rapid breathing (hyperventilation). Both patterns occur with episodic breath holding, incomplete exhalation, and sighs. These patterns may be very obvious or quite subtle. Even in the subtlest forms, these breathing patterns can be harmful to health as illustrated in the **Concept Exercise: Incomplete Exhalation.**

Concept Exercise: Incomplete Exhalation

Sit comfortably in your chair and continue to breathe as you were doing before except reduce your exhalation to ONLY 70% of every inhalation. This means that however much you inhaled, exhale only 70% of the inhaled air. Repeat this 70% exhalation for every breath. If you need to sigh, just do that and then continue to breathe again by exhaling only 70% of the previous inhaled air. Breathe in this pattern for the next 45 seconds, then relax and breathe normally.

Optional: While practicing this breathing, slightly hold in your abdomen.

Observations: *More than 98% of people who do this breathing pattern report uncomfortable feelings and sensations, which include lightheadedness; dizziness; anxiety or panic; tension in the neck, back, shoulders, or face; nervous sensations; heart pounding or increased rate; agitation and jitteriness; feelings of flushing and tingling; breathlessness; gasping and starving for air; upper chest*

> *pressure; and increased symptoms (e.g., headache, joint pain, increased discomfort of an ongoing injury (Peper and MacHose, 1993). If just 45 seconds of breathing can begin to induce these experiences, chronic breathing dysregulation may be a significant contributor to the onset of illness. Conversely, breathing patterns that are effortless and diaphragmatic may promote health.*

Chest (thoracic) breathing includes shallow breathing punctuated by breath holding or gasping. This unconscious pattern is similar to that which is evoked by the alarm and startle reactions or fear. This means that the abdomen tightens and the person inhales into the upper chest. The physiological effects of this pattern include increased heart rate, increased blood pressure, gastrointestinal distress symptoms, asthmatic symptoms, and neck and shoulder tension as illustrated in **Concept Exercise: Threading the Needle**.

Concept Exercise: Threading the Needle.

Act out this demonstration. Sit comfortably and imagine you are holding a small needle between your thumb and index finger of your left hand and in your right hand you are holding a thin white thread. Your task is to bring the thread through the eye of the needle. Raise your hands to eye level as if holding the needle and thread. Focus all of your concentration on the needle and thread. Moisten the thread with your lips and then begin to thread it through the eye of the needle. If you miss the first time do it again.

Observation: *As you acted out threading the needle, did you hold your breath and tense your shoulders? Almost everyone who concentrates intensely becomes vigilant and tends to hold his or her breath. Breath-holding increases stability and auditory acuity, yet, when we do this chronically, we can develop neck and shoulder tension, and remain in a fight/flight/freeze pattern that is ultimately exhausting. We often trigger the same response while mousing at the computer or looking at any visual stimuli, such as computer games. One can reduce the injurious cost of this vigilance by breathing diaphragmatically.*

Habitually breathing in this pattern may foster illness. When we are learning something new, often the anxiety or fear associated with the learning situation may cause dysfunctional breathing. This breathing pattern then becomes associated (conditioned) with the newly learned behavior. For example, one participant observed that each time she wrote in shorthand, she breathed shallowly and remembered how stressful it was to learn shorthand. In your daily logs, you will be asked to observe times when you gasped or held your breath.

Chronic, shallow breathing may lead to hyperventilation that is characterized by rapid, shallow breathing with frequent sighs. When one hyperventilates, too much carbon dioxide (CO_2) is expired, which increases the alkalinity of the blood. Anxiety, phobias, dizziness, and hypertension are all associated with hyperventilation. We commonly think of hyperventilation as an acute and very noticeable state. However, we concur with the observations by the well-known British physicians Claude Lum (1976) and Peter Nixon (1997). They noted that this pattern is more covert and people hyperventilate very slightly so that they chronically blow off a little too much carbon dioxide, which, in the long term, would put their physiological system at risk. Many psychosomatic conditions could be aggravated by chronic hyperventilation as illustrated in Table 2.1 **Symptoms of Chronic Hyperventilation**.

ADVANTAGES OF DIAPHRAGMATIC BREATHING AND DISADVANTAGES OF THORACIC BREATHING

All our physiological processes are controlled by the nervous system. One branch of the nervous system, called the sympathetic nervous system (SNS), is strongly affected by

Table 2.1 Symptoms of Chronic Hyperventilation[6]
Respiratory: Asthma, tight chest, dyspnea (breathlessness), excessive sighing or yawning, dry cough, shortness of breath.
Cardiovascular: Palpitations, tachycardia (rapid heart rate), chest pain or angina, Raynaud's disease (blood vessel constriction in the hands and/or feet).
Neurological: Dizziness, faintness, migraines, numbness, intolerance of bright lights or loud noise.
Gastrointestinal: Dysphagia (difficulty in swallowing), dry throat, gas, belching, globus (lump in the throat), abdominal discomfort.
Muscular: Cramps, tremors, twitches, muscle pain.
Psychological: Tension, anxiety, phobias.
General: Fatigue, exhaustion, weakness, lack of concentration and memory, sleep disturbances, nightmares.

6. Adapted from Lum, L. C. (1976). The Syndrome of habitual chronic hyperventilation. In Hill, V (ed) *Modern Trends in Psychosomatic Medicine*. London: Butterworth, 196-230.

how we breathe. When we breathe rapidly, shallowly, and in our chests (thoracically), the SNS becomes activated. This results in increased heart rate and blood pressure, cool hands and feet, sweaty palms, and other symptoms. People who habitually breathe this way may experience a sense of panic and symptoms associated with hyperventilation; they may even increase their risk of heart attacks. People who suffer from panic attacks almost always have this breathing pattern. Even menopausal hot flashes are more common in thoracic breathers; the frequency of hot flashes can be reduced when the woman practices slower diaphragmatic breathing (Freedman & Woodward, 1992). Emotions have a profound effect on breath patterns. When we are startled, we often gasp and/or hold our breath. The startle or alarm reaction then leads to increased SNS arousal and all the physiological changes associated with that arousal.

Slow diaphragmatic breathing, on the other hand, decreases the SNS activity and encourages regeneration. Slow diaphragmatic breathing has been shown to reduce by half the occurrence of a coronary event in people who have already suffered a heart attack (van Dixhoorn et al., 1987). It also results in lower blood pressure and heart rate, warm hands and feet, a decreased sweat response, and a general sense of relaxation and well-being.

The major physiological effects associated with the different breathing patterns are listed in Table 2.2.

Table 2.2 Physiological Changes Associated With Breathing

Thoracic Breathing		Diaphragmatic Breathing
+	Heart Rate	-
+	Blood Pressure	-
+	Risk for Heart Attack	-
+	Sweat Response	-
+	Gastrointestinal Distress	-
+	Panic	-
+	Hyperventilation Syndrome	-
-	Relaxation	+
-	Peripheral Temperature	+
+	Trigger Point Activation	-
+	Scalene & Trapezius Muscle Tension	-

+ = increases
- = decreases

REMINDERS AND SUGGESTIONS

◆ Breathe "low and slow." Let your awareness be deep in your abdomen, below the navel.

◆ Eliminate "designer jeans syndrome." If you wear constricting clothing, experiment with more loosely fitting style.

◆ Do not alter the use of your medication without consulting your healthcare provider.

◆ If you feel faint as you practice any of these exercises, stop the practice. You might be breathing too fast and too deep. Allow yourself to gently focus on the very slow exhalation. To help you lengthen an exhalation, try letting the air out with a "Ssssss" sound as if exhaling through a very tiny opening. The sound itself will help to remind you to slow your breathing.

◆ Do not try too hard at any time. Practice all exercises at a 70% effort rather than 100%. The purpose is to learn at your own pace, not to be perfect.

◆ If you experience any dizziness or lightheadedness, most likely you were over-breathing. Exhale longer and slower; let the airflow be less. Imagine that as you breathe, your legs and feet contain hollow drinking straws through which the air can flow in and out.

◆ Under stress, always exhale first before taking the next breath.

◆ Do not expect instant success. Be patient. The skills to be learned may take many weeks or even months to master. When you first begin breathing diaphragmatically, you may experience a reduction of skill in some areas. For example, when you first begin to breathe diaphragmatically while speaking, it may feel awkward and impossible. Or when breathing diaphragmatically while performing music, initially you may feel distracted from the playing, and your performance may suffer. This happens because the arm/hand movements involved with playing the instrument were learned (conditioned) with thoracic breathing; you are now relearning the skill in association with the new, healthier breathing pattern. Do not be alarmed; you will find that your new skill level will exceed the previous level in time because diaphragmatic breathing helps you to release dysfunctional muscle tension and lower your stress arousal.

◆ Be gentle with yourself and remember that it is normal to have emotions surface when you slow your breathing. In rare cases, you may find that you experience strong emotions when you allow yourself to breathe diaphragmatically and relax (opening) the abdomen. This may be either an uncomfortable or a positive experience.

◆ If you have difficulty feeling the movement of breath in your abdomen, you might try looking in a mirror while breathing.

◆ To facilitate abdominal movement and reduce chest movement, lock your chest so that the breathing movement can mainly take place in your abdomen. To do this, raise your arms to chest level and cross them so that you can interlace your fingers with palms touching. Then, with interlaced fingers, reach up and behind your head as far as you comfortably can. Practice breathing in your abdomen.

◆ To deepen your awareness, take three slow diaphragmatic breaths before getting out of bed each morning while saying to yourself, "Today is a new day."

SPECIFIC INSTRUCTIONS BEFORE BEGINNING BREATHING PRACTICE

Before beginning this practice, be sure that you will have uninterrupted quiet time for at least 20 minutes in a comfortable room. This practice begins in a sitting posture and progresses to a lying down position.

For the sitting position, sit in a comfortable chair, preferably one providing good lower back support. Place both feet on the floor, with knees slightly apart. (If your feet do not touch the floor, you might put a phone book under them, or whatever is handy.) Loosen your belt or waistband and undo your zipper part way to allow plenty of breathing room.

For the lying position, choose a comfortable surface, such as a bed or a rug. Lie on your back with your feet shoulder width apart and your arms a few inches away from your body. Be sure you are comfortable; you might place one pillow under your knees for lower back support and one under your head. Have a 2 to 5-pound weight to place on your abdomen. This can be a book or a bag of rice or beans. (We recommend a plastic bag of rice or beans because it conforms to the curve of the abdomen and is less likely to slide off.) Using a weight on your abdomen is very helpful as it is easier to allow your attention to stay in your abdomen. In addition, the weight will facilitate exhalation.

As you listen to the tape, allow the suggestions to be your guidelines. Listen to your own rhythm. For example, your exhalations may be longer or shorter than suggested by the script. Many people try too hard at first. Remember, your goal is EFFORTLESS breathing and you are using breathing to help you become quiet and peaceful.

Diaphragmatic Breathing Script

Sit comfortably and begin by stroking your abdomen gently to bring your awareness there and to help you to let go of tense, tight muscles. Let your eyes close as you feel yourself stroking your abdomen... Now, place one hand over your lower abdomen and the other on your chest; breathe comfortably through your nose... Allow your hands to sense your body movements associated with breathing... What part of your body moves when you inhale and exhale? ... What do you feel? ... As you breathe out, make a very soft whispered "Haaaa" sound ... Allow your shoulders to stay relaxed...

At the end of your next exhalation, slightly pull in your abdominal wall to help you exhale a little more while whispering "Haaaa." Then let the air flow in, allowing the abdomen to widen without effort... Imagine that your lungs are located in your abdomen and that the abdomen is like a balloon that, during inhalation expands, and during exhalation deflates.... Slowly and gently inhale through your nose and exhale through your mouth whispering "Haaaa"... Notice any tension in your abdomen and let it go...

Breathe at your own rhythm, gently and slowly... Feel your abdomen moving with your hand... As you breathe out, think of pulling your abdomen in a tiny bit at the end of the exhalation. Do this for the next few breaths....

As you breathe in, feel your whole abdomen widening... the pelvis opening up... Feel the movement in the lower part of your back as you inhale... Then let the air out slowly and comfortably while whispering "Haaaa."... Continue for a few minutes...

Now, as you breathe in, imagine a large beach ball in your abdomen which is filling more and more with air as you inhale... then feel it deflating as you exhale... Imagine this for a few breaths... Notice the internal feelings with the expanding and contracting of the beach ball... Continue to breathe and feel the beach ball for a few minutes...

Now, while you continue to breathe easily, take a moment to notice how your body feels...

Then gently move to your lying down position. Lie on your back with your feet shoulder width apart and, if necessary, a pillow under your knees. Be sure that you are comfortable.... Place a 2 to 5-pound weight on your abdomen, over your navel, and simply observe what it feels like as you breathe in and out....

Feel your abdomen moving as you inhale and pushing the weight up. As you exhale feel your abdomen becoming flat as the weight pushes the air out... Now inhale and push the weight up... and as you exhale allow the weight to push the air out... Allow the air to flow evenly and slowly... As you inhale, feel the weight rising and your abdomen expanding... As you exhale, feel the weight sinking and your abdomen flattening ... Continue this breathing for a few minutes...

Become aware of how slowly you are breathing... Then gradually begin to lengthen the exhalation by silently counting to yourself... Exhaling - 2 - 3 - 4 - ... Let all the air out and then let the breath flow in easily... Let it flow slowly and comfortably... As you count, let the numbers gradually increase without any strain.... Allow the exhalation to lengthen as your body settles into peacefulness... Allow the air to flow in and out your nose for the next few minutes while you count the exhalation...

Allow your breath to relax your body. Just breathe slowly, easily... give yourself permission to let go... Let go of the counting... Just be aware of the movement in your abdomen. As you exhale, imagine the air flowing down and out your legs and feet as if they have hollow straws in them that allows the air to flow freely. As you inhale, imagine the air flowing through your head and into your abdomen... then as you exhale, imagine the air flowing down your arms and out your hands and fingers, as if they contained hollow straws through which the air flows.... On the next breath, imagine the air streaming down your legs and out your feet... Continue to breathe for the next few minutes, imagining the exhaled air flowing out through your arms and legs...

Finally, imagine yourself lying on a beach hearing the rhythmic sound of the waves... Let your breathing be like the waves... flowing in... and out... a timeless natural rhythm... a ceaseless ebb and flow.... receding and moving out toward the horizon....be one with the wave... let all tension flow away from you. Feel a warm wave of relaxation spreading through your whole body...

Allow yourself to relax a few minutes longer, just keeping your awareness on the flow of your breath as it goes in and out...

When you are ready, wiggle your fingers and toes, give yourself a gentle stretch, and open your eyes. Note your feelings of calm; allow them to go with you as you breathe effortlessly through the rest of your day.

Each day, after you have gone through the script, complete **Log Sheet: Breathing— The Mind-Body Bridge: Practice 3**. At the end of the week, answer **Questions: Breathing—The Mind-Body Bridge: Practice 3.** Meet with your group and complete **Group Discussion and Conclusions: Breathing—The Mind-Body Bridge: Practice 3.**

Name: _____ Date: _____

Log Sheet: Breathing—The Mind-Body Bridge: Practice 3

Each day describe: (a) your experience and effects of practicing the script (tape); (b) situations during your daily activities where you gasped or held your breath, such as while driving or chopping vegetables; and (c) your experience of the event or activity when you changed to slow, diaphragmatic breathing.

Day 1   a. _____
Date _____   _____
               _____

            b. _____
               _____
               _____

            c. _____
               _____
               _____

Day 2   a. _____
Date _____   _____
               _____

            b. _____
               _____
               _____

            c. _____
               _____
               _____

Day 3   a. _____
Date _____   _____
               _____

            b. _____
               _____
               _____

            c. _____
               _____
               _____

Day 4

Date _____

a. _____
_____
_____

b. _____
_____
_____
_____

c. _____
_____
_____

Day 5

Date _____

a. _____
_____
_____

b. _____
_____
_____

c. _____
_____
_____

Day 6

Date _____

a. _____
_____
_____

b. _____
_____
_____

c. _____
_____
_____

Day 7

Date _____

a. _____
_____
_____

b. _____
_____
_____

c. _____
_____
_____

Name: _____ Date: _____

Questions: Breathing—The Mind-Body Bridge: Practice 3

1. What benefits occurred as a result of your practice?

_____

_____

_____

_____

2. Under what situations did you gasp or hold your breath?

_____

_____

_____

_____

3. What challenges or problems, if any, did you experience?

_____

_____

_____

_____

4. How did you solve the problems/challenges?

_____

_____

_____

_____

5. In what ways did the shift into diaphragmatic breathing change your experience?

_____

_____

_____

_____

Name: _____   Date: _____

**Group Discussion and Conclusions: Breathing—The Mind-Body Bridge:
Practice 3**

1. What benefits did the group members notice as a result of the practices?
    _____
    _____
    _____

2. What were the common themes associated with gasping and breath-holding and what
    occurred when you shifted to diaphragmatic breathing?
    _____
    _____
    _____

3. What difficulties and or challenges did your group members experience?
    _____
    _____
    _____

4. How did the group members solve the difficulties and challenges?
    _____
    _____
    _____

5. What was the effect of shifting from thoracic breathing to diaphragmatic breathing
    during the day?
    _____
    _____
    _____

6. How did the experiences that occurred during and following the breathing practice
    vary among group members? Was there any correlation to age, gender, medical back-
    ground, or relaxation experience, such as asthma, panic attacks, yoga practice, etc.?
    _____
    _____
    _____

7. Topics or concerns to discuss with the instructor:
    _____
    _____
    _____

List your group members:

_____   _____

_____   _____

_____   _____

_____   _____

✆ Developing A Personal Relaxation Image: Practice 4

Physically creating my personal relaxation scene through watercolors was more impactful than relying solely on imagination. It became a powerful and cathartic exercise pulling up chains of strong affective associations complete with smells, sounds, and feelings that had been blocked off from childhood. These memories felt as strong in my system as certain drugs. These memories were then integrated into my practice and directly contributed to the positive results I had.

Student

I enjoyed regressing back into my childhood, playing in the rain, making paper sailboats with my brother... Placing my fingers in a bowl of water and stroking a paper sailboat enabled me to participate in the total experience... I felt tingling sensations all over my body, much like tiny bundles of energy exploding inside of me. By the end of the week the simple word "rain" could induce these sensations inside my whole being.

Student

Daydreaming! We all know how to do it and it has much in common with imagery practice. When we daydream, we can feel, sense, hear, and taste our daydream—the image almost becomes tangible. A well-developed relaxation image will, also, include colors, scents, sounds, temperature, and so forth. An image of wholeness is essential to an effective relaxation image, as illustrated in **Pavlov's Exercise**.

Pavlov's Exercise

Most of us are probably familiar with the classical conditioning experiment of Pavlov, the famous Russian physiologist. He found that he was able to teach dogs to salivate when they heard a bell ring even if no food was provided to them. Pavlov accomplished this by giving the dogs food immediately after ringing the bell for a certain period of time. Eventually, they became conditioned to expect the food with the bell and simply hearing the bell ring would induce salivation.

There is a story about Ivan Pavlov[7] that illustrates the powerful effects of imagery on our health. As an old man, he became quite ill with heart disease, and his doctors had no hope of curing him. They took his family aside and told them that the end was near. Pavlov himself, however, was not disheartened. He asked the nurse who was caring for him to bring him a bowl of warm water with a bit of mud and dirt in it. All day as he lay in bed, he dabbled one hand in the water, with a dreamy, faraway look on his face. His family was quite sure that he had taken leave of his wits and would die soon. However, the next morning he announced that he felt fine, ate a large breakfast, and sat out in the

---

7. This anecdote was adapted from a talk by Theodore Melnechuk.

sun awhile; by the end of the day, when the doctor came to check on him, there was no trace of the serious heart condition. When asked to explain what he had done, he said that he had reasoned that if he could recall a time when he was completely carefree and happy, it might have some healing benefit for him. As a young boy he used to spend his summers playing with his friends in a shallow swimming hole in a nearby river. The memory of the warm, slightly muddy water was delightful to him. With his knowledge of the power of conditioned stimuli, he decided that having a physical reminder of that water would help him to evoke that time and those blissful feelings, and bring the memories into present time. And that was how he harnessed positive emotions to bring about his healing.

CONDITIONED BEHAVIORS

Each of us performs many conditioned behaviors every day. Some of these behaviors can have significant implications for our health and wellness. For example, some components of certain allergic reactions may be conditioned. One woman developed a severe allergic reaction to a very realistic looking plastic rose. She was not allergic to plastic. She did, however, know she was allergic to roses, and reacted to what she believed was a rose (Mackenzie, 1886).

Another example is an experiment that showed that rats could be conditioned to suppress their immune systems. The rats were injected with a powerful immune-suppressing drug while being fed saccharin-flavored water. Then their immune function was then measured, and it showed an immediate drop. After the drug and saccharine water were paired a number of times, these rats were given just the saccharin water and a harmless injection of salt water. Their immune cells responded exactly as if they had received the drug! The reverse ability, increasing immune cell function, was also shown to be learnable through conditioning (Ader, Cohen & Felten, 1995; Ghanta et al., 1985).

The major concept is that thoughts and images affect our physiology. We often anticipate, react, and form conclusions with incomplete information. Thoughts and images change our physiology and even our immune system. Observe what you experience when you read the following **Concept Exercise: The First Time.**

Concept Exercise: The First Time

The First Time
He pulled my head back,
I know what he wanted.
But I wished that he did not do it.
We were this far and it was the first time.
His hands moved slowly to that place,
I held my breath.

And then I saw him bend over me.
"I'll be careful," he said.
Then he asked if I could open even more,
Then he could get nearer.
It started to hurt,
But I held myself as a woman.
Suddenly, I yelled, " You are hurting me!"
"It is already out," he said.
What a relief.
This was the first and last time
That I have my molar pulled....

SOURCE UNKNOWN

Observations: What did you notice? Did you draw conclusions prior to finishing reading that made you feel insulted, disgusted, or aroused? Whatever your feelings, note how words and images affected your physiology. Hence, be careful what you think and contemplate.

STEPS TO DEVELOPING AND PRACTICING YOUR PERSONAL RELAXATION IMAGE

In this practice, we will reduce the number of steps involved in relaxing by combining muscle groups. You will also begin to use cue words and images to encourage relaxation. If English is not your native language, you may choose to use a word or phase from your mother tongue that elicits, represents, or is associated with a sense of wholeness.

1. **Remember a Time of Wholeness:** Take a few moments to sit quietly and reflect on Pavlov's Exercise. He dramatically changed his health through quiet, positive, and concentrated imagery based upon a personal experience. Now take a moment or two to remember a time in your life when you felt whole; when there was a feeling of joy, peace, and love. For some this might be a short moment, while for others it could be an extended time period.

   Once you have a vivid image, then become very relaxed as you think of that time and the feelings and sensations associated with feeling well, evoking as many senses as possible. Just as unhealthy behaviors can be conditioned, so can healthy responses. The goal is to pair the experience of relaxation with the experience of health and well-being. Think of tangible objects, such as an old teddy bear, a shell from the beach, a favorite song, a certain perfume—olfactory and gustatory cues can be especially powerful—or other items that will help you to remember that time. Describe the specific components of this memory of wholeness on the **Worksheet: Memory**

of Wholeness: Practice 4. If possible, assemble actual objects, pictures, songs, or fragrances from that previous time period to have with you when you practice your relaxation image. These sensory reminders or cues will help evoke the memory and the experience of wholeness.

2. **Develop a Personal Relaxation Image:** Now that you have a vivid memory of wholeness, begin developing your relaxation image. Create a scene for your **Personal Relaxation Image** that you find especially relaxing and one that engenders a sense of wholeness and trust (a warm beach, sitting in front of the fire in a log cabin on a winter evening, floating on a raft on a mountain lake, sailing on a calm day, and so forth). Use significant elements (images, odors, tastes, sounds) from your **Worksheet: Memory of Wholeness**. You may want to jot down notes about what you see that will help you create your **Personal Relaxation Image Script**.

   When you visualize your **Personal Relaxation Image**, picture it in your mind's eye and fill in all the details. See the colors, the shapes, and the textures that you delight in; feel the texture of the ground under your feet and the temperature of the air on your skin. Make it vivid for yourself; so vivid that you can hear the sounds of the place or feel the stillness. Are there any fragrances or aromas that you associate with this beautiful place? Can you smell them? And now see yourself—and feel yourself—strolling easily and slowly through this lovely place, taking in the sights and scents and sounds and letting the peacefulness soak into your being. Imagine yourself settling down in the most comfortable, secure spot.

3. **Create a Personal Relaxation Image Script:** Stay in your image: see it, smell it, taste it, touch it, be it. This may be similar to or different from your memory of wholeness. Stay focused on an image that is particularly relaxing and peaceful. Go with the image and allow the relaxation to deepen. As you sit quietly with your image, begin writing your script on **Personal Relaxation Image Script: Practice 4**. Be detailed about what you hear, feel, smell, and do. The sample image script found later in this practice is a useful example of a detailed script. Insert the scene you create rather than the sample image, where indicated in the relaxation script. (If you prefer, you may use the sample image script.)

4. **Record the Personal Relaxation Script:** Record the script found later in this practice after the **Worksheet: Personal Relaxation Image Script**. Begin with the introductory script with muscle tension and relaxation and where indicated, insert your **Personal Relaxation Image Script**. Finish by recording the closing segment of the script.

5. **Prepare for and Practice Relaxation:** Remember to prepare for relaxation by unplugging the telephone; adjusting the heat to a comfortable temperature; ensuring that you will have uninterrupted quiet time for 20 to 30 minutes; loosening any constricting clothing; removing jewelry, glasses, and so on; and settling into a comfortable chair, bed, or wherever you can easily relax (refer to your **Checklist for Relaxation** found in **Dynamic Relaxation: Practice 2** in Chapter 2).

Optional:

◆ First receive a massage or take a hot bath and then do the practice. Compare your level of relaxation afterwards to the result of this practice.

◆ Practice gentle stretches to loosen some tight muscles or "shake out" your limbs, just before doing your relaxation practice.

◆ Draw or paint the relaxing image or actually go to your "relaxing place" (if possible) and do your practice. Practice outdoors in the most relaxing place you can find. Nature is a healer.

◆ Create an atmosphere that helps evoke and augment your relaxation image (e.g., play background music or have fragrances that you associated with the relaxation image).

◆ Throughout the day, think about your **Personal Relaxation Image** for just a few seconds to evoke a sense of peace.

6. **Keep Logs and Assess Your Progress:** Each day, after you have gone through the script, complete **Log Sheet: Personal Relaxation Image: Practice 4**. At the end of the week, answer **Questions: Personal Relaxation Image: Practice 4**. Meet with your group and complete **Group Discussion and Conclusions: Personal Relaxation Image: Practice 4**.

COMMON CHALLENGES IN CREATING AND PRACTICING YOUR PERSONAL RELAXATION IMAGE

Inability to evoke a memory of wholeness. It is as if one draws a blank. This is common, especially if one has experienced abuse. In this case, just use the model image presented in the script or create a totally imaginary peaceful image.

Positive memories of wholeness evoke a sweet/bitter feeling. The images of wholeness and personal relaxation image include a loved one who has passed on or who has left. On the one hand this may evoke strong positive feelings, while on the other hand, it evokes loss and sadness. In this case, let go and accept that at least you have been loved. For your image, it may be easier to focus and create places in nature that are associated with peace and tranquility.

Lack of experiences with places in nature. Some people have only urban experiences and find nature alien. Use images of sitting by a fireplace, a walled garden, or other images of peace and safety.

Desire to stay in the imagery and not wanting to return to reality. The imagery scene is so much more pleasant than the present. Use this as a trigger to reorganize your life and set new goals and priorities. Begin to explore your purpose for living. Explore some of the practices described by Lawrence LeShan (1994) in his book, *Cancer as a Turning Point.*

Difficulty tensing and relaxing specific muscles. If you're having trouble isolating a muscle: touch it, stroke it with your hands, and then tense it fully (without strain) and feel the tension in your hands; feel the difference with your hands as you let go of the tension. Or you may tighten only as much as is needed to feel the tension.

RECOMMENDATIONS FOR GENERALIZING RELAXATION

Occasionally, practice this and the next few scripts with open eyes. This will help you to transfer the relaxation skills into normal everyday life. Also, notice your posture this week. How do you hold yourself? Do you habitually slump forward while studying or working? Do you create tension in your neck, shoulders, or spine?

Name: _____ Date: _____

Worksheet: Memory of Wholeness: Practice 4

1. Identify a time in your past when you felt joy, peace, love, or a sense of integration/ wholeness.

_____

_____

_____

_____

_____

_____

_____

_____

_____

_____

2. Describe the specific cues or stimuli that could be used to evoke the wholeness image.

_____

_____

_____

_____

_____

_____

_____

_____

_____

_____

3. Describe in detail the image that you associate with wholeness.

_____

_____

_____

_____

_____

_____

_____

_____

_____

Name: _____ Date: _____

Worksheet: Personal Relaxation Image Script: Practice 4

Write out the script for your personal relaxation image.

_____
_____
_____
_____
_____
_____
_____
_____
_____
_____
_____
_____
_____
_____
_____
_____
_____
_____
_____
_____
_____
_____
_____
_____
_____
_____
_____
_____
_____
_____
_____
_____
_____
_____

PERSONAL RELAXATION IMAGE SCRIPT

Begin by getting into a comfortable position for relaxation. Now, tense both arms by making fists, and extend them straight ahead, while continuing to breathe... study the tension... let the rest of your body stay relaxed... now relax and let your arms flop down like a rag doll... and let go and relax... just become aware of any sensations in your arms and hands...

Now hunch up your shoulders towards your ears and tighten your neck, while keeping your legs, buttocks, abdomen, and jaw loose... continue to breathe easily... Let go and relax. Allow your shoulders to drop down... Feel the relaxation flowing from your shoulders, down your arms into your hands and out your fingers... Allow your breath to flow through and down your arms...

Squeeze your eyes shut tight, press your lips and teeth together, and wrinkle up your nose... feel the tightness in your whole face while keeping your neck and shoulders relaxed... notice any tension that may creep back into your upper body and let go of that tension... Let it go completely and relax... Allow your face to soften, feel the sensations of your eyes sinking in their sockets, your cheeks dropping down... Allow your breath to flow effortlessly in and out...

Now press your shoulders backward, and tighten up your chest and stomach at the same time... Let your jaw and thighs be relaxed... Let go and relax... Allow your body to sink comfortably into the surface on which you are resting... Feel yourself being pulled down by gravity... Allow the breath to flow down and through your arms and out your hands and fingers...

Tighten your buttocks, thighs, calves, and feet by pressing your heels down into the floor while curling your toes and squeezing your knees together... Feel the tension as you continue to breathe while keeping your face, neck, shoulders, arms, and hands relaxed... Let go and relax... Allow relaxation to flow through your legs... Imagine exhaling the air through and down your legs and out your feet... Be aware of the sensations of letting go...

Feel the deepening relaxation, the calmness and the serenity.... Observe the ease with which your breath is flowing... Feel each exhalation flowing down and through your arms and legs... Let the feelings of relaxation and heaviness deepen as you relax more... Notice the developing sense of inner confidence... a calm indifference to external events...

Now deepen the relaxation even further by mentally repeating any word or phrase you associate with feelings of calm, wholeness, and relaxation such as, "I am relaxed"... or, "I am loved"... or, just the words "secure" or "peace"... Say the word(s) softly and slowly to yourself as exhale...

Let your entire body become more and more relaxed. Let the feeling of relaxation, calmness, and serenity deepen for a few minutes... Think and feel the words *relax*, *calm*, *serene*, or your own special phrase, as you exhale... Keep repeating the word and if your attention drifts, bring it back to your personal word...

Gently let go of your personal word and enter your **Personal Relaxation Image Script**.

Insert your Personal Relaxation Image Script here or continue with the sample image script

You are walking through a mountain meadow after having emerged from a cool dark forest. Here and there, the green grass is dotted with brightly colored wildflowers in hues of pink, yellow, red, and purple. Touch the delicate petals of a flower and inhale its fresh, sweet fragrance. Remove your shoes and socks and let your feet feel the cool moist softness of the thick grass. Feel the sun overhead warming your shoulders and arms, while a gentle breeze tousles your hair and soothes your forehead. In the distance hear an occasional clear note of a birdsong breaking the silence. A butterfly lazily dips and floats among the flowers and grasses. Smell the grass and a faint scent of pine needles.

As you walk along, enjoying the springy grasses underfoot, become aware of the sound of a brook, which grows louder as you approach. For a while, watch and listen as the water bubbles swiftly over the mossy stones. The sun glistens brightly on the moving water. Leaning over, let your fingers dangle for a moment in the clear cool stream. And now relax and settle back comfortably here, for as long as you like...

After visualizing either the sample image or your Personal Relaxation Image continue with the script

Let yourself just stay in this special place all your own... and know that you can return to this peaceful sanctuary any time you choose to do so.

When you are ready, take a deep breath, gently stretch your body, and open your eyes.

Name: _____ Date: _____

Log Sheet: Personal Relaxation Image: Practice 4

For each daily practice session, (a) describe the "realness" of your imagery and (b) make notes of your mood and physical state before, during, and after the relaxation, as well as the effect of the cue words and your personal relaxation image.

Day 1   a. _____
Date_____   _____
              _____
              _____

           b. _____
              _____
              _____
              _____

Day 2   a. _____
Date_____   _____
              _____
              _____

           b. _____
              _____
              _____
              _____

Day 3   a. _____
Date_____   _____
              _____
              _____

           b. _____
              _____
              _____
              _____

Day 4   a. _____
Date _____   _____
                 _____
                 _____

           b. _____
                 _____
                 _____
                 _____

Day 5   a. _____
Date _____   _____
                 _____
                 _____

           b. _____
                 _____
                 _____
                 _____

Day 6   a. _____
Date _____   _____
                 _____
                 _____

           b. _____
                 _____
                 _____
                 _____

Day 7   a. _____
Date _____   _____
                 _____
                 _____

           b. _____
                 _____
                 _____
                 _____

Additional comments/questions:

_____
_____
_____

Name: _____ Date: _____

Questions: Personal Relaxation Image: Practice 4

1. What benefits occurred as a result of your practice?

   _____

   _____

   _____

2. How did the cue words affect your relaxation experience?

   _____

   _____

   _____

3. How did you experience your personal relaxation image (e.g., did you see it, feel it, taste it)?

   _____

   _____

   _____

4. How did the imagery affect your relaxation?

   _____

   _____

   _____

5. In which ways were this week's experiences different from previous week?

   _____

   _____

   _____

6. What problems/challenges occurred and how did you solve them?

   _____

   _____

   _____

Name: _____ Date: _____

Group Discussion and Conclusions: Personal Relaxation Image: Practice 4

1. What benefits did the group members notice as a result of the practice?

   _____

   _____

   _____

2. Were there common words or images that encouraged or inhibited relaxation?

   _____

   _____

   _____

3. What were the challenges and difficulties encountered doing this practice?

   _____

   _____

   _____

4. What were some successful strategies to counter and deal with the challenges and difficulties?

   _____

   _____

   _____

5. How were the experiences of this week's practice related to the quality of imagery or the type of images (e.g., memories of family or nature scenes)?

   _____

   _____

   _____

6. In what ways did past and/or present health and illness patterns and previous experience with imagery and meditation techniques affect the imagery experience?

   _____

   _____

   _____

7. Topics or concerns to discuss with the instructor:

   _____

   _____

   _____

List your group members:

_____   _____

_____   _____

_____   _____

_____   _____

᦯ Quick and Warm: Practice 5[8]

The secret of health for both mind and body is not to mourn for the past, not to worry about the future, or not to anticipate troubles, but to live the present moment wisely and earnestly.

THE BUDDHA

I did not know it was possible. I opened up my eyes after following the guided instructions and my finger temperature had increased from 78° to 96° Fahrenheit. I literally can feel the warmth in my hands and a slight pulsing in my fingers. I now know I can influence my health. I wonder if I can get rid of my chronic irritable bowel syndrome?

STUDENT

Learning to relax is not just a withdrawal from the world for 20 minutes. It is introducing relaxation into our daily activities. We get locked into a busy, extremely demanding schedule, and we fear that if we take 20 minutes out we'll get behind. We imagine that if we start slowing down in general, we'll become unproductive, get bored, be judged as unintelligent or, worse, we'll start to see more of who we are and even begin to feel some of the emotional pain that we distract from by staying so busy.

It takes time and personal experience to learn that there is more than one possible way to "be" in the world; that by taking our time we allow more creativity, more quality in our work, and feel more whole and happy and less driven to strive for the outward signs of "success;" and that who we really are is very different from what we thought, and worth getting to know.

QR – The Quieting Reflex

While in this transition phase, some quick relaxation methods can be very useful. Dr. Charles Stroebel (1982) developed a brief relaxation practice that he called the "quieting reflex," or *QR* for short. He originally developed it as a result of his own problem with tension headaches. As a busy doctor, he found it hard to take the time out each day for 20 minutes of meditation, progressive relaxation, autogenic training, or other methods that relieved the headaches. He reasoned that since the stress response can take place in a few seconds, why shouldn't we be able to create the relaxation response in an equally brief time?

Remember that during the stress response (fight/flight/freeze), we gasp and hold our breath, clench our jaw, frown, tense our neck and shoulders, and give a general sympathetic response. This reaction occurs many times during the day, often unknowingly (e.g., when the phone rings, during traffic when some one cuts in front of us). This reac-

---

8. Adapted from C.F. Stroebel. (1982) *QR: The Quieting Reflex*. New York: Putnam.

tion carries a significant personal cost because we often have no control over the stressors. All that we know is that at the end of the day, we feel exhausted or have a slight headache or neck and back tension. We need to learn to control or inhibit our own habitual reactions to stress.

The QR response includes the recognition of the stressor and stress reaction, then using these as cues to automatically trigger the opposite body responses. This anti-stress response consists of a smile to stop the frowning and rumination; gentle diaphragmatic breathing to counter breath holding; a gentle exhalation while loosening the tense muscles of the jaw and shoulders to help reduce tension; and imagining and sensing/feeling the breath flowing through the arms and out the hands, which will reduce sympathetic arousal and induce hand warming.

In 6 seconds we can prevent the fight-or-flight response from being activated and, thus, prevent the negative effects of stress. The more frequently it is practiced, the more automatic QR becomes, until it is activated reflexively at a subconscious level whenever we encounter a stressor.

QR can be done in the midst of a stressful situation, with your eyes open, and no one even needs to know you are doing it! With QR you can respond to the situation appropriately without going into an out-of-control stress response. QR can be like a moment of mindfulness, a moment of bringing in space for seeing things differently and for nurturing ourselves when anxious.

QR can be used for preventing anxiety or annoyance, as when preparing for an exam or a confrontation with a problem person. It can help deal with minor stressors, such as stoplights, ringing telephone, waiting in line, or driving in slow traffic. Decide to do a QR each time you encounter one of these daily hassles. (One participant initially had trouble relaxing at the sound of a ringing phone; she then decided to laugh at the sound, and found that this allowed her to relax and lighten up.)

QR can also be used for habit control: To interrupt the craving, do a QR before lighting a cigarette, taking a drink, or reaching for a snack.

If you are angry, you may quietly clench one fist before doing your QR and really feel the anger before letting it go. When you have strong feelings, acknowledge them and ventilate them safely; don't just "QR" them away. Once calm, you may be in a better frame of mind to speak assertively (without blowing up). Assertive action is often the key to resolving issues that generate anger.

By now you are becoming aware of your body's responses to stressors, responses such as shallow breathing and tightening of various muscle groups. Scanning your body helps build awareness, which will be very useful in learning QR. Notice how others respond to stress, especially in their body language. Use those responses as cues to scan your own body and as a trigger to perform a QR. You may indirectly affect the other person as well, since relaxation and peacefulness can be contagious! After you notice a cue for a QR, ask yourself, "What is beautiful or positive about the situation?" Look for the beauty or benefits even in a city traffic jam: buildings, colors, sunlight. See your muscle tension as a "point of control" instead of a spiral out of control; take charge—with relaxation.

Here are the steps involved in QR:

1. Become aware of a *cue* (a worry, a feeling of annoyance or anxiety, or muscle tension). Ask yourself, "Is it life threatening?" If not, go on to the next step.

2. Smile inwardly with your mouth and eyes. Let your eyes move to the left and right. Just moving your eyes side to side can remind you that there is more than one way of seeing any situation, no matter how terrible it seems at the moment. Consider that it might even seem amusing to you 5 years from now. Say to yourself, "Alert mind, calm body." Or you can substitute another coping phrase, such as "I can relax" or "I can choose peace instead of this." Or just repeat your cue words or phrases that you have been practicing.

3. Inhale a slow, deep abdominal breath. Exhale and let your jaw, tongue, and shoulders go loose. Feel a wave of heaviness flowing through your body, all the way down to your toes.

4. Take another easy breath. Exhale and feel a wave of warmth flowing through your entire body, streaming through your arms and legs as though they were hollow tubes; feel the warm air flowing out your fingers and toes.

That is all there is to it! As Thich Nhat Hanh (1987), a well-known Vietnamese Buddhist meditation teacher, said in his book *Being Peace*: "Breathing in, I calm my body. Breathing out, I smile." During your relaxation practice, incorporate this suggestion, with a gentle half-smile.

Optional: *Smile five times today at people you don't usually smile at: service people, checkout clerks, toll takers, classmates, and complete strangers. What was their response? What was the effect on you?*

PRACTICE QR TO GAIN MASTERY

Practice the 4 QR steps: Do role-rehearsal and take yourself through the practice so that it feels comfortable. Although you may have felt some sensations flowing through your arms as you exhaled, some times you may not have noticed it, especially if you take it literally and know that air can only flow out your mouth and nose. As one of our engineering clients said, "I know you are a professor at the University, however, I know air goes out of my nose and mouth and not through my arms!" The air flowing through your arms is really a metaphor of awareness of the sensations down the arm. The intent of the practice is to encourage a conscious awareness of energy (*qi*) flowing through the arms and out the fingers. To deepen and anchor the experience of streaming, do the following **Concept Exercise: QR with Touching**.

Concept Exercise: QR with Touching

This practice takes two people. One person will trigger the QR response by clapping or scaring the other, and the other person will practice the QR in response the clap or scare.

Stand up and face each; keep a distance from each other of about eighteen inches. Identify who will practice and who will trigger the QR. The trigger person then claps his/her hands loudly and, the moment the practice person hears the sound, he/she practices the QR response (awareness of stressor, smile, diaphragmatic breath, exhale down the arms while letting jaw, neck, and shoulders relax). The trigger person gently strokes and squeezes the arms of the practice person from the shoulders down to the hands and fingers in rhythm with the exhalation. The trigger person acts as a role model for relaxation by exhaling at the same time as your partner. The stroking down the arms is performed in rhythm with the practice person's exhalation. You may squeeze down the arms and all the way out of the fingers as if squeezing the toothpaste out of a tube as shown in Figure 2.4. Repeat a few times. Then reverse roles.

Now, sit down and think of a recent stressful situation. The moment you are aware of the stressful situation and your beginning somatic responses, practice the QR exercise. Observe that the stress fades out, as if the stressful event moved away from you.

Observations: Most participants find it much easier to sense the streaming down the arms and out the hands after doing this practice and that the hands are beginning to warm.

Figure 2.4 Illustrations of clapping, squeezing, and stroking motion.

DEEPENING YOUR QR PRACTICE WITH HAND WARMING

In order to receive maximum benefit from your QR practice, it is helpful to have some familiarity and experience with warming your hands. The old phrase "Cold hands, warm heart" might more accurately be changed to "Cold hands, uptight." Peripheral hand temperature is one indication of the level of autonomic arousal. When the sympathetic nervous system is activated, as in the fight-or-flight response, the smooth muscle lining the peripheral arterioles constricts, causing a decrease in blood flow and, thus, a drop in hand and foot temperature. Conversely, when the sympathetic nervous system is quiet, these smooth muscles relax, blood flow increases, and hand and foot temperature rises. This is why you may have already noticed your hands warming or tingling when you did slow diaphragmatic breathing or other relaxation exercises in this workbook. In deep relaxation, the sympathetic nervous system arousal level drops, leading to peripheral vasodilation, and warm hands.

Besides being useful for generalized relaxation, the practice of warming one's hands has been demonstrated to alleviate several other clinical conditions, such as migraine headache, hypertension, Raynaud's disease, and irritable bowel syndrome. Biofeedback training often utilizes a temperature-sensitive indicator for learning the skill of hand warming in order to help people reduce their arousal and relieve these conditions.

Some people react more in certain organ systems than others when under stress. For example, some respond with intense skeletal muscle contractions while others respond with smooth muscle contractions. Smooth muscle is found around the arteries (including the coronary arteries), arterioles, and the digestive tract. Thus, people who are "smooth muscle responders" may, for example, develop gastric discomfort, as smooth muscles in the digestive tract constrict; icy cold hands, as their peripheral blood vessels constrict; and chest pain, as the coronary arteries constrict. Migraine headaches are usually preceded by a vasoconstrictive phase—caused by many factors, including stress—in which not only the peripheral blood vessels but also those in the brain constrict; a "rebound vasodilation" then occurs in the head, with throbbing and pain, sometimes accompanied by nausea and vomiting.

For all of these conditions, therefore, an important component of self-regulation is first to become aware of when the smooth muscles constrict (often associated with cooler hands) and, second, to learn to warm your hands. Many researchers, beginning with the pioneering work of Elmer and Alyce Green of the Menninger Foundation, have demonstrated the efficacy of temperature feedback training for hand warming for the treatment of migraine headache.[9] Temperature training was shown useful for regulating high blood pressure by Fahrion, Norris, Green, Green, and Snarr (1986) and by Wittrock, Blanchard and McCoy (1988); for Raynaud's disease (poor circulation in the hands and feet) by Freedman (1987), and Middaugh, et al (2001); for increasing the healing rate of wounds by Palmer, Tibbetts and Peper (1991); and as part of general stress management and an

---

9. Much of this early work is described in Green, E. and Green, A. (1977), *Beyond Biofeedback.* (New York: Delacorte).

integral part of many relaxation procedures (Schwartz and Andrasik, 1995). Although it can be used as a treatment approach, peripheral hand warming is a strategy to demonstrate passive attention and an individual's ability to achieve physiological mastery. This is a non-striving way of being with the body and of experiencing voluntary influence over an autonomic physiological function. Many people report a reduction in stress after practicing hand-warming.

The practice also calls attention to the fact that awareness and imagery affect peripheral temperature. Explore the implications of the relationship between thinking and body. Be careful what you think and imagine; it may affect your physiology.

Be aware of the Law of Initial Values. That is to say, if your hands start out very warm, you can only warm a few degrees, whereas, if your hands start out quite cold (e.g., 72°F), you can increase your temperature by over 20 degrees. Other important considerations in temperature regulation include:

A. Thermo-regulation (the brain likes to stay at the same temperature). The peripheral blood vessels will constrict to preserve warmth. Hence, one way to warm your hands and feet is to reduce heat loss by wearing a hat (something our grandmothers knew when they wore a nightcap to bed if they had cold feet and could not fall asleep).

B. Chronic arousal and rapid shallow thoracic breathing. When relaxation occurred in the guided exercise and the body was attended to passively and without judgment, the blood vessels dilated, which allowed more blood to flow through the tissue. This process evokes an anabolic state that facilitates regeneration and healing.

C. Pharmaceutical agents and hormonal processes. Certain chemicals such as caffeine and nicotine induce peripheral vasocontriction (hand cooling), while alcohol induces peripheral vasodilation.

Learning that one can warm one's hands—direct one's own blood flow at will—can be an empowering experience. One 13-year-old girl reported that she warmed her hands in the following manner: "I thought to myself that I was in control of everything. Fingers get warm... fingers, I feel them warming.... warm toast, lobsters, ovens, summer.... I would look at the meter. I would be proud of myself because I had succeeded." Having successfully used this skill to overcome her migraine headaches, she spontaneously generalized the learning process to other body systems. She reported that she told her teeth to move faster so that her orthodontic headgear could come off sooner; the result was that she only had to wear it for 4 months instead of 2 years (Peper and Grossman, 1979). This sense of control can be used to enhance the power of imagery and practice in self-healing. For example, Norris and Porter (1987) report in the book *I Choose Life* the remarkable remission of an inoperable brain tumor of a young boy. He had learned to warm his hands and thus came to experience that he could influence his tumor. Each day he then visualized his immune system's attack upon the tumor until he was healed.

Of course, if you are very warm as you begin a relaxation practice (hand temperature of 94 to 96 degrees Fahrenheit), your hand temperature may drop by a degree or so when you relax in a cooler place or it may simply not change. The maximum finger temperature is generally considered to be 96 to 97 degrees Fahrenheit. The temperature card enclosed with this workbook[10] is not as accurate as the more sensitive temperature biofeedback devices; this is not important, however, as the main thing you need to be aware of is the *relative* changes in temperature.

INCREASING AWARENESS OF BLOOD FLOW TO FINGERS

To begin, the following quick exercises can help you gain an awareness of the sensations of blood flow to your fingers.

To observe the blood flow: While seated, place both hands on your lap. Let them rest there for a few minutes. Observe the color of the two hands. Most likely they are the same color. Now raise your right hand straight up, pointing toward the ceiling. For the next minute, hold your right arm up while your left is hanging down at your side. Feel the draining sensation in your right hand and the filling sensation in the left. Then bring both hands to your lap and compare the internal feelings and external color. Note how much lighter your right hand looks. Feel the sensations of blood flowing back into your hand as the color returns.

To push the blood: Stretch your arms up overhead for a moment, and then vigorously swing them in circles. Finally let your hands hang down by your sides. Can you feel pulsations, or tingling? What color do your hands become?

ATTITUDES AND STRATEGIES TO FACILITATE HAND WARMING

The best attitudinal approach to learning the skill of warming your hands is one of passive attention. The more you try to warm your hands or strive for this goal, the more you will arouse your "efforting mode," which means your sympathetic nervous system becomes activated. It's a lot like trying to produce a urine specimen for the nurse; forcing just doesn't work! Nonjudgmental, passive, open awareness is what lowers your nervous system activation. Say to yourself, "If my hands warm up, that's nice and if they don't, that's okay, too."

When learning the skill of warming your hands, and for relaxation in general, always be sure your body is comfortably warm. Be sure the room is, also, comfortably warm. Many people create unnecessary muscle tension just by not wearing warm enough clothes as they go about their daily activities. If you are chilly or the room in which you are attempting to relax is cold, warming will be more difficult. Your goal is not to overcome a cold room, but to practice deep relaxation. Take a relaxed position, sitting in a comfortable chair or lying down, as for your relaxation practices, with belt loose, glasses off, and so on.

Usually, peripheral temperature will increase through passive attention. The more you practice, the easier it will become. Simple cue words, such as *relax* or *warm* are helpful while warming your hands. If you find it difficult to allow your hands to warm, check the following problems and attempt the recommended solutions.

---

10. See the Appendix for sources for additional temperature monitoring devices.

⑤ SOME PROBLEMS AND SOLUTIONS

1. *Striving and/or self-judgment.* Acknowledge that it takes time to learn. If possible, think of a peaceful, warm image. Are you trying to "control" your breath? Allow yourself to release it.

2. *Vigilance.* Be sure you are in a safe environment, where you do not need to check your surroundings and will not be disturbed.

3. *Self-consciousness.* Know you have the right to do what ever you want for yourself as long as it does not hurt other people. Explain to others what you are doing.

4. *Intellectualizing.* Shift your feeling and sensations to your hands and feet. Give or receive a gentle hand massage and just feel the loving sensations.

5. *Excessive heat loss.* Put a scarf and hat on. Much of body heat is lost through the neck and head.

6. *Lack of hand sensations.* Massage your hand or place one of your hands in warm water to experience what the sensation of warmth is. Imagine the other hand warming the same way even though it is not in the water. Or gently tap your fingertips together or on a tabletop 50 times. What do you feel? Or rub your hands briskly to generate heat. Exhale gently into cupped palms to experience warmth on exhalation. Alternatively, sit quietly with your fingers curled as follows: Place your left palm up on your lap, then place your right palm face down on top of it so that the fingers of each hand touch the wrist of the other. Then curl the fingers of both hands so that the fingertips of the right hand are beneath the fingertips of the left hand. Allow your neck, shoulders, arms and hands to relax while sensing the sensations of the inter-curled fingers.*

7. *Hands cool or no change.* Attempt bi-directional control of hand temperature, and begin by perfecting your skill of hand-cooling. Notice what thoughts, images, or feelings help you to cool, such as thinking about an upcoming exam or remembering an unpleasant task or obligation. Then ask yourself: "What is the opposite of these thoughts, images, feelings?" This may give you a clue to the thoughts, images, or feelings that may facilitate warming.

8. *Drafty or uncomfortable location.* Get in a non-drafty location and be sure the chair is comfortable. You might want to turn the heat on in the room to facilitate the peripheral vasodilation. The optimal room temperature for learning is 72° Fahrenheit or higher.

9. *Diurnal rhythms (the body clock).* Practice at different times of the day. Later in the afternoon or in the evening, when you have let go of your daily tasks, often works best. Lack of sleep or exhaustion can inhibit the ability to relax and warm.

---

*Adapted from the work of Dr. Patricia Norris.

10. *Metabolic/dietary factors.* Do not consume caffeine (in coffee, colas, chocolate, and black tea. Caffeine induces vasoconstriction). If you are on medications, check whether they are sympathomimetic (capable of increasing autonomic arousal and thus inducing vasoconstriction). In addition, certain foods and liquids may affect peripheral warming; for example, alcohol often induces hand warming while allergy-causing foods, such as milk, may induce hand cooling. You may also find it will be easier to warm your hands on a day when you have exercised than on a sedentary day, since circulation and metabolic rate are enhanced for hours after exercise. Also, if you have not eaten for a long period of time, warming may be more difficult.

GENERAL INSTRUCTIONS FOR HAND-WARMING EXERCISE

Besides practicing QR at least 10 times a day to imprint the habit so that it starts to become automatic, the following scripts emphasize relaxation, maintenance of easy diaphragmatic breathing, and hand warming during the tension and relaxation phases of the exercise. This warming relaxation practice also facilitates the mastery of hand warming as part of QR. Increase mastery of hand warming by practicing the following hand-warming scripts each day.

For your first experience with temperature observation, hold the temperature card enclosed in this book between your thumb and forefinger of your dominant hand. You will need to wait about a minute in order for the temperature card to equilibrate from the cooler room temperature to the temperature of your fingers. Meanwhile, familiarize yourself with how to read the temperature. After 1 minute, while still holding the device, record your pre-baseline temperature on your log sheet. Then do the following exercise, which was adapted from the practice by Norman Cousins (1989). If no temperature-monitoring device is available, touch your fingers against your throat to the side of your Adam's apple and observe how warm or cool your fingers are as compared to your throat.

Suggestions: Usually this will work better if either you first tape record the script and then listen to it, or you have some one else read it to you.

Script for Hand-Warming Exercise[11]

Day 1

Hold the temperature card between your dominant index finger and thumb for a minute and record the temperature or, if you don't have a temperature card, touch your fingers to your throat to observe the temperature.

Wiggle around…. Sit comfortably in the chair and let your weight just rest against the back and seat of the chair… Allow your eye to close; if you want to keep them open, that is all right, too.

---

11. Adapted from Cousins, N. (1989). *Head First: Biology of Hope.* New York: Dutton, pp, 88-89.

Now, press together your ankles, then knees, and continue pressing while tightening your buttocks, raising your shoulders, and frowning. Hold this for the count of 10.... Now, let go and relax and let your eyes be closed... Feel your body relaxing and being supported by the chair... Just keep gently holding the temperature card between your thumb and index finger. In case you relax so much that the card drops, just pick it up again and continue with the exercise.

Now, think back on a nice memory. Think of the nicest thing that happened to you—something that made you feel very good at that time. When you think of this memory, just nod your head.... (Usually, it takes no more than 30 seconds for a memory to be summoned.) In case no memory comes up, which is very common,[12] just create a peaceful and secure imaginary place or event...

Allow this memory to be as real as possible, so real you can almost taste it. Imagine that you are reliving that experience. Go slowly, breathe easily.... Feel the way you did during that experience... Let everything about that experience give you the same pleasure now as it did then... Enjoy the feeling... Breathe evenly and easily.... (Allow this to continue for a minute or so.)

Now, let go of the memory, and imagine that you can focus your concentration and attention so that it is like the tip of a blackboard pointer that you can move from place to place inside your head. Let this point of consciousness and focus of attention slowly move and come to rest toward the front of your face, just behind your nose. Then, concentrate on the tip of your nose... Keep focusing on the tip of your nose. Imagine the sensation of touching the tip of your nose with your mind... (Allow this to continue for about 30 seconds)

Now, elevate this point of consciousness until it comes to rest just behind your eyes. Bear down at that point... When you are bearing down on the point just behind your eyes, gently nod your head. (Use the nod response to pace the sequence of the instructions.) In a little while, you may experience a pulsing sensation behind your eyes... (Allow this to continue for about 1 minute).

Now, raise your point of consciousness even higher until it comes to rest just under your scalp in the middle of your head. Concentrate on that point. Concentrate hard.... (Allow for about 90 seconds.) In a little while, you may experience slight tingling sensations. When you feel those sensations, gently nod your head...

Now, bring your attention to your hands and allow blood to flow into them. Just visualize your heart pumping your blood up to your shoulder, across your shoulders, and then down your arms, past your elbows, down your forearms, past your

---

12. Sometimes, a history of abuse or depression can interfere with thinking of and feeling a positive memory.

wrists, and into your hands... Let this flow of warmth into your arms and hands continue.... (Allow this to continue for about 30 seconds.)

Allow your breathing to go slowly and easily. Each time you exhale imagine your breath flowing through your shoulders, down your arms, and out your hands.... Imagine your breath streaming through your arms as though they were hollow tubes.... As you are breathing, allow your exhalation to go slower.... Allow each exhalation to flow through your arms... If your attention wanders that is okay, just gently bring it back to an awareness of feeling the air flow down your arms and out your fingers. As if you can feel someone stroking down your arms ... Continue to allow the air to flow down your arms... (Allow this for about two minutes.) Feel the warmth flowing out through your fingertips.... You may want to repeat to yourself, "My arms are heavy and warm.... My arms are heavy and warm....." You may notice gentle pulsation and tingling in your fingers.... Be aware and feel the sensations while you continue to exhale slowly and allow the air to flow down your arms and out your hands and fingers... (Continue for one minute.)

Now, let go of breathing down your arms, become aware of the room, take a deep breath, stretch, open your eyes, and look at the color of the temperature card held between your thumb and index finger or touch your throat with your fingers and observe the change in color/temperature. Note your experience and color/temperature change on your daily log.

Observation: *This exercise almost always results in increased hand temperature with concurrent reduced subjective level of stress. For example, when physical therapists were guided through this practice, the average hand temperature increased from 85.3° to 95.4° Fahrenheit, as illustrated in Figure 2.5. University students reported an average increase of 8.8° Fahrenheit in hand temperature with a reduction in subjective stress levels from 4.3 to 2.2 (on a scale from 0-relaxed to 9-tense) as shown in Figure 2.6.*

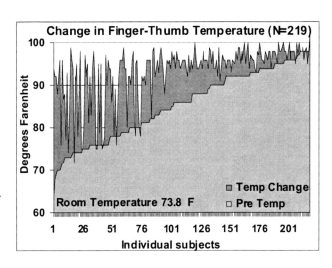

Figure 2.5. Change in temperature for each individual subject.

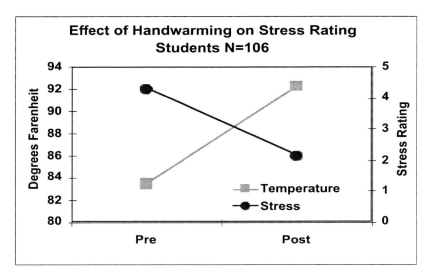

Figure 2.6. Change in subjective stress levels with hand warming (ambient temperature was 74.1° Fahrenheit).

I feel incredibly relaxed right now, and somewhat surprised that I raised my hand temperature 26 degrees.

STUDENT

DAYS 2 - 7[13]

Begin by taking a comfortable posture. Either tape the thermometer to your index finger or gently hold your temperature device between the thumb and forefinger of your non-dominant hand. Observe your temperature after 1 minute and record you "PRE temperature on the log sheet. (If it is taped in place, let it stay on for the whole exercise. If you are holding the temperature card, put it down at this time. You will pick it up again at the end of the exercise.)

Allow your eyes to close and feel yourself sinking into the chair. Tighten up your whole body: feet, legs, stomach, buttocks, back, shoulders, jaw, face, fists. Hold it. . . Let it go and relax… Take a slow deep breath and let it out with a sigh of relief, "Haaaaaa." Continue to leg go and relax….

Now, just tighten your jaw… Does this feel familiar? Does it remind you of any tense situations? Feel the jaw muscles with the fingertips of one hand, just in front of your ears and at your temples. Open and close your mouth a couple of

13. Adapted from Stroebel, C.F. (1982). *QR, The Quieting Reflex.* New York: Putnam.

times and notice the movements of these muscles... Inhale, exhale, and consciously let your jaw go loose... Feel it with your fingertips... Imagine a feeling of heaviness in your jaw. . . Let your arms return to a resting position. . . Now, raise your shoulders; hold and feel the tension. . . As you let them go, exhale and imagine a sense of heaviness in your shoulders.

Now, inhale and cup your hands, placing them over your mouth and nose. . . Exhale gently and slowly, and feel the *flowing* of the warm air; imagine it's streaming down and through your arms and out your fingertips. Do this for two or three breaths. Now, allow your arms to relax in a resting position; let them just stay relaxed.... With the next exhalation, imagine the flowing warmth down your arms and out your fingertips... Continue with this image for the next few breaths.

Mentally scan your body, playing "body detective" and looking for those places where there is muscle tension. Briefly tighten any area that feels tense, then let it go and relax... Breathe easily and imagine feelings of heaviness throughout your whole body... Allow your chest and abdomen to relax more and more as you breathe slower and slower... Feel your abdomen expanding outward and filling with air as you inhale... Give yourself plenty of time; let the breath move easily in and out at your own pace... If any thoughts or concerns arise, just let go and refocus your attention on your breath... You may think of these thoughts as attached to clouds that drift briefly across your consciousness and then away... Allow your exhalation to lengthen... Repeat your special relaxation cue words for the next minute or so.

Whenever you're ready, inhale very slowly, easily, and deeply into your abdomen, going at your own comfortable rate (which may not be the same rate at which the suggestions to breathe come in this script)... Feel how your stomach, hips, and lower back expand outward as you inhale, almost like a balloon filling... Feel the movement of your abdomen as you inhale. Then exhale... Imagine the breath flowing out through your shoulders, down your arms, and out your hands and fingers... As you exhale, imagine the relaxation flowing like a gentle warmth through your arms as though they were hollow tubes... Feel the warmth flowing out through your fingertips as you repeat to yourself, "My arms are heavy and warm; my arms are heavy and warm"... Continue to breathe regularly and slowly... For the next few minutes, feel the movement of breath deep in your abdomen while letting the air flow down your arms with each exhalation... Become aware of gentle pulsations, tingling in your fingers, or whatever else you sense.

And now as you breathe easily and slowly, imagine having breathing holes in the bottoms of your feet... Imagine the air flowing through your feet as you inhale, coming up through your ankles, knees, and thighs, filling your abdomen slowly and gently. As you exhale, imagine the warm air flowing from your abdomen through your legs and out of your feet and carrying away any remaining tension... Breathe in this way for a few moments, while you repeat to yourself, "My legs are heavy and warm; my legs are heavy and warm. "

Imagine your blood vessels widening and dilating, as your heart pumps warm blood down your arms into your hands and through your whole body into your abdomen, legs, and feet. Imagine the warm pink glow of each finger and toe as your blood pulsates through your arterioles, bringing warmth, oxygen, nutrients, and healing to each cell... Stay with this image as long as you like, and add other details to it if you wish, picturing and feeling the subtle pulsations. And now, imagine the space inside each finger and the space around each finger... Feel the peace and quietness.

When you are ready, take a deep breath, gently stretch your body, and open your eyes. Then observe your temperature.

If the thermometer is taped on, you can record it instantly. Otherwise, hold the temperature device between your thumb and index finger, wait for one minute while you continue to feel the warmth sensations flowing down your arms and hands, and then record your "POST" temperature on the log sheet.

Each day, after you have gone through the script, complete **Log Sheet: Quick and Warm: Practice 5**. In addition, your log sheets for the next two weeks include questions about the QR practice. At the end of the week, answer **Questions: Quick and Warm: Practice 5**. Meet with your group and complete **Discussion And Conclusions: Quick and Warm: Practice 5**.

Optional: Smile 5 times today at people you don't usually smile at: service people, checkout clerks, toll takers, classmates, or complete strangers. What was their response and how did you feel?

Name: _____ Date: _____

Log Sheet: Quick and Warm: Practice 5

I.   After each practice, describe your experiences and record your PRE and POST color/ temperature.

II. During the day practice QR and describe at least two different experiences before, during, and immediately after practicing QR.

III. Describe the triggers or cues to practice QR. These are the inner and outer stressors (e.g., a ringing phone, a tightness in your jaw, a craving for a cigarette or snack).

Day 1   I. _____

Date _____   _____

Temperature Pre _____ Post _____

II. QR   _____

experiences   _____

III. Cues   _____

for stress   _____

Day 2   I. _____

Date _____   _____

Temperature Pre _____ Post _____

II. QR   _____

experiences   _____

III. Cues   _____

for stress   _____

Day 3   I. _____

Date _____   _____

Temperature Pre _____ Post _____

II. QR   _____

experiences   _____

III. Cues   _____

for stress   _____

Day 4   I. _____
Date _____   _____
Temperature   Pre _____ Post _____

II. QR   _____
experiences   _____

III. Cues   _____
for stress   _____

Day 5   I. _____
Date _____   _____
Temperature   Pre _____ Post _____

II. QR   _____
experiences   _____

III. Cues   _____
for stress   _____

Day 6   I. _____
Date _____   _____
Temperature   Pre _____ Post _____

II. QR   _____
experiences   _____

III. Cues   _____
for stress   _____

Day 7   I. _____
Date_____   _____
Temperature   Pre _____ Post _____

II. QR   _____
experiences   _____

III. Cues   _____
for stress   _____

Name: _____ Date: _____

Questions: Quick and Warm: Practice 5

1. What benefits occurred as a result of your practices?

    _____

    _____

    _____

    _____

2. What changes in your hand (foot) temperature occurred?

    _____

    _____

    _____

    _____

3. What were the stressors and what were the common themes that were the triggers to practice QR?

    _____

    _____

    _____

    _____

4. In which situations was it the most useful? The least?

    _____

    _____

    _____

    _____

5. What challenges occurred during the week and how would you change your future practice to overcome these challenges?

    _____

    _____

    _____

    _____

6. Comments and observations:

    _____

    _____

    _____

Name: _____ Date:_____

Discussion and Conclusions: Quick and Warm: Practice 5

1. What benefits did the group members notice as a result of the practices?

    _____

    _____

    _____

2. What factors influenced the hand warming?

    _____

    _____

    _____

3. What physiological factors, medical background, etc., related to the ease or difficulty in mastering hand warming?

    _____

    _____

    _____

4. What were the common stressors used to trigger the QR?

    _____

    _____

    _____

5. How did practicing QR affect the experience of the stressors?

    _____

    _____

    _____

6. Topics or concerns to discuss with the instructor:

    _____

    _____

    _____

List your group members:

_____   _____

_____   _____

_____   _____

_____   _____

⑤ Generalize Relaxation: Practice 6

I personally learned quicker in the context of movement as opposed to learning differential relaxation while remaining still. The movement gave me more contrasts, thus maximizing my ability to recognize tense states from loose states. I experimented with just how loose I can become and still execute the task.

STUDENT

Generalizing relaxation into daily life requires mindfulness. It means doing quick body scans several times a day to search for muscles that are being tightened unnecessarily and letting the tightness go. It means becoming aware of your breathing, noticing if it becomes short or shallow, or if you are holding your breath, and then returning to effortless diaphragmatic breathing. This takes practice and patience with yourself, so start with the simplest things.

Often, bracing is embedded in our habitual daily behaviors. For example, while driving in traffic we clench our jaws, hunch up our shoulders, and grip the steering wheel for dear life. This excessive bracing is part of the startle and/or orienting responses that we evoked when we first learned to drive and have not yet unlearned.

In order for relaxation training to have the greatest impact on one's life, it is necessary to learn to generalize the skills. In other words, while it is valuable to know how to relax and let go in a quiet, private space, it is equally important to be able to relax and let go of unnecessary tensions during the activities of daily life. As a step toward learning these skills, this script encourages relaxation during simple movements. With practice, you may learn to stay relaxed while performing increasingly complex and stressful tasks, such as doing dishes or driving a car in traffic. Athletes, dancers, and other performers use differential relaxation for peak performance. It allows for more fluidity and grace, besides conserving precious energy by relaxing all muscles except those needed for their performance.

Suggestions For Generalization

1. Find the place, posture, time, and setting where you *think* you are most relaxed (watching TV in a recliner, sitting in bathtub, etc.) and observe where in your body you're still tight. Then, let the tension go. A few minutes later, check again: Are you still relaxed? How is your breathing?

2. Have as a goal the ability to keep a part of your awareness on your muscles. When you find unnecessary tension during the day, let it go.

3. Continue breathing as you go about your other activities; check in on your breath frequently, especially when concentrating or under stress.

4. Do simple artwork while concentrating on breathing and relaxation. What do you notice about your artwork?

5. Be a relaxed role model for your children.

6. Practice letting go of any unnecessary muscle tension while walking. Before you start, visualize yourself staying relaxed during the movement; look for creative ways to allow your walk to be more relaxed. For example, if you carry books or other things in a heavy shoulder bag, try using a backpack. Notice how you breathe while walking. Be aware of your rhythm. Let walking be a kind of moving meditation.

7. Use your cue word and/or any part of your ritual for relaxation to help you let go. For example, while driving in traffic you might loosen your belt a notch or two as a cue to relax.

8. Progress gradually from relaxing during simple, rhythmic activities to relaxing during more complex ones, like cooking, shopping, eating, talking with a friend, or doing yoga.

9. Do the differential relaxation as a part of any new activity or behavior that you begin at this time. For example, starting a yoga class or an aerobic dance class or even beginning to drive a car that's new to you is a perfect opportunity to build in the new relaxation skills. Or if you have a new job or job assignment that requires you to walk up and down a flight of stairs, you could decide that every time you do this particular flight of stairs you will practice your generalization skills. This way you will build up an associative process that quickly becomes automatic.

10. Keep a chart or notebook and give yourself a checkmark (or a gold star!) each time you remember to generalize relaxation.

11. Use a stressor to remind you to breathe slowly and relax, such as the ringing of the phone.

12. You might want to set aside one day a week to practice mindfulness of breathing and relaxing muscles. Go about your activities while giving attention to your breathing and your body. Be aware of your breath and body relaxation while conversing with another person, washing dishes, driving, and so on. Taking one day a week for mindfulness will gradually extend into greater self-awareness every day.

13. Use mental rehearsal. Plan situations where you will release unneeded tension, and visualize which muscles you might need to relax; feel the relaxation. Then check your visualization against the real-life situation. Which other muscles tightened up that you had not anticipated? Revise your imagery and keep practicing with it.

Optional: Fill out the Generalization Reminder Chart and use it to remind yourself to perform in more relaxed and effortless patterns in the different situations.

Generalization Reminder Chart

Situation (1) _____

Muscles/ breathing to be aware of: _____

Recommended muscle/breathing pattern: _____

_____

Situation (2) _____

Muscles/ breathing to be aware of: _____

Recommended muscle/breathing pattern: _____

_____

Situation (3)_____

Muscles/ breathing to be aware of: _____

Recommended muscle/breathing pattern: _____

_____

GENERALIZING RELAXATION SCRIPT

For this exercise, have a book or magazine near the chair you will be sitting in and have adequate light for reading.

Get comfortable in a sitting position, allow your eyes to close, and let your body relax and rest. For the next few minutes, recreate the sensations you have experienced in your previous relaxation practices... Tighten all your muscles and hold... Let go and relax... Relax all over... Allow a pleasant heaviness to develop... Allow the comfortable sensations of warmth to flow through your entire body... Take a few moments to scan your body for areas of tension and holding and gently release those areas.

Feel your muscles yielding and relaxing all over. Let the contractions loosen ... Feel more at rest... Let your breathing flow freely and easily without any effort... Imagine your blood vessels widening as you relax so that circulation increases without strain or effort... Feel the pleasant pulsing and throbbing sensations in your fingers. Feel the movement of the abdomen as you breathe... Let the exhalation lengthen...

Enjoy the serenity of being enveloped by restfulness, heaviness, and warmth... Nothing can disturb you... Feel the inner restfulness deepening and know that as you relax and enjoy these sensations, you will gain a sense of strength and confidence from the inner peacefulness. Continue to allow the air to flow in and out. Each time you exhale imagine the air to flow through your arms and hands and out your finger... Imagine the air flowing outward like a gentle ocean wave washing and carrying away any tension or strain.

With each exhalation, think your cue word or phrase, such as "I am at peace" or "I am relaxing." Think about the words and their meaning to you and feel them more and more... Just let the words reverberate inside you. Notice the pleasant feelings you associate with them... Experience the feelings as you relax more and more... Feel the sensations of relaxation and calm... heaviness, warmth, peace... Surrender to the good feelings all over.

Now, imagine yourself as you sit in the chair. Notice any area of lingering tension and let go and relax... Picture yourself raising your right arm and holding it up while you stay quite relaxed. What sensations can you imagine feeling in that shoulder and arm?... Now, actually raise your right arm and hold it up using the minimum muscle tension necessary for the task. Let the rest of your body stay relaxed... Feel the slight tension in your right shoulder and arm... Study the contrast in feeling and notice how it differs from the mental image you had formed... Now, let your right arm fall to your side and relax it further and further, feeling the difference as the tension drains from your shoulder and arm.

Now, visualize yourself raising your left arm and feeling the sensations of tension... Now, actually raise your left arm up and hold it with the minimum effort, feeling the tension in that shoulder and arm as distinct from the relaxation in the rest of your body... Continue to breathe... Feel the tension. Let your arm fall to your side; relax your left shoulder and arm further and further... Notice the difference between relaxation and tension.

Imagine raising both arms using the minimum of muscle tension. Now, actually raise both arms. Study the tension... Where do you feel it?... Let both arms fall limply and notice the tension evaporating.

Visualize yourself standing up in a very relaxed way and walking slowly. Notice which of your muscles tighten up just by imagining this movement... Notice how your breathing changed as you imagined yourself moving... Breathe, let go of any tension, and relax.

Open your eyes and maintain the relaxed feelings. Let your eyes move lazily around the room, adjusting to the light... When you are ready, stand up slowly while exhaling easily and stand with your feet planted firmly on the floor and shoulder-width apart... Breathe, and relax as much as you can... Drop your shoulders while imagining the back of your head extending toward the ceiling, loosen your stomach and knees, let your arms hang loosely... Relax and stand still for a few minutes.

Begin to walk slowly back and forth. Let your arms swing gently... Let go as much as you can while walking... Study your body and release any tension you don't need... Be aware of your breathing as you walk.

Stand still, again, and relax those parts of your body that are not needed for standing and walking—face, scalp, eyes, jaw... Have your tongue rest against the upper palate and loosely in your mouth. Breathe easily, with your neck, throat, and shoulders fully relaxed and your stomach relaxed... Feel the relaxation in your legs as best you can while standing.

Again, think of your cue words or phrase. Just think each word and let each word enhance your overall relaxation... Develop the feeling of relaxation while standing.

Now, sit down again. Relax comfortably and fully, closing your eyes... Rapidly go back into that heavy, comfortable feeling all over and feel the good sensations of warmth throughout your entire body... Feel an inner restfulness that deepens and gives you inner strength and confidence... Feel all the muscles yielding and letting go as you release contractions everywhere... Let yourself feel completely at rest, with your breathing coming freely and easily.

Slowly open your eyes and, again, allow them to adjust to the lighting in the room... Pick up your book or magazine and hold it without reading it yet. Just become aware of the muscle tension involved in holding it and adjust your position as much as you need to in order to let go of unnecessary muscle tension... Now, while keeping your eyes and forehead as relaxed as possible, begin to read... Monitor your breathing and muscle tension every few words or so... What tension can you let go of while still having full comprehension? Relax your jaws, lips and tongue... Relax your neck, shoulders, and abdomen... Breathe freely and easily and go back to your reading.

After you have read a page or so, put the reading material aside, close your eyes, and let go and relax. Tell yourself, "I can carry relaxation with me throughout the day."... When you are ready, take a deep breath, gently stretch your body, and open your eyes.

Each day after you have gone through the script, complete your **Log Sheet: Generalizing Relaxation: Practice 6**. You will also be asked to describe one situation each day where you generalized the relaxation skill into an activity. At the end of the week, answer **Questions: Generalizing Relaxation: Practice 6.** Then meet with your group and complete **Discussion And Conclusions: Generalizing Relaxation: Practice 6.**

Name: _____ Date:_____

Log Sheet: Generalizing Relaxation: Practice 6

I.   After each practice, describe your experience.

II. Describe a situation where you generalized the relaxation skill. Describe how your experience of the situation changed when you added the relaxation component to the activity.

Day 1
Date
_____

Generalize:

Day 2
Date
_____

Generalize:

Day 3
Date
_____

Generalize:

Day 4

Date

_____

Generalize:

Day 5

Date

_____

Generalize:

Day 6

Date

_____

Generalize:

Day 7

Date

_____

Generalize:

Name:_____ Date:_____

Questions: Generalizing Relaxation: Practice 6

1. What benefits occurred as a result of your practices?

    _____

    _____

    _____

2. What problems/challenges occurred and how did you solve them?

    _____

    _____

    _____

3. In what ways did your ability to perform activities while staying relaxed change during the week?

    _____

    _____

    _____

4. How have your experiences while reading and walking changed as a result of the practices?

    _____

    _____

    _____

5. When generalizing the relaxation into different activities, what factors and components of the activities made it easier or more difficult to relax?

    _____

    _____

    _____

6. If you could change how you did the generalization practice this week, how would you do it differently in future?

    _____

    _____

    _____

Name: _____   Date:_____

Discussion and Conclusions: Generalizing Relaxation: Practice 6

1. What benefits did the group members notice as a result of the practices?

    _____
    _____
    _____

2. Were there common situations where group members found it easy or challenging to generalize relaxation?

    _____
    _____
    _____

3. Were there differences among group members in the ability to stay relaxed during the simple movements and generalization? Was there any pattern to past experience with relaxation, meditation experiences, practice of sports or music, or medical conditions?

    _____
    _____
    _____

4. What did you learn from the group discussion that you could apply to yourself?

    _____
    _____
    _____

5. Topics or concerns to discuss with the instructor:

    _____
    _____
    _____

List your group members:

_____   _____
_____   _____
_____   _____
_____   _____

✿ Creating Your Own Relaxation Practice: Practice 7

Writing Your Own Script

In this practice you can create your own integrated script that incorporates the most beneficial components of the previous experience to enhance relaxation. Go back over your notes on the previous weeks of practice. At this point you may want to reflect upon your experiences and write about it as suggested in the section **Reflection And Integration: Summarizing your Experiences** in Chapter 1. This process allows an opportunity to integrate your experience and to be a witness to your own experience.

What were the parts or aspects of these practice scripts that appealed to you the most or helped you relax most easily? Use these components to create your own relaxation script. For example, if you found that imagery (**Developing A Personal Relaxation Image: Practice 4**) was especially helpful to you, you might want to incorporate imagery when you write your own script.

You can also use this script to increase relaxation in areas of your body where you may hold habitual tension or experience discomfort. For example, if you are a woman who has painful menstrual cramps (dysmenorrhea), you might want to include a few instructions, suggestions and/or images concerning relaxation and warmth in the pelvic area. Or if you hold chronic tension in your neck and shoulders, you might include specific instructions to tense and relax different muscles (e.g., Roll your shoulders forward...Let go and relax...Pull your shoulders down...Let go and relax...Pull your shoulders back...Let go and relax.... Raise your shoulders... Let go and relax...). If you tend to gasp, include more slow diaphragmatic breathing instructions (e.g., Let each exhalation become slower and longer... While exhaling count during the exhalation—one, two, three, four, five... Slowly increase the count with each exhalation).

First, write down your own relaxation script on the **Worksheet: Creating Your Own Relaxation Practice: Practice 7**. Record the script, then practice it each day for the next week. Obviously, to optimize the experience you can make changes and adapt the script after having practiced it. Each day after you have gone through your script, complete **Log Sheet: Creating Your Own Relaxation Practice: Practice 7**. In addition, continue to describe one situation each day in which you have generalized the relaxation skill into an activity (e.g., relaxing your shoulders while driving, breathing calmly while mousing). At the end of the week, answer **Questions: Creating Your Own Relaxation Practice: Practice 7**. Then meet with your group and complete **Discussion and Conclusions: Creating Your Own Relaxation Practice: Practice 7**.

Optional: Teach a script in practice 2 or 3 to a friend or family member. What was it like to be the trainer? What did it do for your own commitment level?

Name: _____ Date: _____

Worksheet: Personal Relaxation Script: Practice 7

In the space below create your own personal relaxation script.

_____

_____

_____

_____

_____

_____

_____

_____

_____

_____

_____

_____

_____

_____

_____

_____

_____

_____

_____

_____

_____

_____

_____

_____

_____

_____

_____

_____

_____

_____

_____

_____

_____

_____

Name: _____ Date: _____

Log Sheet: Creating Your Own Relaxation Practice: Practice 7

After each practice, describe your experience.

Day 1
Date _____

Day 2
Date _____

Day 3
Date _____

Day 4
Date _____

_____
_____
_____
_____
_____
_____
_____
_____

Day 5
Date _____

_____
_____
_____
_____
_____
_____
_____
_____

Day 6
Date _____

_____
_____
_____
_____
_____
_____
_____
_____

Day 7
Date _____

_____
_____
_____
_____
_____
_____
_____

Name:_____ Date: _____

Questions: Creating Your Own Relaxation: Practice 7

1. What benefits did you experience?

    _____

    _____

    _____

2. Looking back over week six, what parts of your script were helpful to you in encouraging relaxation? Were there components that inhibited relaxation?

    _____

    _____

    _____

3. How was your experience with your personalized relaxation script different from the previous guided practices?

    _____

    _____

    _____

4. What components of your script did you find most helpful?

    _____

    _____

    _____

5. What problems/challenges occurred and how did you solve them?

    _____

    _____

    _____

6. How did you feel about creating your own script? If you could revise and write your script again, what improvements might you make in light of this week's experience?

    _____

    _____

    _____

7. If you could do the practice over, how would you do it differently?

    _____

    _____

    _____

8. Comments.

    _____

    _____

    _____

Name: _____   Date: _____

Discussion and Conclusions: Creating Your Own Relaxation: Practice 7

1. What were the common benefits experienced by the group members?

_____
_____
_____
_____

2. Were there differences among group members in the scripts they developed? What
    creative parts of their scripts would you incorporate in your script?

_____
_____
_____
_____

3. Looking back over the past week, were there parts of your script that encouraged or
    decreased relaxation that were common among group members?

_____
_____
_____
_____

4. What were common pitfalls and challenges and how were they resolved?

_____
_____
_____
_____

5. Topics or concerns to discuss with the instructor:

_____
_____
_____
_____

List your group members:

_____   _____
_____   _____
_____   _____
_____   _____

—————————————————————————————————————— *Chapter 3* ——

COGNITIVE BALANCE

A human being fashions his consequences as surely as he fashions his goods or his dwelling. Nothing that he says, thinks or does is without consequences.

NORMAN COUSINS

We are what our thoughts have made us; so take care about what you think. Words are secondary. Thoughts live; they travel far.

SWAMI VIVEKANANDA

⑨ INTRODUCTION TO COGNITIVE BALANCE

Beware of psychosclerosis: the hardening of the attitudes.

Through the process of learning dynamic relaxation, you may have observed that bodily tensions are connected to mental tensions. The process of somatic relaxation encourages awareness, mindfulness, and passive attention. Thinking patterns are intertwined and are part of the somatic body patterns. This process is more easily observed when you become quiet. When the soma is quiet, the effect of thoughts and feelings can be more easily felt in the body. The content of the thoughts can have a dramatic effect on our body tensions; just notice how differently your body feels when thinking about an anger-provoking incident as compared to thinking about a peaceful scene or a lover.

For profound and lasting changes in body tension to take place, usually some rearranging of thinking patterns is necessary. This awareness and changing of thinking patterns we call "cognitive balancing." For example, a constant judgmental thought of "I am not good enough" by itself can create both mental and physical tension. Dynamic relaxation may help to undo some of this tension. However, the tension will always return whenever such negative thoughts are present. Hence, we need also to learn to change the thought patterns.

129

Often, we resist letting go of our dysfunctional and irrational thought patterns, since we may use these thoughts as part of our self-identity. For example, thinking, "I know I can't learn Japanese" or "I am stupid" may confirm a belief that we lack intellectual capacity. Or thinking, "I never let any SOB cut in front of me on the freeway" may confirm an image of being aggressive and a fear of not being a pushover. We may fear that if we changed our patterns we would have to accept, face, or let go of who we are. Or we may believe that these ways of thinking are necessary for generating our best performances or that it is impossible to change the thought patterns.

Thoughts seem to occur automatically and beyond our control. We often forget how potent thoughts are: They are the production orders for our brain's pharmaceutical company to produce different neurotransmitters. The effects ripple through our whole being and, if repeated enough, will contribute to our health and achievements. The potency of how thoughts can affect our body is illustrated in the following **Concept Exercise: Thoughts and Muscle Resistance**.

Concept Exercise: Thoughts and Muscle Resistance

◆ This exercise is done in pairs. Begin by standing facing each other. Identify who is the subject and who is the experimenter.

◆ Begin by testing the strength of the subject's arms (see Fig. 3.1). The subject extends his left arm straight out to the side and holds it in a horizontal position. The experimenter places his right hand on top of the subject's left wrist and gently applies downward pressure while the subject resists. The experimenter slowly increases the pressure until he senses when the subject can no longer hold the arm in a horizontal position. Relax, and repeat the test with subject's right arm.

◆ Identify which arm appears stronger and more able to resist the downward pressure.

◆ Now, with both arms hanging at his side, the subject is to mentally evoke a past memory or experience in which he felt either: (1) Hopeless, helpless, and powerless; or (2) Empowered, positive, and successful. (If the subject is unable to quickly remember an experience, he can just make one up.)

◆ Do not reveal to the experimenter which memory is chosen.

◆ After choosing one of the above, think about the memory and make it as real as possible—feel it, hear it, and so forth. The goal is to quickly have a felt-sense of that memory. Then, when the experience is felt, extend the stronger arm straight out to the side. The experimenter, once again, tests the strength of the arm by pressing down on the wrist.

◆ After being tested, without saying anything or describing the experience to each other, the subject let's go of the memory and drops his arm to his side.

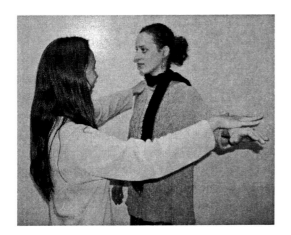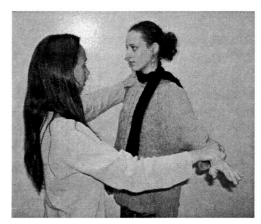

Figure 3.1. Pressing arm down at the wrist.

He then evokes the opposite memory, making it as real as possible. When the subject feels the experience, he raises his strong arm again, and the experimenter tests the strength of the arm by pressing down on the wrist.

◆ When done, reverse roles and repeat the same exercise.

◆ Now compare your experiences.

Observation: *In almost all cases, when people thought of the hopeless, helpless, and powerless memory, they had significantly less strength than when they thought of the empowering, positive, and successful memory. With the hopeless, helpless, and powerless memory, the arm is much easier to press down, the subject experienced "a lack of oomph," and a sense of not being able to resist; as if the whole body just collapsed and let go. With the empowering, positive, and successful memory, the experimenter needed to apply more pressure to the subject's arm, while the subject experienced a sense of energy and ability to resist the pressure.*

Our thoughts and images form the template of future activity and are derived from the many hypnotic suggestions given covertly by our family and social culture—suggestions that set the limits on our potential. If we become aware of, accept, and change those habitual thinking processes that act as hypnotic suggestions, we may be able expand our health and potential. It is truly amazing to witness the tenacity of a thought pattern. Deepak Chopra, a well-known Ayurvedic physician, states in his book *Quantum Healing* that our mental patterns are largely responsible for creating our bodies: "...memory must be more permanent than matter. What is a cell, then? It is a memory that has built some matter around itself, forming a specific pattern. Your body is just the place your memory calls home."

Life is change. Thoughts, even though they may seem permanent, can change as we grow. Yet, making changes in habitual thought patterns requires patience with oneself, an experimental attitude, flexibility, openness, and, above all, a sense of humor. Observing and changing our thought patterns to mobilize health are basic approaches of rational emotive therapy (Ellis, 1988) and cognitive-behavioral psychology (Meichenbaum, 1977) as well as a component of many meditative practices. The underlying principles of most cognitive therapies are the following:

1. All humans are irrational at times in our assumptions and expectations of the world, self, and others. Most likely, it is delusional to believe that the world can be rationally understood. For example, how do we rationally understand birth, death, love, art, or music?

2. Cognitive activity (thought) affects behavior. We are mainly disturbed by our absolutist beliefs and demands about events rather than by negative events themselves. It is not the events that disturb us, it is our perception of the events: The sound of footsteps can evoke fear, if it is late at night on the street, or pleasant expectancy, if it is the approach of a loved one.

3. Distorted thinking patterns can be observed, challenged, and transcended. We can change our demands to preferences, using cognitive and behavior change methods. Desired behavior change will be effected through cognitive change.

Thoughts and Posture

Thoughts and feelings are linked to our energy level, attitude, and posture. Negative and depressive thoughts will arise more easily if one is tense-tired or following snacking on sweets (see **Log: Responses to Stress: Practice 1** in Chapter 1). Thought patterns are not independent of our soma. Exhaustion and low blood glucose levels may allow negative and impulsive thoughts to come forth—supporting the perspective that we are a system in which mind and body interact.

Similarly, our posture reflects our emotions and our thoughts. When we feel happy, we sparkle and walk erect with a bounce to our step; when depressed, we tend to slouch and may actually have a gray hue to our vision. Emotions and thoughts evoke a posture and energy state and, conversely, posture and energy states evoke emotions and thoughts. The popular phrases *put on a happy face* or *whistle a happy tune* reflect this belief as illustrated in the following **Concept Exercise: Thoughts and Posture**.

Concept Exercise: Thoughts and Posture

◆ Sit comfortably at the edge of a chair and then, collapse downward so that your back is rounded like the letter *C*. Let your head tilt forward and look at the floor between your thighs.

◆ While in this position, think of many hopeless, helpless, powerless, and depressive thoughts for 30 seconds.

◆ Then, let go of those thoughts and, without changing position, think of many empowering, positive, and happy thoughts for 30 seconds.

◆ Shift position and sit up erect with your head tall while looking straight ahead or slightly upward.

◆ While is this position, think of many hopeless, helpless, powerless, and depressive thoughts for 30 seconds.

◆ Then, let go of those thoughts and, without changing position, think of many empowering, positive, and happy thoughts for 30 seconds.

◆ Ask yourself: In which position was it easier to evoke hopeless, helpless, powerless, and depressive thoughts? In which position was it easier to evoke empowering, positive, and happy thoughts?

Observations: *Most people find that the collapsed position facilitates negative and hopeless thoughts while the upright position encourages positive thoughts.*

INTERNAL DIALOGUE

Our thoughts or cognitions are often similar to a pair of glasses or contact lenses through which we perceive reality. They are so close to us that we are usually unaware of possible distortion. Do we see through rose-colored glasses or charcoal-tinted ones? Another way to say this is that we are constantly bombarded by sensory inputs and must learn to interpret and filter out a large portion so that we can create a sense of order and meaning. We tend to let in those experiences that support our belief systems and discard the rest. We generally hate to be wrong and prefer to be "right," even if it makes us miserable. We often focus on negative experiences and disregard positive ones in order to support our beliefs, which may be generalizations like "The world is a dangerous place," "Men are no good," or "This government serves only the rich." Thus, our emotional distress may be due less to an event than to our interpretation of it.

How do our thoughts distort reality? Depression, mood swings, and anxiety are often due to a negative view of oneself, the world, and/or the future (e.g., "There is no hope... I failed the exam; now I won't be able to graduate. No one will hire me"). By replacing maladaptive or irrational *automatic thoughts* with more rational, positive ones, and by identifying and questioning underlying negative beliefs, many people can overcome depression, mood swings, and anxiety. The events and circumstances in our lives may not change but as our perceptions and beliefs become less distorted, our emotional experiences improve.

Perhaps language is the most important means of shaping and structuring our perception of reality. How we experience reality is determined, in large part, by how we talk to ourselves about it. This is one reason why talking about our troubles or even writing about them can be so helpful in understanding and integrating our experience. Putting events and emotional responses into language (by speaking or writing) seems to provide distance, perspective, and structure on what would otherwise be overwhelming and chaotic. Even keeping log notes helps build the "witness" part of us, which observes without emotional attachment.

When we listen in to our automatic inner language, it may also become easier to identify any distortions and shift them. In addition, we can train ourselves to shift from negative self-talk to positive reinforcements (self-instructions). For example, if we are about to give a speech, we can say to ourselves, "I always stammer and say 'ummm' when I pause to think; the audience will get bored." Or we can learn to say positive statements such as, "The audience will be attentive. I am breathing slowly; I can smile and relax." Simply substituting *I choose* for *I have to* can change our experience.

This inner language is not only the overt phrases and statements we use, it is often the background worrying that continues as we are doing other things. So often we are only partially present while performing specific tasks. A large part of us is ruminating. We could activate much more potential if we channel the worry energy spent in rumination into performance of the task at hand.

The language we use both creates and describes our images. Hence, imagery is an important tool for changing thoughts. Going over a mistake strengthens the chance of repeating it; imaging success builds a better performance. A form of mental rehearsal is used to help improve performance on an exam or in music or sports. It is often used in a process called *systematic desensitization*, which helps people overcome phobias. For example, a person who fears snakes learns to relax. Then, he imagines the steps involved in getting closer and closer to the snake without fear. When he can imagine relaxing while holding a snake, the final step will be a structured, safe, real-world experience with a snake.

Frequently, we are covertly conditioned to respond to stimuli outside and inside ourselves. The cognitive balance process allows us to increase our freedom through reducing automatic, conditioned thought patterns. Instead of getting our buttons pushed by events, we can take control by observing and changing our inner dialogue about those events. The inner dialogue, made up of cultural and familial injunctions that have held us with hypnotic power, can be transformed into a positive tool for self-change. Expressing our secrets (through writing) can be another way to dissolve those constraining injunctions, thus freeing more of our intrinsic potential.

Finally, our patterns of thinking about illness are shaped by strong cultural and family traditions. Moreover, we create our own reality to bring order into a complex world. Many of us learned at a young age that getting sick was a guilt-free way to avoid obligations, such as school or social gatherings, as well as to receive extra care and attention. Such rewards can reinforce the pattern of getting sick. The *shoulds, oughts* and *musts* of our cultural and familial conditioning are so strong that, often, it takes an illness to allow us the freedom to put them aside. Why not learn to challenge these constraints so that we can get our needs met without having to get sick? By exploring the advantages of illness, we can develop alternative approaches to getting needs met without having to become ill.

✪ CHANGING THE INTERNAL DIALOGUE: PRACTICE 8

We are formed and molded by our thoughts. Those whose minds are shaped by selfless thoughts give joy when they speak or act. Joy follows them like a shadow that never leaves them.

THE BUDDHA

Life consists in what a man is thinking of all day.

RALPH WALDO EMERSON

I took a different attitude toward my illness... I looked at it as necessary or as a learning experience and refused to say things to myself such as "I am never going to get better"... I got better faster than usual. I feel that this was due in part to controlling the panic I usually feel when I get sick during the school year.

STUDENT

I approached illness in a non-judgmental, welcoming way, seeing symptoms as messages to be understood, not suppressed. I found that blame-free language helped me to eliminate my guilt, too.

STUDENT

Sometimes our internal language (self-talk) is the main place where *should* and *can't* appear. Does your internal dialogue empower or undermine you? Do you perceive yourself as a helpless victim, boxed into a set of obligations and struggling to be barely acceptable, or as a powerful person with many choices? Every time we say, "I should," we make ourselves wrong or not good enough. As you rewrite your self-talk you will be rebuilding your self-esteem.

REFRAMING

Reframing, a term used in neuro-linguistic programming, is the process of voluntarily shifting perception, usually from a negative image to a more positive one. For example, changing from powerlessness to choice, from threat to challenge, and from nuisance to blessing in disguise. It can also refer to revising a memory of the past in order to correct a mistake. By changing our internal language we change reality and possibility as is illustrated in the following **Concept Exercise: Changing Language.**

Concept Exercise: Changing Language

Sit comfortably and gently close your eyes. Now think of a task or a skill you want to do, about which you might automatically say, "I can't do that" or "I can't learn that" (e.g., "I can't learn Japanese because I could not even learn Spanish" or "I just can't learn Excel, I can't even do email" or "I can't fix the dryer"). Pick a realistic situation and just keep repeating the phrase, "I can't learn/do......," for about one minute. Stop and observe how you feel.

Now, thinking of the same task, change the phrase to, "I haven't taken the time to learn/do....." or "I choose not to learn/do.....," and repeat the phrase for about one minute. Stop and observe how you feel. Compare the feelings evoked by the different phrases.

Observations: *Most people observe that with the negative, helpless phrase, their posture collapsed slightly, they felt withdrawn and somewhat hopeless, and the world appeared bleaker. On the other hand, when they repeated positive the phrase that indicated choice, they felt more energized, slightly more hopeful, and more optimistic.*

In studies done by Kobasa, Maddi and Kahn (1982), people who coped well with stress and stayed healthy were compared with others in similar situations who became ill. The researchers identified three characteristics of the hardy personality: commitment (rather than alienation), sense of control (rather than helplessness), and viewing change as challenge (rather than threat). This means that a large part of coping is how we "frame," or talk to ourselves about our experience.

For example, in doing Dynamic Relaxation practice, *powerless* self-talk would be, "I have to (should, ought to) do my Dynamic Relaxation practice;" *Choice/control* self-talk would be, "I deserve to have a break; I choose to do Dynamic Relaxation" or "I have the opportunity to do Dynamic Relaxation."

As another example, suppose everyone with whom you live and work has been coming down with colds or flu. *Threat* self-talk would be, "I always catch everything that's going around" or "I know I'll be next; I can't avoid it." On the other hand, *challenge* self-talk would be "In the past I might have caught that bug. Now, I will build up my immune system with extra rest, eating well, drinking more fluids, more vitamin C, and I'll stay healthy."

Our feelings of helplessness can easily shift to feelings of strengths and resourcefulness if we reframe the situation. For example, a young boy with migraines was reluctant to practice his hand-warming skills at home. When his therapist asked him if he would be willing to help to make a video in order to show other children how to learn to warm their hands, the boy practiced with great enthusiasm in order to be a movie star. Similarly, a nursing instructor who had a multicultural group of students felt upset by their behavior that she considered to be rude and disrespectful at times. Deciding she could write a book about strategies other teachers could use for teaching culturally diverse students offered her a new viewpoint. Now she could experiment with new teaching strategies in order to become an expert and have something valuable to share with others. To learn more about her students was no longer just a way of helping herself, but a way of making a contribution to others in her profession.

Einstein once remarked that the most important question we much each answer for ourselves is "Is the universe a friendly place?" If your answer is yes, then even seeming catastrophes can be viewed as opportunities or challenges.

Dr. Bernie Siegel, a well-known surgeon who works with cancer patients to enable their self-healing, illustrates this point with the following story: A man is on his way to the airport, rushing to make the plane, when he has a flat tire. Imagine his feelings as he sweats and struggles to put the spare on; anger at himself for not leaving earlier, anger at the tire, anger at the whole world. When he finally arrives, his plane has just taken off. In disgust, he drives home, flipping the radio on for a bit of distraction. On the news he hears that the plane he missed has just crashed shortly after take-off. He kisses the flat tire!

Is it possible that the things you thought were a nuisance or a curse could turn out, when viewed from a broad enough perspective, to be a gift or blessing? "To accept the things we cannot change" as in the Alcoholics Anonymous Serenity Prayer does not mean passivity or resignation, but something closer to trusting that, while we do our best to deal with what *is* within our power to change, all will be well.

EXPLANATORY STYLES

The language we use often reflects how we feel about ourselves and how honestly we are willing to communicate with others. Such common phrases as *but*, *I should*, and *I can't* may be replaced with phrases that reflect a greater degree of self-confidence and/or honesty.

Martin Seligman (1998), a well-known psychologist at the University of Pennsylvania, has codified explanatory styles into three categories. The following is a brief outline of his concept of internal language and learned optimism.[1]

1. *Stable versus unstable* language describes an experience as a permanent versus a transient situation (e.g., "It's *always* this way").

2. *Global versus specific* language describes an experience as affecting the person's entire life versus affecting a specific aspect of his or her life (e.g., "It's the story of my life").

---

1. For more detailed background, self-assessment, and strategies for change, read Seligman, M.E.P. (1998). *Learned Optimism*. New York: Pocket Books.

3. *Internal versus external* language describes a situation as being caused by the person versus being caused at least in part by the situation or circumstances (e.g., "It's all my fault"). A systems approach assumes that all phenomena are interdependent; thus, there is a balance between personal responsibility and the system in which we are embedded.

The distinctions in these explanatory styles have important health implications. Somatic and psychological symptoms of helplessness and depression may be correlated with stable, global, and internal explanatory styles for negative events. (In animal studies, Visintainer, Volpicelli and Seligman, 1982, showed that rats that were conditioned to experience helplessness were more likely to develop cancer and die than rats that were not similarly conditioned.)

The following suggestions may be used to guide you in your practice this week:

1. *Shift "always" to "at this time."* For example, instead of saying, "I always make mistakes on exams," say, "I have made mistakes in the past on exams" or "I am making mistakes today on this exam." This does not imply that you will always make mistakes in the future on exams. Absolute statements have a self-hypnotic effect. The first step in changing self-image and internal dialogue is to change the way we describe ourselves and our past experiences to others. This leaves the door open for change. Otherwise, because we don't want to break our predictions, we will stay stuck.

2. *Change "I can't" to "I haven't taken the time to learn to" or "I haven't chosen to learn to."* "I can't ski" can be changed to "I have not chosen to take the time to learn how to ski." Sometimes, "I can't" may really means "I prefer not to" (as in, "I can't baby sit tonight") or "At this time I don't see a way to."

3. *Change "should" to "choose" or "choose not."* This language change implies assertiveness rather than passivity or aggressiveness. "I should do my home practice" becomes "I choose to do my home practice." The attitude and expectancy of rewards are different in these two statements. "I could" also implies choices. Sometime, the "should" is stated as "I have to;" this too can be rephrased using "choose" or "could". When you hear yourself saying, "I have to," you might also try substituting "I get to," as in "I get to dress up for the party."

4. *Change "but" to "and."* When you say, "I really like your new haircut, but it could be a little longer" what you are really saying is that you don't like her new haircut because it's too short. If you say, "I really like your new haircut and it could be a little longer," you are communicating that you are used to their hair longer and you like it that way and you also like it the way it is cut now. Of course, another option is that you may not actually like their new haircut at all. You may choose to say nothing about the new haircut rather than to criticize it.

5. *Change absolute statements to relative statements.* This suggestion relates to our conceptual framework rather than specific words or phrases. For example, during a

standoff in an argument with his spouse, a man at first thought, "We're stuck", which meant to him that there was no hope for change. He then reframed it to, "We are pausing," which implied that the disagreement would be resolved. Another example: "I am an asthmatic" can be changed to "On certain occasions, I wheeze."

6. *It is important to avoid rehearsing a bad experience in your mind as you think about it or retell it.* Professional athletes use this concept. For example, one of the authors asked a professional world-class skeet shooter what she does when she misses. She replied that she assesses what she did wrong, sees herself correcting the mistake, and then pictures herself doing it again in her mind perfectly. That way she never rehearses the mistake again.

CHOOSING NEW PHRASES

Be aware of your language. Whenever you think, intend to speak, or actually speak, change self-defeating words and phrases to self-enhancing ones:

From	*To*
but...	and...
I can't...	I haven't taken the time to learn to...
	I prefer not to...
I have to...	I will or I want to...
I should...	I choose or I could...
I'm afraid to...	I'm afraid to and I'll do it anyway...
	I want to...
	I am excited about...
I never...	I seldom...
I always...	I sometimes/often...

Thoughts sometimes seem to have a life of their own. Even when we have decided to stop thinking about something or are wishing to substitute a positive phrase, the old negative phrases often keep circulating in our head. Even when we say or yell, "Don't think this.....," the thoughts keep going. One useful behavioral strategy that often works is to use a snapping rubber band to stop the thought and then substitute the new positive phrase. If you decide to do this, wear a loose rubber band around your wrist and the moment the undesired thought bubbles up, pull the rubber band and let it snap against your skin. Then think or image the newly desired positive thought. Do this every time the thought or image comes to awareness.

WRITTEN EXERCISE

To practice changing your habitual self-statements, write out your old statement and then substitute a new empowering phrase. On the **Worksheet: Changing the Internal Dialogue: Practice 8**, complete the sentence with your most habitual thoughts or statements. Then, say the empowering sentences to yourself (or to a partner) and notice the effect it has on you (and/or your partner).

Optional: With a partner, practice using positive phrases while talking about topics in which have to, should, *and* must *are typically used, such as in areas of obligation. The partner who is the listener makes a note on paper each time a negative phrase is accidentally used and gives feedback after a few minutes. Then partners reverse roles.*

Ask friends and family members to help you become aware of your use of these phrases. Agree with a friend to monitor each other's use of but, should, can't, *and so forth, for one week. The one who uses these words most treats the other to dinner.*

Tape-record your own conversation, then play it back and listen to how you speak. Each time you observe yourself using limiting phrases, restate them and speak them out loud.

The objectives of this home practice are the following:

1. To increase awareness of language patterns

2. To develop the ability to change these patterns

3. To observe the effects of these changes

During the week whenever you think, intend to speak, or actually speak, monitor your language and, if you find that you are thinking of self-defeating statements, immediately substitute an empowering phrase whenever possible. Each day complete **Log Sheet: Changing the Internal Dialogue: Practice 8**. At the end of the week answer **Questions: Changing the Internal Dialogue: Practice 8**. Meet with your group and complete **Discussion and Conclusions: Changing the Internal Dialogue: Practice 8**.

Name:_____ Date: _____

Worksheet: Changing the Internal Dialogue: Practice 8

1. I should _____

_____

_____

Empowering phrase: _____

_____

_____

2. I have to _____

_____

_____

Empowering phrase: _____

_____

_____

3. I should have _____

_____

_____

Empowering phrase: _____

_____

_____

4. I can't _____

_____

_____

Empowering phrase: _____

_____

_____

5. I'm afraid to _____

_____

_____

Empowering phrase: _____

_____

_____

6. I always _____

_____

_____

Empowering phrase: _____

_____

_____

7. I never _____

_____

_____

Empowering phrase: _____

_____

_____

Name: _____ Date: _____

Log Sheet: Changing the Internal Dialogue: Practice 8

Each day note: (a) Situations in which you changed your *old* phrases into new empowering phrases; (b) factors that affected the use of the new phrases (your emotional state, the presence of others, etc.); and (c) your subjective experience when you used the new phrases.

Day 1   a. _____
Date _____   _____
               _____

          b. _____
               _____
               _____

          c. _____
               _____
               _____

Day 2   a. _____
Date _____   _____
               _____

          b. _____
               _____
               _____

          c. _____
               _____
               _____

Day 3   a. _____
Date _____   _____
               _____

          b. _____
               _____
               _____

          c. _____
               _____
               _____

Day 4   a. _____
Date _____   _____
           _____

           b. _____
           _____
           _____

           c. _____
           _____
           _____

Day 5   a. _____
Date _____   _____
           _____

           b. _____
           _____
           _____

           c. _____
           _____
           _____

Day 6   a. _____
Date _____   _____
           _____

           b. _____
           _____
           _____

           c. _____
           _____
           _____

Day 7   a. _____
Date _____   _____
           _____

           b. _____
           _____
           _____

           c. _____
           _____
           _____

Name:_____ Date: _____

Questions: Changing the Internal Dialogue: Practice 8

1. What benefits occurred as a result of your practices?

_____

_____

_____

2. Describe common situations where it was easy to be aware of and substitute the new phrases.

_____

_____

_____

3. Describe common situations where it was challenging to be aware of and substitute the new phrases.

_____

_____

_____

4. Describe the process in which you intercepted the limiting phrases and substituted the empowering ones. How often were you able to choose the empowering phrase?

_____

_____

_____

5. How did changing your language change your experience of yourself and/or the world?

_____

_____

_____

6. What problems/challenges, if any, occurred?

_____

_____

_____

Name: _____ Date: _____

Discussion and Conclusions: Changing the Internal Dialogue: Practice 8

1. What benefits did the group members notice as a result of the practice?

   _____
   _____
   _____
   _____

2. Describe common situations where it was easy to be aware of and substitute the new phrases.

   _____
   _____
   _____
   _____

3. Describe common situations where it was challenging to be aware of and substitute the new phrases.

   _____
   _____
   _____
   _____

4. How did the experience of substituting empowering phrases instead of the habitual ones differ among group members?

   _____
   _____
   _____
   _____

5. Topics or concerns to discuss with the instructor:

   _____
   _____
   _____
   _____

List your group members:

_____   _____
_____   _____
_____   _____
_____   _____

↺ Changing Energy Drains and Energy Gains[2]: Practice 9

I just hated doing the weekly data entries; I dreaded the boring task and post-poned it to the end. I talked to my co-worker at the next desk and I found out that he did not mind doing this. We traded tasks, he does the data entry and I do the filing.

Although I talked to Sharon very infrequently, each time I feel as if a 25-pound weight was lifted. Now we talk nearly every day and the deepening connection gives my life a sparkle.

This morning when you woke up did you feel alive, joyous, happy, energized, and looking forward to the day? Or did you drag yourself out of bed to once again go back on life's treadmill? Remember how you felt when you anticipated meeting a new date? In many cases there was anxiety and butterflies in your stomach yet, at the same time, an anticipation of opportunity. To believe that life is worth living—that beyond and throughout the daily mandatory tasks and occasional drudgery, there is optimism and an opportunity to attain what one wants—facilitates health. The opposite experience—that life is only drudgery that regardless how good it is or can be, life is living the myth of Sisyphus (pushing a rock uphill and just as the end is within reach, losing control and having to repeatedly start over at the bottom ... without ever being able to achieve success)—con-tributes to illness. Having purpose and hope are common themes associated with cancer survivors and with those who live longer with HIV (LeShan, 1994 and Solomon, Temoshok, O'Leary & Zich, 1987).

An important aspect of staying healthy is that daily activities are filled more with activities that contribute to your energy than with tasks and activities that drain your energy. Energy is the subjective sense of feeling alive and vibrant. An energy gain is an activity, task, or thought that makes you feel better and slightly more alive—those things you *want to* or *choose to do*. An energy drain is the opposite feeling—less alive and almost depressed—those things you *have to* or *must do*; often something that you do not want to do. An energy drain can be an energy gain for another person and vice versa. Energy drains can be doing the dishes and feeling resentful that your partner or children are not doing them, or anticipating seeing a person whom you do not really want to see. An energy gain can be meeting a friend and talking or going for a walk in the woods, or finishing a work project. Energy drains and gains are always unique to the individual. The challenge is to identify your energy drains and gains and then explore strategies to decrease the drains and increase the gains.

Begin this week's practice by first identifying your specific energy drains and gains at home and at work/school and then developing a detailed behavior program to increase

2. This practice was adapted from the presentation by Arnold Bakker, Ph.D., Preventie en behandeling van RSI bij beeldschermwerkers, at the NPI Cursus, Arnhem, The Netherlands, October, 2001.

the energy gains and decrease the energy drains on **Worksheet: Changing Energy Drains and Energy Gains: Practice 9**. Each day keep a log of the energy drain you have decreased and the energy gain you have increased on **Log Sheet: Changing Energy Drains and Energy Gains: Practice 9**. At the end of the week answer **Questions: Changing Energy Drains and Energy Gains: Practice 9**. Meet with your group and complete **Discussion and Conclusions: Changing Energy Drains and Energy Gains: Practice 9**.

Name: _____ Date: _____

Worksheet: Changing Energy Drains and Energy Gains: Practice 9

List your energy drains and energy gains (sources) at work:

Energy Gains (Sources)	Energy Drains

List your energy drains and energy gains (sources) at home (outside of work):

Energy Gains (Sources)	Energy Drains

Identify one energy gain that you will increase and one energy drain that you will decrease this week:

Energy Gain (Source)	Energy Drain

On the reverse side, describe your detailed behavior program that you will implement to increase an energy gain and decrease an energy drain. Describe in complete detail so that the reader can picture how and where you are doing it. Include how, where, when, with whom, under which situations, what may interfere with your plan, and how you will overcome the obstacles.

Detailed behavioral description for increasing an energy gain:

_____

_____

_____

_____

_____

_____

_____

_____

_____

_____

Detailed behavioral description for decreasing an energy drain:

_____

_____

_____

_____

_____

_____

_____

_____

_____

Describe possible factors that would interfere with implementing your plan and then describe how you will overcome those obstacles or change your plan.

_____

_____

_____

_____

_____

_____

_____

_____

Name: _____ Date: _____

Log Sheet: Changing Energy Drains and Energy Gains: Practice 9

Describe the specific energy drain you wish to decrease and the energy gain you wish to increase. Keep a daily log of your experience with increasing the gain and decreasing the drain.

Energy drain: _____
Energy gain: _____

Day 1

Date

_____

_____

_____

_____

_____

_____

_____

_____

Day 2

Date

_____

_____

_____

_____

_____

_____

_____

_____

Day 3

Date

_____

_____

_____

_____

_____

_____

_____

Day 4
Date

_____

_____
_____
_____
_____
_____
_____
_____
_____

Day 5
Date

_____

_____
_____
_____
_____
_____
_____
_____
_____

Day 6
Date

_____

_____
_____
_____
_____
_____
_____
_____

Day 7
Date

_____

_____
_____
_____
_____
_____
_____
_____

Name: _____ Date: _____

Questions: Changing Energy Drains and Energy Gains: Practice 9

1. What benefits occurred by increasing energy gains?

    _____

    _____

    _____

2. What factors impeded increasing energy gains?

    _____

    _____

    _____

3. What benefits occurred by decreasing energy drains?

    _____

    _____

    _____

4. What factors impeded decreasing energy drains and how did you cope with that?

    _____

    _____

    _____

5. What strategies did you use to remind yourself to decrease the energy drains and increase the energy gains?

    _____

    _____

    _____

6. If you could have done the practice again, how would you have done it differently?

    _____

    _____

    _____

    _____

Name: _____ Date: _____

Discussion and Conclusions: Changing Energy Drains and Energy Gains: Practice 9

1. What benefits did the group members notice as a result of the practices?

    _____
    _____
    _____

2. What challenges did the group members encounter as a result of the practices?

    _____
    _____
    _____

3. Describe the common energy drains.

    _____
    _____
    _____

4. Describe the common energy gains.

    _____
    _____
    _____

5. What were the common strategies to implement the energy gain/drain practice?

    _____
    _____
    _____

6. Topics or concerns to discuss with the instructor:

    _____
    _____
    _____

List your group members:

_____   _____
_____   _____
_____   _____
_____   _____

ॐ Transforming Failure Into Success: Practice 10

During the slalom race, I was going too fast. I was thrown by a bump and exploded on the slope at fifty miles per hour. The ski patrol got me, put me in the toboggan and took me down the slope and then to the hospital. All the time I was asking why and how come this happened. Every time someone came to visit, they again asked, "What happened? How did you get injured?" Each time I recited the accident.

Finally, when I got back to competitive skiing, I had lost the edge. Each time I went fast or hit a bump, I got scared and felt just like I did when I was injured. Then I realized that I had rehearsed how to ski with failure. I had rehearsed the accident scene hundreds of times. First when I kept asking why, and then when I retold the event to my coach, parents, friends and any one who asked. I had over learned the bad habit of stiffening whenever I was going fast.

Once I realized this, I asked myself, "How could I have skied differently so that I would not have been hurt?" The answer was obvious: The moment I was going too fast, I would have exhaled, flexed my knees and retracted my legs as I hit the bump. Then I would have slowed down. At this point, I started to rehearse this new image. In fact, every time I thought of skiing or the accident, I imaged this new scene. I continued this process even when friends asked me about my accident. Instead of telling them about it, I now answered, "I got injured, and let me tell you how I would ski it now."

After practicing this for a few weeks, my skiing improved remarkably. It taught me an important lesson. Instead of going over failure, I now ask, "What can I learn from it? How would I do this differently?" I now spend my time rehearsing how I would like to do it instead of how not to do it.

What we think about and rehearse is the template for future actions. Our past rehearsal prepares us for future action. We all stumble, make mistakes, and repeat old negative behavior patterns that do not work for us. We can change the thoughts and images of failure into learning moments to create a successful future, a major process of changing our future behavior. Through changing our previous self-defeating or limiting patterns we can correct our errors and, thereby, learn from the past. Mistakes and errors are feedback, and feedback is essential for growth. Therefore, errors, mistakes, or wrongdoings are *opportunities* to learn from. When we think about the past event we need not remember how it actually happened, since that would just encourage the same pattern to occur again. Instead, we can image how we could have done it differently, thereby creating a new template for future action. Remember, making mistakes is not a bad thing; in fact, it is the major source of learning. However, *repeating* mistakes is a waste of time.

What happens when we act foolishly, make a mistake, or get into a fight? Often we look back and feel guilty or bad about ourselves. We may try to analyze and ask why the behavior occurred. Perhaps we used the image of failure to beat ourselves up, repeatedly chastising ourselves for what we did: "I shouldn't have done ...." or "I can never seem to ...." We may even believe that this process of reminding ourselves again and again of not doing the wrong thing is a good strategy to *make sure it won't happen again*. Unfortunately, this strategy of reminding yourself of what not to do only strengthens the memory of the mistake, since you mentally rehearse it each time you think of not doing it. Hence, what is frequently rehearsed is more likely to be repeated.

The alternative is simple: *Learn from your mistakes*. Ask: "With the wisdom I now have, how could I do things differently in that situation?" We can all play Monday morning quarterback, since hindsight is "20/20 vision." This means that we have the wisdom and resources to change and not repeat our mistakes. When you notice yourself thinking, "I wish I'd done that differently," stop. Give yourself credit for being aware of the thought. Breathe and relax, then ask yourself, "If I could do this over, what would I do?" Then imagine yourself doing it in the new way.

Whenever we visualize or mentally rehearse in our minds, we are strengthening behaviors. We are reinforcing *engrams*. Engrams are well-established pathways in the nervous system along which information flows, making certain thoughts and behaviors habitual. In the process of conditioning, there appears to be no difference between actual rehearsal and imagined rehearsal; both strengthen the engram. The rehearsed behavior then occurs, which in turn reinforces the mental pattern. The major question is: Which pattern would you like to reinforce?

We consciously or unconsciously mentally rehearse so that our real lives will go more smoothly. For example, you may anticipate questions that might be asked at a meeting. As you think of the questions, you also practice the answers. In a more structured form, you may at some time have done role-playing, such as pretending that your friend is a prospective employer who is interviewing you for a job; you practice how you would introduce yourself and even the responses you want to give. Role rehearsal makes the actual behavior much easier, especially if you do it a few times; in the role-playing you are reinforcing a desirable behavior. Most, if not all, politicians, from President downward, role rehearse their answers to possible questions to be asked at a press conference before they actually have the press conference; it's no wonder that they appear to proceed so smoothly.

Mental rehearsal is role-playing done in your imagination. The more you imagine yourself performing the desired behavior, the more likely it is that you will actually perform that behavior. Almost all athletes and performers mentally rehearse their performance as the major tool in enhancing their optimal performance. The golfer who miscalculated at the fourth hole and hit the ball into the pond illustrates this. Instead of cursing himself and feeling dumb, the wise golfer acknowledged that a mistake occurred and then asked himself, "What was the problem?" He then considered that he might not have hit the ball hard enough or that he might not have accounted for the cross winds—or that he did not know and needed to ask a consultant for suggestions. He decided that he did not account for the cross winds and then asked, "How could I have done it differently to get the outcome I wanted?" He then imagined exactly how hard and in what direction to hit the ball. He mentally rehearsed the appropriate swing a number of times, each time seeing the ball landing on the green just a short putt away from the fifth hole. As he imaged this perfect swing, he felt it in his body. A bit later when his golfing partner asked him what happened when his ball went into the pond, he answered, "It went into the pond, and let me now tell you how I would hit it now." Thus, the past error became the cue to rehearse the desired behavior. To make the mental rehearsal even more useful, the golfer would continue this mental practice after every swing. In addition, he might imagine a slightly different situation coming up in the future and imagine himself performing perfectly also in that situation. For example, he might imagine that he will be confronted by a large sand trap; again, he calculates the force necessary to clear the obstacle, feels himself doing it perfectly, and watches the ball sail across to the green on the other side.

We all have more wisdom and resources at our command when we are relaxed and in a positive frame of mind. Mental rehearsal gives us an opportunity to take charge and change situations in which we have made mistakes. It is a process of accepting what is and what happened without blaming, judging, or criticizing ourselves. The past memory of the personal failure or poor coping behavior becomes an opportunity and trigger to imagine ourselves acting more wisely, compassionately, or in whatever manner we would prefer. Thus, we rehearse and strengthen the desirable behavior. Even the language by which we describe our potential goals will affect the outcome. For example, a person who desires to stop smoking can describe himself as a *non-smoker* or as a *smoker trying to stop*. Generally, the concept of the non-smoker leads to more success than of a smoker trying to stop. In the later case, the person continuously evokes the image of smoking and attempts to stop.

Consider the problem of overeating, especially at parties. Often, would-be dieters look back with chagrin on how they wolfed down cookies and cakes. They conclude that they have no will power, which makes them feel bad about themselves. The internal language is something like, "I shouldn't have eaten that stuff—the shrimp toasties, the egg rolls, the chocolate mousse; I can never control myself at parties." If you are an overeater, try an alternative approach instead of self-blame and continued mental rehearsal of eating the wrong things. Visualize yourself first relaxing at the party by doing QR (see **Quick and Warm with QR: Practice 5**), then picking up a handful of baby carrots, slowly chewing each one and tasting its sweetness, and then drinking a sparkling soda water with a twist of lemon.

Similarly, if your goal includes more exercise, do you find yourself saying, "I shouldn't have watched TV yesterday" or "I'm such a lazy bum"? Guilt does not produce the results you want. Instead, say, "I choose to run" and visualize yourself first walking to the TV to turn it off, then turning away from it, putting your running shoes on, and heading out the door, breathing in the cool air, and feeling invigorated.

To practice rewriting the past, it is best to begin with relatively easy things. For example, suppose you are often impatient when waiting in long lines; the last time that happened you felt yourself becoming annoyed, tense, and angry. When you reached the checkout clerk, who seemed to be very slow, you growled and gave her a dirty look. Now you have decided you would like to behave differently, that it is not helpful to get upset over such an event. Imagine yourself again in the long line, feeling the first twinges of irritation; then remember your decision and say, "This is silly." Next, take a deep breath and relax, realizing that this is a lovely opportunity to let go. As the clerk begins your order, say to him, "It sure must be a drag to have such long lines." As you leave, congratulate yourself for the ease with which you kept control and for being kind to the clerk.

GENERAL GUIDELINES

Image in total detail: see and feel the experience. Imagine every small step, sensation, and thought—everything that would occur when you actually do the task. How you image the task is not important. Some people see it in living color while others only have a sense of it. Just take yourself through the new activity. Rewriting the past takes practice. During the mental rehearsal the old pattern often reasserts itself. Just let it go and practice again. If it continues to recur, ask yourself, "What do I need to learn from this; what is my lesson?" The following is an example rewrite of coming home at night and pigging out by drinking two beers and eating half a cold pizza.

> *I walked to the door, inserted the key into the upper lock and turned the handle. I pushed the door open, flung my coat over the chair and kicked off my shoes. I walked into the kitchen and as I started to go to the fridge, I stopped, took a gentle breath, and exhaled. I checked inside; what was I feeling? I paused. Then I turned to the sink, got a glass, filled it with water and drank it. I took another breath, pulled up the chair and reached for the phone. I felt lonely. I called Frank and we talked for a few minutes. Then, I hung up the phone, walked to the bathroom, squeezed peppermint toothpaste on my toothbrush, brushed my teeth and went to bed.*

You can only change yourself. Remember that others have the freedom and the right to react in their own way. In your imagery, see yourself changing. Others may also change in their response to your change; however, they have the right NOT to change. Finally, there are many settings in which we have no control and, regardless of our behaviors, nothing would be different (e.g., being abused as a young child). In such cases, acknowledge what happened, reaffirm that you are no longer the same person as when the experience occurred, then take a deep breath and relax, and let go while knowing that this personal experience has taught you a set of coping skills that have nurtured your growth and development.

Specific Instructions

Begin by thinking of a past behavior you would like to change. Take time to observe the problem and identify new solutions. Then write out the new behavior pattern that you would like to rehearse using the wisdom you now have on **Worksheet: Behavior Rewrite: Practice 10.**[3] Follow this by daily practicing the **Transforming Success into Failure Script.** During the visualization, you might elaborate upon or even change your new pattern. Finally, each day observe an action you experience as an error (however small) and at that moment mentally rewrite how you would like to have behaved. Use the following five-step process:

1. Think of a past conflict or area of behavior with which you are dissatisfied.

2. Ask, "How could I have done this differently?"

3. See yourself in that same situation but behaving differently, using the wisdom you now have. (You might want to rehearse this step a number of times.)

4. Picture a possible future situation where you might react in the old pattern and see yourself doing it differently, with the desired behavior.

5. Smile and congratulate yourself for taking charge of programming your own future.

Remember, you will strengthen your new behavior pattern even more when you also practice it in real life!

You can also use the **9-Step Problem Solving Approach** to brainstorm the best solution to your behavioral problem or other problems that may contribute to your behavior (see pages 169-174). Write out the problem process on **Worksheet: Problem Solving: Practice 10.**

Optional: Do this with a partner. Think of a time when you acted in a way you would now like to change. Mentally rehearse the new strategy. Then share your new strategy and pattern as if that really had *happened; that is, describe to your partner not the actual event that happened but how you wish you had behaved—as if the desired behavior had actually occurred in the past.*

Repeat the exercise by switching roles.

Notice to what extent you still want to explain what actually happened versus truly allowing the new pattern to be presented as if that had already taken place in the past.

Note: In most cases, people first begin by explaining in detail the failure episode to offer the reasons for the new script. In many ways, the intensity with which you feel that you have to describe an old failure experience indicates how strongly this pattern of behavior is conditioned and continues to be the template for future actions.

---

3. Although it is usually possible to generate a new pattern to change the undesired behavior, some people report that when they rehearse the new pattern, it feels like a lie. If you experience that, just say, "I learned from this past behavior and now I will just imagine a situation in the future where I can rehearse the new desired behavior."

Name: _____ Date: _____

Worksheet Behavior Rewrite: Practice 10

Behavior to rewrite:

_____

_____

_____

Detailed description of new behavior pattern:

_____

_____

_____

_____

_____

_____

_____

_____

_____

_____

_____

_____

_____

_____

_____

_____

_____

_____

_____

_____

_____

_____

TRANSFORMING FAILURE INTO SUCCESS SCRIPT

Get into a comfortable position. Tighten all the muscles in your body; feel the tension.... Let go and relax; feel the relaxation spreading... Let you eyes be closed... Focus on your breathing, letting it become very relaxed, very low in your abdomen... Allow your abdomen to expand with your breath as you inhale; feel your pelvis widening... Exhale and feel the tension leaving your body as your abdomen comes in... Let the breathing be slow and effortless...As you exhale, imagine a blue wave going out further and further.... Let the relaxation deepen as your breathing deepens, allowing yourself to sink into a pleasant relaxed state... Use your own personal relaxation image to deepen your relaxation...

Allow the memory of the past event where you would like to have acted differently to come into your mind now... Observe it from beginning to end from a detached point of view, as if watching a movie... Ask yourself, "Given the wisdom I have now, how might I have behaved differently?"... Examine your options; there may be many different ways of responding.... Let the answers and images flow into your awareness, or use the previously written desired pattern.

Now go back to the behavior you would like to rewrite. See yourself in it once again, only this time go through it in a new way... Rerun the movie, imagining the event, the people, the whole situation in detail, except this time, see and feel yourself behaving in the new way... See yourself acting with confidence and control, breathing comfortably and easily the whole time... Remember, you cannot change others; the only person you have control over is yourself. See how others respond to your new behavior.

When you have finished reliving the scene, focus on your breathing; feel the widening and narrowing of your abdomen as you inhale and exhale... Allow the feelings of relaxation and peacefulness to be present.

Now either repeat the scene once more or picture a similar situation that could occur in the future... See and feel yourself behaving with the new pattern.

When you have finished experiencing this scene, return to your slow, easy breathing.... Feel the peacefulness and calm; let the relaxation occur as your breathing slows. Let your exhalation lengthen.... Be aware of the change in feelings about the event. Note the sense of control and autonomy...Feel the feelings and remember that the more you mentally practice, the more likely it is that you will achieve the desired outcome... Then take a deep breath, stretch, gently open your eyes, and feel peacefully alert.

Each day after you have gone through the script, complete **Log Sheet: Transforming Failure Into Success: Practice 10**. At the end of the week, answer **Questions: Transforming Failure Into Success: Practice 10**. Meet with your group and complete **Discussion and Conclusions: Transforming Failure Into Success: Practice 10**.

Name: _____ Date: _____

Log Sheet: Transforming Failure into Success: Practice 10

1. After each practice, describe the experience of rewriting your past in your imagination while being relaxed (you may use the same or a different rewritten image each day).
2. Each day describe one situation or experience that you chose to rewrite mentally. Do this right after the occurrence of the event. Describe how it changed your feelings about the event.

Day 1   1. _____

Date _____   _____

_____

_____

2. _____

_____

_____

_____

Day 2   1. _____

Date _____   _____

_____

_____

2. _____

_____

_____

_____

Day 3   1. _____

Date _____   _____

_____

_____

2. _____

_____

_____

_____

Day 4
Date _____

1. _____
_____
_____
_____

2. _____
_____
_____
_____

Day 5
Date _____

1. _____
_____
_____
_____

2. _____
_____
_____
_____

Day 6
Date _____

1. _____
_____
_____
_____

2. _____
_____
_____
_____

Day 7
Date _____

1. _____
_____
_____
_____

2. _____
_____
_____
_____

Name: _____ Date:_____

Questions: Transforming Failure into Success: Practice 10

1. What benefits occurred as a result of your daily mental rehearsal practice?

   _____

   _____

   _____

   _____

2. What were the benefits of rewriting your experience right after it happened during the day?

   _____

   _____

   _____

   _____

3. In what ways did your feelings change as a result of the practices?

   _____

   _____

   _____

   _____

4. What helped you remember to rewrite your experience right after it happened?

   _____

   _____

   _____

   _____

5. How might this practice affect your reaction in future events?

   _____

   _____

   _____

   _____

6. What problems/challenges occurred and how did you solve them?

   _____

   _____

   _____

Name: _____ Date: _____

Discussion and Conclusions: Transforming Failure into Success: Practice 10

1. What benefits did the group members notice as a result of the practices?

_____
_____
_____

2. What challenges did the group members encounter as a result of the practices?

_____
_____
_____

3. What situation or conditions facilitated or hindered the rewriting of experiences during the day?

_____
_____
_____

4. Describe common themes that the group members chose to rewrite.

_____
_____
_____

5. Among group members, how were the experiences of this week's practice related to ease of the practice, belief in efficacy of mental rehearsal, or other factors?

_____
_____
_____

6. Topics or concerns to discuss with the instructor:

_____
_____
_____

List your group members:

_____   _____
_____   _____
_____   _____
_____   _____

9-Step Problem Solving Approach

Rewriting our behavior may also involve changing conditions within our environment. Our behaviors may impact or be influenced by conditions over which we have control but may not have thought to change. The **9-Step Problem Solving Approach** is useful in identifying problems in our lives and in developing strategies to foment change.

Using this strategy you will select the problem you want to address, generate possible solutions, identify one or more workable solutions, implement a plan, and follow-up on your progress. Problem solving includes a willingness to explore and take risks so that more can be achieved. Most problems have a solution even though it may not be obvious at first. Finding a solution may demand that we think outside the box. For example, if you are working at the computer and the monitor is too low, you could purchase a stand to raise the monitor or, by shifting perspective, you can insert a telephone book underneath it to serve the same purpose. All it takes is a willingness to explore, experiment, and play. This 9-step process is useful in resolving most problems. First, read through the general procedure and the example. Then set aside at least 30 minutes to complete steps 1 through 7 using the **Worksheet: Problem Solving: Practice 10** to help you organize your thoughts. When you have implemented your plan, complete steps 8 and 9.

1. **Define problem.** List all your problems, allowing them to flow freely on the paper without editing them. When you are done, rank order them and identify the one problem you want to work on *now*. Describe this problem in detail—a concrete and specific form. Describe: How, when, how often, where and what. A common challenge in this step is specificity; framing the problem in a non-specific and diffuse form can prevent us from effectively addressing it. If we see the problem everywhere, or in most daily situations, it can appear overwhelming and unsolvable. For example, if the problem is that I am timid, I can narrow it down to being timid at work, rather than everywhere. Then I can begin to address the problem in that one situation. It is usually easier to learn to solve problems by beginning to work on a small one.

2. **Brainstorm solutions**. Write down all solutions however silly, crazy, or ridiculous. Make a list of all solutions as they pop-up—just write them down one after the other in order. At this stage do not *judge* or *criticize* the possible solutions. Allow a free flow of ideas. Common pitfalls in this stage of problem solving are:
   - *Judging the solutions as they occur* (e.g., thinking "This is silly" or "What a stupid idea" or "It can't be solved"). Postpone judging until after brainstorming; just acknowledge those thoughts and the internal critic and put all judgments to the side. Then continue to allow other childlike and crazy ideas to come forth.
   - *I cannot think of any solutions* (e.g., feeling blank or frozen). In this case, acknowledge the block and then bypass it by asking yourself what someone else would suggest (e.g., your best friend, therapist, mother, politician, dog or supervisor).

◆ *I think the problem is beyond my control* and therefore I will not even try to generate solutions. If the problem is beyond your control and there is nothing you can do, there are really only two solutions: Accept the situation (e.g., it happened and there is nothing I can do about it) or remove yourself from the situation or problem (remember that environment can be stronger than will power).

After generating all possible solutions, take a break and see if other solutions pop up. If possible, ask your friends, family members, or colleagues for help and suggestions for solutions.

3. **Review and evaluate brainstormed solutions.** List all the pros (benefits) and cons (problems, difficulties) for each solution.

4. **Identify the best solution**. Review your assessment of the solutions, then rank order and select the best solution. Pick the solution that can work in the face of all the constraints. Common pitfalls that may occur are the absence of any viable solution or that the brainstormed solutions will not solve the problem at this time. If no solution appears viable, accept that for now you are still working on a resolution; keep the problem in writing where you can continue to think of a resolution (do not get down on yourself for not resolving it immediately). Schedule a future time to review the problem and/or request help from others. If feasible, hire an outside consultant to help with the problem solving.

5. **Develop an action plan to implement the solution.** Make this action plan very specific. It should include answers to: what, when, where, how, with whom, and under what conditions. Be sure you include a time-line. Define the action plan in total detail. Common pitfalls are:
   ◆ *Lack of specific details*. If you think, "I will just do it," instead of creating a detailed plan, you may not achieve the desired results.
   ◆ Believing that I do *not have the resources to implement the action plan* (e.g., it is too expensive, too difficult, or too daring). Solve this by taking the time to review your solutions and ask for assistance from others. Appeal to your family, friends or coworkers for help or enlist the services of an outside consultant. Remember, two brains are often better than one.

6. **Mentally rehearse the action plan**. Imagine seeing yourself executing the plan; identify any barriers or blocks that would prevent success. Then develop strategies to overcome the barriers and blocks. A common pitfall is the thought that the barriers and blocks are overwhelming (e.g., my family, boss or co-workers will block it). Investigate the validity of the barriers and blocks. Often, the blocks are in our own minds and may not be actual limitations and constraints imposed by others. Communicate your needs to your co-workers, family, and friends.

7. **Revise the action plan in response to imagined barriers**. Incorporate procedures to bypass and overcome the barriers. Be sure the plan is very specific. You know exactly what you want, when you want it, and how and when it is to be done.

8. **Implement the plan and keep detailed notes on the progress.** Keep a detailed log of what actually happened when you carried out the action plan. Also, schedule a time to review the outcome of the action plan. The most common pitfalls are:
   ◆ *Not documenting what actually happened* so that later it is challenging to know exactly why it was or was not successful.
   ◆ *Not scheduling a time to review the outcome* of the plan.

9. **Follow-up assessment of the action plan.** Review the outcome of your action plan. Continue if successful or stop if your goal has been achieved. If less than successful, go back to step 1 of the problem solving process and develop a new action plan in response to the barriers that occurred. Common pitfalls are the lack of time to implement the plan, other work/activities took priority or interfered with the plan, or social pressure.

The following is a detailed example of the 9-step process.

1. **Define problem**

   The keyboard is too high and causes my shoulders to go up when I work on the computer. This contributes to discomfort: shoulder tightness and slight tingling in my arms by the end of the day.

   Observation: This problem needs more specificity since it consists of two parts: The keyboard is too high and having shoulder and arm discomfort. It is best to redefine the problem very specifically:

   a. Keyboard is too high.
   b. Problems with neck and shoulders at the end of the workday

   Determine the one *problem that you want to resolve, even though resolution of one may result in the resolution of the second. In this example,* the keyboard is too high *is the problem to brainstorm.*

2. **Brainstorm solutions**
   a. Get a keyboard tray
   b. Saw part of the legs off the desk so that the whole desk is lower
   c. Find another job that does not include keyboard work
   d. Get a pillow and sit on it.
   e. Buy a voice activated data entry program
   f. Hire an assistant to do the data entry
   g. Get a lower desk
   h. Get a leg operation to make me taller

3. **Review and evaluate brainstormed solutions**
   a. Buy and install a keyboard tray. It is possible, however it costs money and takes time to install, and it may not provide enough room for a mouse.
   b. Saw part of the legs off the desk so that the whole desk is lower. It is possible on this desk since the legs are wooden. Do I have the tools? What will other people

say? I will need to check with my supervisor if it is okay—it is usually easier to ask for forgiveness than for permission.

    c. Find another job that does not include keyboard work. No, I like my job. I just need to change the keyboard height.

    d. Get a pillow and sit on it. That is a possible solution until something better comes up. It may not look neat in the office.

    e. Buy a voice activated data entry program. It is a possibility, however, it will take money. Then I will be talking all day, which I don't want to do. It does not really solve the problem.

    f. Hire an assistant to do the data entry. Yes, this and retiring would be great, although not yet realistic since I do not have the budget for it.

    g. Get a lower desk. This is a possibility, however it may cost too much money.

    h. Get a leg operation to make me taller. Oh well, it's fun to be silly!

4. **Identify the best solution.** First, I will begin to use a pillow as a temporary solution and then in the next few days lower the height of the desk by either trimming the legs or by buying a new desk.

5. **Develop an action plan to implement the solution.** I have a pillow at home that is on the couch and I will bring it in tomorrow. This afternoon I will speak with my supervisor about the need for a lower desk. I can trim the legs of the desk. I have a saw and I could do this on Thursday after work. I will ask Michael to help me move the computer from the desk so that I can do it.

6. **Mentally rehearse the action plan.** (Mentally rehearse the plan and identify any blocks that would prevent implementation. Take yourself through all the steps.) I saw myself talking to my supervisor and needed to demonstrate that the height of the desk was the problem. I better suggest that the office engineer shorten the legs of the desk. It might take a bit longer but I won't be stepping on any political toes.

7. **Revise the action plan in response to imagined barriers.** I will still bring the pillow and will propose three options to my supervisor: buy a lower desk, I shorten the legs of the desk, or I request that the office engineer does this work.

8. **Implement plan and keep detailed log of its actions.** Tuesday, I brought the pillow from work. It helped however, my feet could not reach the floor so I had to put a phone book under my desk to serve as a foot stool. Tuesday afternoon at 3:17 pm, I talked with my supervisor and she agreed that the desk could be lowered. She called the engineer and he came Thursday at 10 and trimmed 8 cm off the legs.

9. **Follow-up assessment.** The keyboard is lower; however, I still have discomfort in my shoulders. I will make that my next problem to solve.

Name: _____ Date: _____

Worksheet: Problem Solving: Practice 10

1a. List problems:

1b. Select problem you would like to solve and describe the problem in detail.

2. Brainstorm solutions. Write down every solution without judgment, however ridiculous.

3. Review and evaluate brainstormed solutions.

4. Identify best solution and then describe it.

5. Describe the action plan in detail.

6. Mentally rehearse action plan and describe possible barriers.

7. Describe the revised action plan to bypass barriers and blocks.

8. Implement action plan and write down your experiences.

9. Follow-up assessment. Describe the outcome of your action plan.

✆ Freeing the Hidden Secrets: Practice 11[4]

A human being has so many skins inside, covering the depths of the heart. We know so many things, but we don't know ourselves! Why, thirty or forty skins or hides, as thick and hard as an ox's or a bear's, cover the soul. Go into your own ground and learn to know yourself there.

Meister Eckhart

I wanted to tell my girlfriend that my father was crazy, yet I could not. Would she suspect me? What would she think? How could I talk about the shame in my family? I can tell no one. I can't even talk to my family. Definitely not my father; he just drifts away. Not my mother; she just does not want to hear it.

I must keep it a secret so no one will know. The myth of my perfect family must continue at any cost. Yet, how can I be truly close to my girlfriend, if I cannot share my life? Each time I talk I have to edit, I block, I pull a curtain down, I tighten up.

Student

We are inhibited whenever we keep secrets or don't express our true thoughts and feelings about an emotionally upsetting experience in our lives. This inhibition occurs when we are ashamed, guilty or afraid to express ourselves because our family or we might be judged by the disclosure. The rules of what is acceptable to share are covert and culturally determined. Disclosure depends upon cultural rules as well as idiosyncratic family rules.

Inhibition takes energy; it is a type of dysponesis (misdirected effort). Inhibition affects all parts of our physiology and functioning—from the blood vessels, the breathing pattern, and the immune system to the striate muscle system. When it involves the muscles, a person may brace and unknowingly tighten muscles such as those in the neck and shoulders. Holding back words and thoughts can easily become a pattern of holding (bracing) in the body. It takes effort to hold back, to distract ourselves, to not think or not feel. This causes both short-term biological changes and longer-term health consequences. Inhibition prevents us from truly understanding and assimilating the traumatic event. Talking or writing about a trauma offers the opportunity to reframe, to accept, to integrate, and to gain insight so that healing may occur. Sometimes just seeing, remembering, and experiencing the event from another perspective may evoke the wisdom we need to integrate and let go of the feelings and thoughts around the event. This is true whether the event is childhood sexual abuse, an earthquake, the loss of a spouse, or entering college.

James Pennebaker, a professor at Southern Methodist University in Dallas, Texas, has documented the health-promoting effects of "confession" (writing or talking about

---

4. Adapted from the research of James Pennebaker, 1991.

traumas) in a series of ingenious experiments. Typically, subjects were assigned to write (or talk into a tape recorder) for 20 minutes on 4 consecutive days. In one study, subjects who were asked to disclose previously inhibited traumas showed pronounced improvement in immune function. The effects persisted for 6 weeks. College students who wrote about the trauma of coming to college decreased their health center visits by half in the 6 months following the experiment. (Subjects assigned to simply write about trivia showed no such changes.) Given the opportunity to unburden, some subjects revealed a lot (high disclosers) while others did not (low disclosers). The high disclosers gained the largest health benefits. Those writing about traumas felt sad or depressed immediately afterward (and, for some, even throughout the whole 4-day period); these feelings soon gave way to feelings of increased well-being, however.

After disclosure, many people experience a sense of "freeing up." Most of us experience this when we come to a decision we have been wrestling with. During the period when we are mulling over the pros and cons, bodily discomfort, anxiety, and sleeplessness are common. Once we have made a decision, there is a sense of release—as if a burden has been lifted—even when the choice made will result in discomfort.

Another interesting finding is that when people are actively inhibiting unwanted thoughts and feelings, they tend to engage in mindless activities requiring mindless or low-level thinking, such as housework, watching TV, eating, and strenuous exercise, rather than creative thinking or analytical problem solving. Pennebaker calls this "getting stupid and avoiding pain." Of course, drugs and alcohol may be used in the effort to numb pain and avoid thought, too. (Of all these strategies, physical exercise is undoubtedly the best alternative.) If there are unexpressed traumas and unwanted thoughts, you may have difficulty with high-level thinking. Perhaps this explains why 20% to 30% of the college students who wrote freely about traumas also showed slight improvements in their grades. In other studies, subjects who had written about traumas showed increased congruence of brain waves between right and left hemispheres. Thus, writing seems to decrease the physiological work of inhibition and to increase the ability to understand, find meaning, manage situations, and complete unfinished business. It seems that by externalizing an event through writing or talking we gain a kind of distance from it, as if the expression allows a new reorganization to occur.

WILL WRITING BENEFIT YOUR ABILITY TO COPE?

People vary in the degree to which writing (or talking) about traumas will assist them. Consider writing if you can answer yes to any of the following questions:

◆ Do you have any issue you have never shared with another person, or have prevented yourself from thinking about, no matter how long ago it occurred?

◆ Do you have unwanted thoughts that crop up, including in your dreams?

◆ Are you still upset, grieving, or obsessed about a traumatic event a year and a half or more after it occurred?

◆ Are you currently undergoing a stressful situation or adjustment, such as being a college freshman or returning to college after years of being away?

◆ Do you sense you have "unfinished business"?

◆ Do you have trouble finding meaning in some traumatic events in your life?

Although letting go of hidden secrets through writing is a powerful mechanism, for some participants there may be other strategies to be free from, open up, integrate, accept, and transform present and past conflicts. For example, sometimes we continue to act as if we are still a vulnerable and hurt child while at other times we automatically react strongly to a situation or person without knowing why. Almost instantaneously, we may feel intimidated, angry, or loving. As we learn to be relaxed and centered, we may sometimes be able to become an observer of our process—the first step to being freed from the past bonds. Resolving past conflicts, letting go of resentment, or making peace with a past traumatic situation may liberate us so that we can avoid these automatic reactions. The following are a series of optional complementary practices to mobilize understanding, compassion, and wholeness.

Optional Practices

If you have an early experience of loneliness, isolation, hurt, or lack of love (e.g., your mother died when you were 8, you were hospitalized for 3 months, your parents got divorced), practice **Writing and Receiving a Loving Letter.** *If you react strongly with resentment, fear, anger, or frustration to a certain person or event (e.g., you like babies yet you feel anger and rage toward a specific baby or you dislike a person or your roommate without any reason), practice* **Creating a Past Connection**. *If you want to let go of anger and resentment (e.g., a coworker, former spouse), practice* **Projecting Goodwill.**

1. **Writing and Receiving a Caring Letter**[5]

   Think about an experience when you were young where you felt lonely, isolated, hurt, and unloved. Now imagine that you had an aunt or uncle or other adult who truly understood and loved you. Imagine this person writing you a letter that, when you received it, helped you cope with the situation and feel at peace.

   In this exercise, take the role of the person who truly understood and loved you when this loss or difficulty occurred. Sit down and write a letter that would help the little boy or girl—use language that is appropriate for the age of the child—so that when the child receives it and reads it, it brings peace and he or she feels supported and loved. After you have finished writing the letter, place it in an envelope, address it to yourself, and mail it.

---

5. Adapted from a practice taught by Dr. Lawrence LeShan.

When you receive this letter, read it as if you are the little child again.

Observation*: Writing this letter is challenging. However, you can write about any-thing you choose and be as detailed as you feel comfortable. Often this letter only begins the process of healing and resolution. If this is the case, repeat the process of writing a letter to yourself until you experience a sense of peace and letting go.*

2. **Creating a Past Connection**

Think of someone to whom you automatically react strongly or unreasonably, espe-cially in specific situations. Imagine that you have lived previous lives—that you and that person have had previous relationships in which your sex, age, and respon-sibilities were quite different than in this life (e.g., imagine that you lived in the 18th century and that you are the spouse of that person). Now create imaginary past-life situations in which you and that person interacted (e.g., he/she could have killed you, beaten you, loved you, or fought in battle with you). Write a short story in detail about this imaginary relationship. After writing the story, set it aside. Each day repeat the same exercise except imagine a different setting, relationship, and time period. After a week, reread each of the short stories. As you read them, ask your-self if you intuit a theme that may explain and offer understanding in freeing your automatic reactivity.

Observation*: Through the creative process, one often develops a sense of peace, which allows us to react less to situations and people. The major challenges to writing the stories are the thought that this practice is silly because you do not be-lieve in past lives, and experiencing a creative writing block where you cannot imag-ine different relationships. This practice does not require a belief in reincarnation; it is a creative metaphor to allow exploration of the problem from many perspec-tives. If you experience a creative writing block, just begin and identify a time pe-riod (e.g., the American Revolution) and arbitrarily assign yourself a person (e.g., Paul Revere).*

3. **Projecting Goodwill**

Think of a person for whom you feel strong resentment, frustration, fear, or anger. Each time you begin to think about or anticipate meeting the person, take a gentle diaphragmatic breath and then, as you exhale, imagine that you can exhale the air outward like a blue wave rippling towards the person. At the same time wish the person goodwill. Even if the person hurt you badly or is cruel, hypothesize that within each person there is some part, however hidden, which represents the positive human potential (Christ or Buddha nature). As you project this blue wave of good-will, imagine it supporting that positive quality within the person.

Each time you become aware of the thought of, or anticipate meeting, or just before actually meeting the person to whom you feel strong negative emotions, practice a

QR (see **Quick and Warm: Practice 5** in Chapter 2) and follow it by projecting goodwill. In addition, do this practice as you wake up. Project goodwill as your first thought. Repeat for four weeks.

Observation: *If you practice sending goodwill consistently for three months, there is usually a significant change in your feelings toward this person. In the duration of the practice, the feelings slowly dissipate. The major challenge is that changes occur very slowly and often people expect a radical change in a day. By allowing time, change does occur.*

A Few Cautions Before You Start

Writing is not a substitute for friends or a good therapist. Friends can provide emotional support and grounding in reality. Although friends and family members may sincerely want to support and help you, a therapist may be better suited for the listening role. If you are distraught, see a therapist. If you decide to talk to a confidant, be sure that your listener is nonjudgmental; that you can trust him or her to keep your secrets; that you, too, are open and willing to listen to and to safeguard his or her confidences; that you are not editing or distorting your expression to suit your audience; and that you are not doing this out of a desire to hurt your confidant.

Don't use writing as a substitute for action in situations over which you do have control. Don't write just to complain; that is counterproductive. Instead, express your deepest feelings and thoughts about the event. Beware of writing with intellectual detachment; try for self-reflectiveness. Notice feelings and ask yourself what makes you feel this way.

Instructions

1. Ideally, have a unique setting which is conducive to opening up. (People who rarely travel often open up to a complete stranger on an airplane, not only because they feel safely anonymous but because of the novelty of the situation.) Evening hours, dim lighting, candlelight and complete privacy will all be helpful for letting go of inhibitions for your writing or tape-recording session. Set a specific time and location and keep it the same for each day's writing. Be sure there are no distracting sounds, smells and sights.

2. Have complete privacy. Be sure that you KNOW that you will not be seen, overheard, judged, or interrupted. For some people, anonymous public places such as a library are ideal locations; for others, sitting in the car with the doors locked offers a sense of security and privacy.

3. Decide whether you prefer to write or talk into a tape recorder and prepare by having a blank tape or plenty of paper and a pen available.

4. Set a timer for 20 minutes.

5. Once you begin, write or talk continuously for the whole 20 minutes about an upsetting or traumatic experience. Don't worry about grammar, spelling, or sentence structure. *Discuss your deepest thoughts and feelings about the experience.* You can write about anything you want but, whatever you choose, it should be something that has affected you very deeply. Ideally, it should be about something you have not discussed in detail with others. Let yourself go and touch the deepest emotions and thoughts you have. Write about what happened and how you felt about it, as well as how you feel about it now. You can write about different traumas during each session or the same one over the entire 4 days. If you run out of things to say, just keep going at the same pace and repeat what you have previously said or written. Write or speak it for *yourself,* not for anyone else or any audience. This helps prevent you from editing it even subtly and rationalizing or justifying yourself to another person.

6. Don't be surprised if your writing style or voice on tape seems different from usual; this is normal.

7. Ask yourself the following questions while writing: What are my thoughts? How do they make me feel? Why do I feel this way?

8. If, for example, you choose to write about coming to college, you might consider addressing your thoughts and feelings about leaving your friends and parents, about adjusting to the various aspects of college, or even about your feelings of who you are or what you want to become.

9. Keep or destroy the written or audio material. Be sure if you keep the material that it is in a safe place and not left for others to discover and read or listen to.

10. Do not write for anyone but yourself. Do not turn in any of your writing or tapes. These are for you alone. However, please be prepared to write about how you felt before and after the experience for each day of your writing, along with any thoughts you have about the usefulness of the whole exercise. For that purpose, complete **Log Sheet: Freeing the Hidden Secrets: Practice 11**, in which you simply describe your emotional and mental states without revealing anything confidential. After one week, reflect upon your experience and complete **Worksheet: Integration: Freeing the Hidden Secrets: Practice 11**.

One month after completing the practice, describe how the practice changed your perspective on the experience. What other shifts in perspective took place? Although the instructions encourage either writing or talking about a hidden secret, there are numerous additional approaches to release and shift perspectives. Instead of writing or talking, express the experience in dance, photography, music, drawing, sculpture, sand painting, and so on. In each case, be sure the focus is the expression of something that has affected you deeply. This nonverbal expression involves the intuitive and creative component that is within each of us. It is in connecting with this intuitive and creative force that healing occurs.

Name:_____ Date:_____

Log Sheet: Freeing the Hidden Secrets: Practice 11

For each of the 4 days you write, describe how you felt before and after the experience. (Reminder: you are *not* being asked to disclose any of the contents of your private writing.) Or, describe your experience with the optional exercises.

Day 1 Before: _____

Date _____   _____

                        _____

                        _____

                        _____

                        _____

      After: _____

                        _____

                        _____

                        _____

                        _____

                        _____

Day 2 Before: _____

Date _____   _____

                        _____

                        _____

                        _____

                        _____

      After: _____

                        _____

                        _____

                        _____

                        _____

Day 3 Before:

Date _____

       After:

Day 4 Before:

Date _____

       After:

Comments:

Name: _____ Date: _____

Worksheet: Integration: Freeing the Hidden Secrets: Practice 11

One week after completing the exercise, describe how the writing or the optional practices changed your perspective on the experience you wrote about. What other shifts in perspective took place?

_____

_____

_____

_____

_____

_____

_____

_____

_____

_____

_____

_____

_____

_____

_____

_____

_____

_____

_____

_____

_____

_____

_____

_____

_____

_____

_____

_____

_____

ᔐ CONVERTING THE ADVANTAGES OF ILLNESS: PRACTICE 12

Now when my eye fuzzes up, I know that it is telling me to slow down, stop judging people and not be so hard on myself.

CLIENT WITH MULTIPLE SCLEROSIS

My heart attack made me ask myself was my work worth dying for. It made me realize how estranged I had become from my children. Looking back it gave me a second chance with life and my family.

CLIENT WITH HEART DISEASE

Each of us would like to be well and healthy; however, health-promoting practices may at times be more difficult, demanding, and/or painful than continuing our present illness-producing or maintaining patterns. When we look back at a past illness, we can often see that the illness brought with it certain benefits and/or advantages. For example, being sick may have allowed us to excuse ourselves from work or family obligations and to experience love and care. Being ill may allow time for reflection or breaks from boring routines. A major or life-threatening illness may force us to make changes in relationships, work, and life direction. After all, if our survival is at stake, why put up with what is killing us?

It is interesting to consider that our bodies may be wiser than we are and that when we get off track—for example, by making the wrong decision, by overworking, or by staying in a dead-end job or abusive relationship—our bodies let us know and demand that we stop doing whatever it is. Have you ever wondered why, if your job demands a lot of speaking or telephone work, you seem to get laryngitis (rather than, say, a broken ankle)? Rather than getting angry at our "uncooperative" body parts, we might ask them, "How do I need to take care of you better?" or even "How are you taking care of me?" To quote Norman Cousins: "When we have a health disorder, we should ask what our bodies are doing right to adapt to a situation, and not what is wrong with our bodies." Sometimes when we experience a pain in the neck, we could ask, *who* or *what* is the pain in the neck? By identifying the advantages of illness, we may be able to change our behavior, learn from the illness experience, and mobilize our innate healing potential.

Sometimes, we develop illness as a conditioned response to certain events or stressful situations. One theory of allergic reactivity is that when a young, sensitive and vulnerable child is subjected to a traumatic event, such as parental fighting, his or her body reacts dramatically. The child's immune system goes on the alert to find the antigen that might be responsible for the reaction but finds, say, only cat dandruff in the child's sinuses. The immune system mounts an all-out attack on the antigen, leading to sneezing, wheezing, and so forth. If this combination of events happens a few times, the immune response becomes conditioned and will activate whenever cat hair is around—and/or whenever emotional stress occurs. In addition, if the child's allergic response leads to the parents dropping their argument and uniting to care for him or her, the response is further reinforced. When such children grow up, this allergic response is no longer so useful in getting their (or their family's) needs met, so it may disappear naturally. Or, if the adult gains understanding of the origin and pattern of the allergy, it may disappear.

We live in a culture that places little importance on inner development and, indeed, tells us there is too much else to do to take any time for it. Regular time set aside for reflection and expression—for example, journal writing or an emotional support group or creative artistic expression—is not a part of most people's lives. Yet this type of inner work may well be vital for our health, both emotional and physical. When we stray too far from the path of the heart, getting caught up in a rat race of "have to's" and "shoulds," we get sick. There are many wonderful stories of people healing—even from usually fatal illnesses—when they rediscover and begin to pursue what is truly meaningful to them. Evy MacDonald has graphically described this in her lectures and public appearances. She is a remarkable nurse administrator who completely recovered from amyotrophic lateral sclerosis (ALS). After receiving the gloomy prognosis for this usually fatal disease, she decided that before she died she wanted to learn to love herself unconditionally. Previously, she had always been too focused on outward achievement to be aware of her inner pain; having a life-threatening illness enabled her to turn her life around. She views the illness as a gift that enabled her to heal her self-hatred and transform her life.

Evy MacDonald emphasizes that each person's path of healing is unique. From her perspective, illness is complex and multicausal. In almost all cases, it is the interaction of genetics, environment, psychosocial variables, and the like. Even when we take responsibility to mobilize our self-healing, it may *not* result in improved health. It may, however, help us to grow. Dr. Lawrence LeShan who successfully worked with patients with cancer to explore and find their *own song* also describes this same theme. When patients started to sing their *own song*—their personal reason for living—their cancer some times ameliorated and regressed (LeShan, 1994).

The purpose of this exercise is to explore the advantages and benefits associated with some past or possibly present illness and to develop a strategy by which we can experience the benefits associated with the disease process without having the disease. For example, if an illness allowed me time to be by myself or to read or to watch TV without feeling guilty, how can I develop a strategy that would include some time out—a time period in which I take care of my own needs?

Begin by identifying the advantages of illness and then develop a strategy by which you may experience this advantage without being sick; use the worksheet entitled **Converting the Advantages Of Illness: Practice 12**. Each time you create the benefits, complete **Log Sheet: Converting the Advantages of Illness: Practice 12**. At the end of the week review your experience and answer the **Questions: Converting the Advantages of Illness: Practice 12**. Then meet with your group and complete **Discussion and Conclusions: Converting the Advantages of Illness: Practice 12**.

Optional: *After having completed Chapter 3 of this workbook, review your experiences. Write about them as suggested in the section **"Reflection and Integration: Summarizing Your Experiences"** in Chapter 1. This process allows an opportunity to reflect and integrate your experience.*

Name:_____ Date: _____

Worksheet: Converting the Advantages of Illness: Practice 12

1. Describe some past or present illness:

_____

_____

_____

_____

2. List the advantages or benefits gained when you were ill:

A. _____

_____

_____

_____

_____

B. _____

_____

_____

_____

_____

C. _____

_____

_____

_____

_____

3. Select one of the advantages you gained when you were ill and develop a strategy by which you can continue to experience that benefit. (For example: An advantage of being ill was having my mother cook for me. My mother lives a long way away, so it's not practical to go home for a meal. Instead, I can either ask my best friend to cook for me or take myself out for dinner. I don't have to get sick in order to enjoy the dinner; in fact, I might enjoy it more if I'm NOT sick!) Describe the advantage you picked and how you are going to implement the strategy to gain that advantage during the week. Be sure you include how, when, where and with whom.

_____

_____

_____

_____

_____

_____

_____

_____

_____

_____

_____

4. How might you try to talk yourself out of doing the exercise during the week and how will you counter your own self-talk?

_____

_____

_____

_____

_____

_____

_____

_____

_____

5. Now share and role-play your strategy with the members in your group and ask them to play devil's advocate. The role of your group members is to help you finalize your procedure and discover possible ways by which you may fail to implement your strategy. With their help, describe the restructured procedure you will practice during the week.

_____

_____

_____

_____

_____

_____

_____

_____

_____

Name: _____ Date: _____

Log Sheet: Converting the Advantages of Illness: Practice 12

Describe when, where, and what you experienced when you practiced your advantages-of-illness exercise. (For some, this exercise needs to be done only once or twice.)

Date _____

_____
_____
_____
_____
_____
_____
_____
_____
_____
_____
_____
_____

Date _____

_____
_____
_____
_____
_____
_____
_____
_____
_____
_____
_____

Date _____

_____

_____

_____

_____

_____

_____

_____

_____

_____

_____

Date _____

_____

_____

_____

_____

_____

_____

_____

_____

_____

_____

Date _____

_____

_____

_____

_____

_____

_____

_____

_____

_____

_____

Name: _____ Date: _____

Questions: Converting the Advantages of Illness: Practice 12

1. What were the benefits of illness you received without having to be sick?

   _____
   _____
   _____
   _____
   _____
   _____
   _____

2. What insights from this exercise might you incorporate into your life in order to reduce the "need" for illness?

   _____
   _____
   _____
   _____
   _____
   _____
   _____

3. What problems/challenges occurred and how did you resolve them?

   _____
   _____
   _____
   _____
   _____
   _____
   _____

4. How would you have done this exercise differently?

   _____
   _____
   _____
   _____
   _____
   _____

Name: _____ Date: _____

Discussion and Conclusions: Converting the Advantages of Illness: Practice 12

1. What benefits did the group members notice as a result of the practice?

   _____
   _____
   _____
   _____

2. Describe common themes in the strategies that the group members adopted to achieve the advantages of illness without being sick.

   _____
   _____
   _____
   _____

3. What were the common challenges experienced and how did the group members cope with them.

   _____
   _____
   _____
   _____

4. Among group members, how were the experiences of this week's practice related to past and/or present illness patterns and beliefs about responsibility and/or control over health?

   _____
   _____
   _____
   _____

5. Topics or concerns to discuss with the instructor:

   _____
   _____
   _____
   _____

List your group members:

_____   _____
_____   _____
_____   _____
_____   _____

SELF-HEALING THROUGH IMAGERY AND BEHAVIOR CHANGE

Movement in the depth of being is the manner in which the psyche performs its directive role in man. The content of this movement is imagery.

IRA PROGOFF

Imagination is a good horse to carry you over the ground, not a magic carpet to take you away from the world of possibilities.

ROBERTSON DAVIES

⑤ MOBILIZING HEALING WITH IMAGERY AND BEHAVIOR CHANGE

I am part of the world—the universe. I am connected to the yellow healing energies and the blue peaceful calm. All flow through me and around me. I am whole. I am good. I am part of the world. The dark clouds are also part of the world—they will be there but only along with the blue and yellow.

I see myself as a seed. The roots have been growing for a long time but I feel like I've just cracked the seedpod and am reaching for the light. The drought, the rain, the wind, the calm—all are parts of life that affect the seed—all help it to become stronger in some way. These things are not so much to be feared—as to be understood.

JANICE METTLER

We believe that all of us can mobilize our self-healing potential, although this does not mean that we will get physically healthier. In fact, we will all die. Nor is it possible to resolve all psychological and social conflicts or problems. However, we are all capable of moving toward wholeness and integration.

In beginning the self-healing process, there are two important components: imagery and behavior change. Imagery is very important because of its potential for bringing insights from the unconscious mind into awareness. Whenever illness or other forms of imbalance are present, we could go to someone outside ourselves, such as a doctor or therapist, to get a diagnosis and prescription for how to get well; or we could choose to tap into that part of ourselves that truly understands what the problem is and how to resolve it. Insights gained through imagery exploration may then direct us to make certain behavior changes involving rest, diet, exercise, work/career, relationships, and so on. Sometimes there are surprises, sometimes not. Often the insights that come from imagery sessions help provide the truly inner-directed motivation to make the necessary lifestyle changes.

WHAT IS IMAGERY?

Imagery is the direct language of the unconscious and the autonomic nervous system. Although most people associate imagery with the visual domain, we use the term in a broader sense. Images can be visual, olfactory, tactile, kinesthetic, or auditory. They may be directly descriptive or allegorical. Imagery can be passively observed or overtly acted out, guided or spontaneous. It is the medium of intuition and creativity. Imagery is the symbolic communication of body/mind/spirit. It is our belief that through imagery, we can access the deepest levels of our self-knowledge and awareness. Bodily symptoms can be thought of as communications from the unconscious. Decoding these symptoms into messages that we can understand can occur through imagery.

When we use the term *imagery* in this workbook, it usually means spontaneous rather than guided or preconceived visualization. Visualizations are images that are consciously created and directed; they can be very helpful. The exercises in this section emphasize tapping creative and healing potentials by means of unedited spontaneity in the imagery. Often, visualization and imagery may be combined. For example, a guided visualization may suggest that you are about to meet a wise being, without telling you anything descriptive about this being, such as gender, age, or even whether this being is an animal or a human. All the specifics are allowed to arise spontaneously in your mind.

The right and left hemispheres of the brain seem to have somewhat specialized functions. While the left hemisphere is responsible for speech, analysis, and logic, the right hemisphere is involved with images, emotions, the larger picture, and relationships between events and between people. In our society, we tend to value the rational, linear, logical thought of the left hemisphere; therefore, we are usually not in touch with the insight and wisdom that the right hemisphere can provide. However, when we become deeply relaxed in body and mind, the censorship of the left hemisphere loosens and we can access insight and wisdom from the right hemisphere by tuning into images. "Imagery lets you communicate with your own silent mind in its native tongue" (Rossman, 2000). Ideally, in this simplified model the right and left hemispheres work as a team.

The right gives guidance and the left creates the will, intention, and real-world behavior changes.

Imagery is used as a tool to become aware of the meaning of illnesses or to enhance the healing process. Imagery, like dreams, offers insight into patterns underlying the messages of the body. In addition, it is one of the approaches by which people can actively, and in a self-accepting way, participate in their own reintegration. Moreover, in the act of imaging you may rehearse and make easier the new behavior. Benefits usually accrue if the imaging is practiced often and with openness to new insights. It is used in a wide array of areas—from psychotherapy, personal goal setting, and self-healing to enhancing peak performance. (Athletes often call this type of practice "visual motor behavior rehearsal.")

Imagery, combined with acting on our goals, gives us the experience and confidence that change is possible. In the act of doing, we *know*—not just believe—that we can grow and change. Athletic, theater, and musical performers mentally rehearse exactly how they will act. They create in their minds visual, kinesthetic, auditory, and olfactory sensations as they imagine themselves performing perfectly. As they mentally rehearse, their bodies react as if the performance is occurring in that moment. The actual performance is the next step.

Imagery is usually practiced after relaxation has been mastered. For many people, a regular relaxation practice is all that is needed to relieve or prevent the majority of symptoms; for others, relaxation sets the stage for a deeper exploration of problem areas through imagery. Healing can include reduction of physical symptoms, accepting who and what you are, transforming negative mental and emotional patterns, or integrating new behavior patterns, such as increasing exercise or improving diet.

If you have led a sedentary life and have no particular illness problems, you may simply feel that your life would be healthier if you exercised. Exercise, then, can be your self-healing practice. Mental rehearsal of you exercising and enjoying it can be a motivator. Some people include imagery as a complement to their medical treatment, such as chemotherapy for cancer. Many have reported that by taking care of one symptomatic area in a holistic way they improved their general health and well-being. When we begin to trust and follow our inner promptings (intuition), rather than acting from "shoulds" and expectations, we encourage healing. How do we know whether to trust an impulse? Is it intuition or conditioning/habits/desires? Follow those "gut" feelings and look at the results! If the results enhance your wholeness, that is good evidence that you followed your intuition.

The self-healing process is based upon a sequence of steps. These steps will first be listed and then described in detail.

1. *Imagery Exploration: Answers from the Unconscious.* For one week allow spontaneous images to come each day. Either ask the question "What do I need to know or do for my own self- healing?" or hold conversations with an inner guide (see sections **Exploration Script** and **Inner Guide Script** in this chapter).

2. *Developing a Self-Healing Strategy.* On the basis of information you discover during imagery exploration[1], include some or all of the following steps:
    a. Reviewing the insights from imagery
    b. Reading up on the area of concern
    c. Setting goals and priorities
    d. Monitoring baseline data
    e. Arranging new behavioral cues
    f. Selecting reinforcers
    g. Planning ahead for relapses

3. *Imagery for Self-Healing.* Begin with the image of illness and then develop a process for healing that is ongoing and prevents relapses. Finally, imagine yourself integrated and whole.

4. *Carrying Out and Adapting Your Strategy.* Using self-devised forms, maintain an ongoing evaluation of your success or failure in achieving your goals; modify your strategy when necessary.

5. *Integrating Your Experience.* Summarize what you have learned.

OBSERVATIONS FROM STUDENTS AND PATIENTS

In follow-up surveys, most participants after 4 weeks of practice reported that their conditions improved and that they reaped significant benefit from the self-healing practice as shown in Figure 4.1.

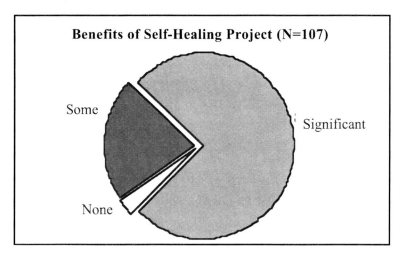

Figure 4.1. Participants' self-rating of successfully achieving self-healing goals after practicing for four weeks.

---

1. The behavioral approaches have been adapted from. Watson, D.L. & Tharp, R.G. (1992). *Self-Directed Behavior: Self-Modification for Personal Adjustment* (6th ed). Monterey: Brooks/Cole. We recommend this text to anyone desiring to change his or her behavior.

Some of the areas that participants explored and developed successful self-healing strategies included: increase in daily exercise, weight loss, changing internal thoughts to eliminate depression; breathing and cognitive change for reduction of anxiety, anger, and jealousy; relieving and reducing headaches, back pain and stiff necks; stopping itching and eczema, stopping smoking, decreasing caffeine intake, stress reduction and time management.

Participants reported that the following common themes were associated with success:

◆ Making the project a priority, which meant making **ME** a priority (e.g., commitment to help myself and I wanted to do it).

◆ Having clear, obtainable goals.

◆ Taking responsibility for my actions.

◆ Doing it daily—all of a sudden after four weeks there was a real change (e.g., I stuck with it despite all odds; my perseverance and continuity of my daily practices).

◆ Realizing that I had the power to make changes in my health that would affect my world forever.

◆ Pushing myself out of my comfort zone (e.g., trusting that I could face my weakness and get over it).

◆ Receiving support from group members, family and/or roommates.

◆ Understanding that my old habits made me worse and that I could change my behavior (e.g., the infection got worse by scratching; breathing and imagery made it better).

◆ Experiencing that through the imagery I gained the self-control and self-esteem (e.g., now I know I do have the power for self-healing and I no longer think of myself as a helpless being).

◆ Having constant reminders of my inner power to be healthy and the power to choose my interpretation of the world (e.g., I learned a variety of things of which I was unaware, taking time out for myself reduced tension/stress. Being organized and well prepared is a key contributor in my stress and pain reduction. Opened doors in my life that I was unwilling to open).

✆ IMAGERY EXPLORATION-ANSWERS FROM THE UNCONSCIOUS: PRACTICE 13

Imagery exploration is based upon the observation that our unconscious can communicate and be accessed through imagery or dreams. This communication may be more accessible when we are quiet (centered) and not distracted by external cues or internal emotions and desires. Imagery is then a communication from our intuitive and creative self. At times, symptoms and problems are messages that prod us to make changes in our lives.

As you explore, do not have an agenda or try to construct images. Be open to novelty and surprise. Remember, images need not be visual. They may be kinesthetic sensations or auditory sensations or a felt sense. Don't judge your experience. If your attention wanders, bring it gently back to the question. Even fleeting images or feelings may be important, so record them faithfully. Some things that are puzzling to you now may later make sense. You can explore the previous day's images by asking open-ended questions about them during the practice. It may be useful to ask, "When did this problem develop? Why do I have it?"

Many healing traditions call upon a wise inner guide or advisor. The form does not matter. This being may appear as a friendly animal, a guardian angel, a religious figure, a wise old man or woman, a radiant light, or simply a voice. It is compassionate and loving and understands everything about your problem or symptom and how to heal it. This wise being is actually a part of you: the part that truly knows how you can assist in your own healing. You may also have more than one guide. Accept whatever image comes to you. The insight or images you access may direct you to something other than what you would have chosen for the self-healing project. For instance, a woman who thought that her self-healing would involve dieting to lose weight discovered through her imagery that the most important thing was learning new ways to nurture the child within her and treat herself well. These new ways did not involve food but included long, hot bubble baths, drawing, and going to the beach.

Accept the spontaneous images. They are meaningful, although they sometimes appear to come from left field. For example, one woman wanted to use imagery to enlarge her breasts. The image that came up—large, droopy breasts like her mother's—surprised her. She felt disgusted by the image. As a small child, she might have thought: "I do not want droopy breasts when I am my mother's age. Therefore, my breasts will stay small and not grow large!" For her, self-healing was accepting the images of her own and her mother's body.

Another woman observed that each time she explored ways to reduce her sugar intake, an image of her ex-lover appeared:

My relationship with this man and our consequent separation involved a lot of emotional turbulence, and I soon realized that although our connection ran very deep, on one level he was a means of filling a void within myself, like sugar was. Furthermore, I would often find myself stuffing my face with sweets whenever I was feeling hurt over this relationship. This realization helped me to gain an increased awareness of my thoughts and feelings surrounding my sugar habit.... The objects of our addictions take many forms, but they all seem to be a means of connection to something we don't find in our lives. I have begun to probe more deeply into the spiritual question that is the human condition: How can we find love, how can we feel connected?.... Meditation has helped me to address this question by awakening an awareness in me that enables me to go into each experience fully, to be completely present in the moment, and to observe how I am feeling in the moment.... I feel that, as I bring more awareness to my life through the integration of mind/body and spirituality, my compulsive behaviors, including my sugar addiction, will eventually disappear.

INSTRUCTIONS

Each day, begin either with your favorite relaxation practice, which you synthesized in **Creating Your own Relaxation: Practice** 7, or use the printed relaxation script. After you have relaxed and feel peaceful, continue either with the **Exploration Script**, which consists of a series of open-ended questions, or with the **Inner Guide Script** (both are presented in the next section of this chapter). You may want to adapt the questions in the exploration script to the area you have selected for healing. These two sample scripts were adapted from a very helpful book, *Healing Yourself*, by Dr. Martin Rossman (2000). Allow images to arise spontaneously for 10 to 15 minutes. In some cases, nothing comes up. That is equally OK. Just continue with the practice. We suggest you try out each of these imagery explorations at least once and go with the one you find most helpful. After each practice draw, sketch, or in some other way express the images. At the end of this week's practice, integrate the observations and develop your self-healing project.

If an uncomfortable, unfriendly, or critical figure arises with the inner guide imagery, ask it to go away and request another guide.[2] If you choose to draw or paint your image, be sure to have your materials available before starting your relaxation.

EXPRESS THE IMAGES

Each day after you have gone through the script, find a way to express the important images. You can draw or sketch them in color, compose music, act them out in dance, and so forth. Remember, not everyone receives visual images. If your information came as words, sounds, or feelings, these are fine. Describe the images briefly in your log notes.

If you do draw or paint, you might consider using your non-dominant hand, which is in closest communication with the non-dominant (right) hemisphere of the brain. This technique has been taught by Lucia Capacchione and is beautifully described and illustrated in the books *Recovery of Your Inner Child* and *The Power of Your Other Hand* (Capacchione, 1988 & 1991). You might also write next to your drawing a few words that seem appropriate, while still using your non-dominant hand. Be sure not to judge these drawings or writings as clumsy or childish. These are powerful ways to enhance the imagery experience. To clarify the insight gained from imagery, write a single sentence that most clearly expresses that insight.

When beginning to pay more attention to spontaneous imagery, many people report that their nighttime dreaming becomes more vivid and meaningful and that they remember their dreams more easily. This may be because through imagery explorations we are

---

2. For more detailed instructions see: Rossman, M.L. (2000). *Guided Imagery for Self-Healing.* New York: New World Library.

encouraging and increasing our access to previously unconscious material. Although the instructions may appear to imply that the images are visual, in many cases they can equally be experienced in words, kinesthetic sensations, sounds or music, or just a sense of knowing. Remember, each person has his or her own unique expressive communication channel with the intuitive process.

ANSWERS FROM THE UNCONSCIOUS: SCRIPTS

Have drawing or painting materials ready. Get comfortable in a sitting position, and let your body relax and rest. Allow your eyes to close. For the next few minutes, recreate the sensations you experienced in your previous relaxation practices.

Insert your Personal Relaxation Script (from Practice 7) or continue with the following relaxation script

Relax all over; allow a pleasant heaviness to develop... Take a couple of deep, full breaths and feel yourself letting go with each exhalation... Allow the comfortable sensations of warmth to flow through your entire body... Let go of any unnecessary tension and take the time to attend to each part of your body... Invite your feet and legs to relax, gently noting any areas where there is tension and just releasing it... Allow your thighs and buttocks to relax, and then your pelvis and lower back... Feel your abdomen expand with your slow, easy breaths... Let go of tension, being aware of any area of your body where there is a need for healing... Relax the organs within your abdomen and chest... Relax your back... Feel more and more comfortably relaxed, letting go of your shoulders and neck, relaxing your arms and hands... Feel the warm relaxation flowing, allowing your forehead and eye muscles to let go, and your jaw, throat, face, to relax... Feel your breath flowing easily in... and out.

Now, find yourself in a special inner place of relaxation and healing, a place where you feel calm, safe, and secure... Notice what your senses are taking in: colors, sights, sounds, textures, aromas... Breathe in the peacefulness, the quiet, soothing atmosphere of this place, and find a spot in which to settle down, where you feel centered and comfortable... You might say to yourself: "I am now deeply relaxed, in a calm, peaceful state of mind. My body feels comfortable and quiet. My mind is clear and open to images that will be helpful to me."

CONTINUE WITH EITHER THE EXPLORATION OR INNER GUIDE SCRIPT

Exploration Script.

When you feel ready, bring your awareness to your own area of concern, the symptom or problem that you would like to heal. Explore this as if it is totally new to you... Allow any image to emerge that represents this symptom or problem, while you remain comfortably relaxed, and accept whatever image comes up whether it is symbolic or realistic, familiar or strange... Observe, feel, touch it from different perspectives and note how large it is... what shape it has... how it moves or not... what colors you observe... Notice where the problem seems to be... how and where you feel it inside yourself... Does it have a sound or vibration... a smell or a taste...?

And now, ask: "What do I need to know?" or "What can I learn from this?" or "What do I need to do to mobilize my own self-healing?"

When you ask the questions, gently wait for the answer. Trust that an image, thought, sensation, or association will occur. After a little while, ask the question again. When an image, thought, or sensation arises, observe it and then let it go... Then, repeat the question.

Now, let an image arise that represents the process of healing... Allow this image of healing to become vivid and bright and clear... see it, feel it, experience it... What part do you need to play in this healing process?...

Observe this process for as long as you like... and then slowly, gently, begin to feel yourself as you rest on the chair... become aware of your toes and wiggle them... gently move your fingers... give yourself a slow, comfortable stretch... breathe fully... and open your eyes when you feel ready.

Inner Guide Script.

As you relax and rest in your peaceful place of healing, you now become aware of another being who is approaching, yet waiting to be invited to join you... It could be a person, an animal, or a light... Just accept whatever image comes as long as it feels safe for you... As this being comes nearer, you notice that it appears to be kind and gentle and wise... This guide knows you very well... And so, if it feels right to you, invite this being to be with you awhile in your special place... Take a moment to study your guide, noticing everything about it... Feel the loving presence... And now, with your area of concern in mind, ask your guide any question that comes up... You might want to ask about why you have this problem, or what steps you can take to assist your own healing... And wait for an answer to come... Allow your guide to communicate with you in what ever way seems natural, which may not be in words... Answers may also come at a later time, such as in a dream or while relaxing... You may ask any other question you wish, to gain more clarity... And again, be open to the answer in whatever form it may come... If you receive advice that you feel hesitant to follow, know that you can ask the guide for further explanation, either now or later, and that you can ask for reassurance that the advice will be helpful.

And now, thank your guide, and say good-bye, knowing that you can make contact again at any time when you are relaxed... Watch as your guide leaves and once again, feel the beautiful serenity of your special place enfolding you... Breathe easily and become more aware of your body... Slowly wiggle your fingers and toes, breathing deeply... Open your eyes when you are ready.

Each day right after your imagery exercise (and drawing), complete **Log Sheet: Answers from the Unconscious: Practice 13**. At the end of the week, answer **Questions: Answers from the Unconscious: Practice 13**. Meet with your group and complete **Discussion and Conclusions: Answers from the Unconscious: Practice 13**.

Name: _____ Date: _____

Log Sheet: Answers from the Unconscious: Practice 13

After each daily practice session, (a) describe your questions from the exploration or dialogue with the internal guide, (b) describe your imagery, and (c) write the sentence that most clearly describes the insight gained from the imagery.

Date _____   a. _____
Day 1   _____
                  _____

          b. _____
             _____
             _____

          c. _____
             _____
             _____

Date _____   a. _____
Day 2   _____
                  _____

          b. _____
             _____
             _____

          c. _____
             _____
             _____

Date _____   a. _____
Day 3   _____
                  _____

          b. _____
             _____
             _____

          c. _____
             _____
             _____

Date _____   a. _____
Day 4   _____
                  _____

              b. _____
                  _____
                  _____

              c. _____
                  _____
                  _____

Date _____   a. _____
Day 5   _____
                  _____

              b. _____
                  _____
                  _____

              c. _____
                  _____
                  _____

Date _____   a. _____
Day 6   _____
                  _____

              b. _____
                  _____
                  _____

              c. _____
                  _____
                  _____

Date _____   a. _____
Day 7   _____
                  _____

              b. _____
                  _____
                  _____

              c. _____
                  _____
                  _____

Name:_____ Date: _____

Questions: Answers from the Unconscious: Practice 13

1. What benefits occurred as a result of your practice?

_____

_____

_____

2. What were the common themes of your imagery?

_____

_____

_____

3. What were the themes of insight derived from the imagery?

_____

_____

_____

4. Which approach, exploration or inner guide, did you find more helpful and why?

_____

_____

_____

5. What did the drawing show? What other forms of expression did you use?

_____

_____

_____

6. What problems/challenges occurred?

_____

_____

_____

7. How did you resolve the challenges?

_____

_____

_____

Name: _____ Date: _____

Discussion and Conclusions: Answers from the Unconscious: Practice 13

1. What benefits did the group members notice as a result of the practice?

    _____

    _____

    _____

2. How did the images offer insight to the explored questions and problems? Share draw-
    ings and other productions with others in the group for feedback.

    _____

    _____

    _____

3. Describe the common challenges encountered and strategies used to resolve them?

    _____

    _____

    _____

4. What were the differences or similarities between exploration and internal guide prac-
    tices?

    _____

    _____

    _____

5. What personal factors contributed to experiencing spontaneous answers from the ex-
    ploration and wise one (e.g., past practice with meditation, hypnosis, day dreaming)?

    _____

    _____

    _____

6. Topics or concerns to discuss with the instructor:

    _____

    _____

    _____

List your group members:

_____   _____

_____   _____

_____   _____

_____   _____

✥ DEVELOPING A SELF-HEALING PLAN: PRACTICE 14

Scientific discovery is 1% inspiration and 99% perspiration.

This next phase involves transforming insight from your imagery exploration into an action plan. Having insight is fun and inspiring, but it is through action that we truly transform ourselves. If we do not act upon insights, we tend to disconnect from our inner knowing. Taking charge and developing a self-healing strategy means that you are becoming the master of your own ship. No longer are you adrift, pushed around, and buffeted by myriad thoughts and stimuli. The aim of this section is to develop an action plan and begin the self-healing practice. Read the background material carefully and then develop your plan. Many of these concepts have been derived from an outstanding text by Watson and Tharp (1992), *Self-Directed Behavior: Self-Modification for Personal Adjustment (6th ed)*. We recommend that you look at this text if you would like additional information.

REVIEW THE INSIGHTS FROM IMAGERY

Go over your responses from the previous section and list a few ways by which you might translate these insights into practical action. Brainstorm by writing down as many ways as you can think of to put your plan into action. Use the **9-Step Problem Solving** procedure (see Chapter 3, Practice 10). You might want to do this with your small group or a friend. Brainstorming means that even the wildest ideas are allowed and written down, with the aim of generating many possibilities in a short time. Then, look over your options. Which would be the simplest, easiest, most practical, most fun? Choose one or two.

READ UP ON THE AREA OF CONCERN[3]

Become informed about the problem to which you plan to apply your self-healing practices. For example, if your imagery guided you to work with your sore back, research both standard, or allopathic, medical approaches (e.g., orthopedics and physical therapy) and complementary, or alternative, approaches (e.g., dietary, chiropractic, Naturopathic Medicine, Feldenkrais, or massage). By exploring and investigating appropriate treatment approaches, you can begin to make informed choices. You can question your allopathic or alternative health care provider on the risks and benefits of any proposed strategy. You will then be in a good position to devise your self-healing strategy, which may or may not use allopathic approaches.

---

3. For specific information, we recommend that you search relevant databases such as PubMed, a service of the National Library of Medicine, provides citations back to the mid-1960's and additional life science journals. PubMed includes links to many sites providing full text articles and other related resources. See: http://www.ncbi.nlm.nih.gov/entrez/
Most libraries have access to this and other databases (e.g., Psychological Abstracts) in printed form, CD-ROM, or direct computer access.

SET GOALS AND PRIORITIES

> *If you want your dream to be*
> *Build it slow and surely*
> *Small beginning, greater end*
> *Heartfelt work grows purely.*
>
> "STONE BY STONE" BY DONOVAN,
> FROM THE FILM *BROTHER SUN, SISTER MOON*

Set realistic and, if possible, quantifiable goals. Define your goals clearly in terms of particular behaviors in particular situations. As one participant stated, "The major reason for success was that my practice was based on clear, obtainable goals." That will make your progress much easier to measure. After all, being able to see measurable evidence of change, even if it is small, is a wonderful incentive to help keep going in a new (and perhaps less comfortable) behavior. If, for example, you would like to be more outgoing, you'll first want to decide what outgoing behavior means to you. Perhaps it means smiling and making eye contact with an increased number of people each day or speaking up in class more times each week or starting more conversations with people at work.

It's easier to increase desirable behavior than to decrease undesirable behavior. For example, if you'd like to stop biting your nails, increase the number of times you engage in different behaviors with your hands, such as using an emery board or giving yourself a brief hand massage. Choose a behavior that is incompatible with the problem behavior to enhance success. For example, saying something pleasant to yourself or another person is incompatible with saying something critical or practicing QR (Quieting Reflex—rapid relaxation—see Practice 5 in Chapter 2) is incompatible with frowning.

Set as a goal behaviors that you can monitor and control. For example, if your goal is to lose weight, break that down into several sub-goals that are expressed as specific behaviors in particular situations such as, getting up from the table and going for a walk instead of staying for dessert; relaxing and acknowledging emotions when anxious or upset, beginning an exercise program, or substituting more vegetables for high fat foods. If you get stuck on what your sub-goals need to be, try brainstorming, that is, writing down any and all ideas, no matter how wild or impractical, and selecting later.

If your goal is to remove a wart from a finger using imagery, your behavioral sub-goals may include daily relaxation and visualization of the wart shrinking. You could also count every time during the day you remember the thought and image of the wart dissolving and your finger being smooth and totally healthy. You may want to monitor thoughts that are self-defeating and those that are supportive of healing.

Remember to start with small, easy to achieve goals; then move on to more challenging ones. Start with the behavior change that is most fun, easiest, and most appealing; the others will follow more easily when you have already gotten yourself moving. For example, exercise leads to a better self-image and a happier body, which then makes it easier not to eat compulsively.

COLLECT BASELINE DATA

Before beginning the self-healing project, establish a baseline of where you are now. Whatever behavior or other data you decide to monitor, attempt to be as specific as possible. Ask when, where, what, and with whom the behavior occurs; what preceded it; and how it changes your or others' behaviors afterward. For example, if you have a migraine headache twice a week, record the time and place of occurrence along with all the other situational and behavioral information you can come up with. Your notes might read as follows: "Finished a 10-page paper, what a relief, after 4 days of intense effort. Migraine, pain about 8 on a scale of 1 to 10. Began the night after I turned in the paper and lasted until the next day at 1:00 P.M., family tiptoed around and didn't disturb me."

In order to establish a baseline and later monitor progress, you may want to devise your own log format. For example, one woman who was monitoring negative self-talk carried a small notepad around with her at all times and jotted down each negative thought; then she immediately rephrased it in a more positive and rational way. She also used the notepad to record affirmations and looked at them a few times each day. One person devised a food diary with spaces for recording his emotions and thoughts about the food, as well as how hungry he was, the time, and so forth.

These measures can be divided into objective and subjective categories. Objective measures tend to be quantifiable and include such variables as weight, number of laps run in 10 minutes, pulse rate, and so on. Subjective measures tend to be ratings and description of feelings, such as intensity of depression, alertness, or pain. For some projects, one can collect and measure both objective and subjective data, while for other projects, only subjective measures can easily be collected (e.g., daily subjective pain rating).

Here are a few more examples of baseline and continuing measurement strategies that others have used:

◆ Simple tally sheet of marks to register each time a problem behavior occurs per day, with a graph at the end of the week (e.g., nail biting)

◆ A mood-rating chart (used by a woman working on overcoming depression)

◆ Ink prints of a wart on a fingertip, showing its shrinkage each week

◆ A series of pictures of body image, beginning with a whale and ending with a small fish

◆ Measurements of range of motion in an area of the back that did not move normally

◆ Self-rating scales for pain intensity (important to rate and record because when you're not in pain, it's hard to remember how it felt when you were, and vice versa)

◆ Testimonials from friend, roommate, or spouse concerning an objective view of changes observed in you. If your behavior is quite automatic or unconscious, you may want to enlist the help of others to point out when you do it (gently and tactfully, of course, not punitively!)

During the period in which you record your baseline data, which is typically a week, you are just observing. However, the mere act of recording may also change the behavior in the desired direction by making it less automatic. Remember that statements you make to yourself are also a form of behavior. You may be monitoring a symptom, to begin with; in addition, you may decide to observe your own behavior and/or inner language that precedes or in some way seems to support the symptom. (See Sample Daily Log, used by a student with multiple sub-goals.)

```
                    Sample Daily Log
                          Date: Thurs., Nov. 24
Diet:        Water (glasses) 2
             Salty foods  yes
             Wine  Champagne III      wine III
             Caffeine  coffee  HHT I    Coke III
             Fats  yes
Exercise:    Type      dance
             How long?    20 minutes
             Heart rates
             Time of day
Relaxation:  Type
             Time of day
             How long?          none
             How effective?
Sleep:       Bedtime  2 AM
             Wake time  8 AM
             Hours      6
             Quality    ok
Other:       Any symptoms?   still PMS
             If so, what and when?
             Idea of nature of symptom
General      Moods     moody
well-being:  Physical  very tired
             Spiritual  down
Comments                           20 people to dinner
on today:     dress rehearsal 3         busy day
                            11 3        ate far too much
```

If your goal is to stop smoking, collect data first. Discover how many cigarettes you smoke a day and in which situations you want the cigarette most (with coffee, with alcohol, with certain friends, when others light up, when you're bored, tense, angry, etc.). In other words, what are your triggers or cues?

If your goal is to control your temper, ask yourself, "Is there a chain of events that leads inevitably to the problem behavior?" For example: "I come home from work tired and cranky, the kids are whining or fighting, I start hurrying to fix dinner without taking a break, I feel hassled and pressured, and then I yell at one of the kids. If I interrupt this chain by taking even a few minutes to relax before I jump into fixing dinner, there is less likelihood that I'll lose my temper. If I can catch myself feeling pressured and substitute another thought, I can break the chain." Observations such as these will provide valuable information to help you devise a strategy for success.

If it is some form of compulsive behavior—such as overeating, alcohol use, smoking, or drug use—that you are seeking to decrease or eliminate, be aware that the behavior may take place in order to suppress some unpleasant or unacceptable feelings you are having. By keeping good records of the thoughts and feelings that typically precede this behavior, you can discover their nature; then ask yourself how you might accept yourself for having those feelings and take care of yourself in a better way. Get emotional support; avoid guilt. A student observed, "Obsessions are ways to remove yourself from yourself because you're not comfortable with who you are and what you're feeling" Acknowledge your feelings; nourish yourself emotionally.

In this self-observation period, also make note of the consequences of your problem behavior or symptom. Honestly list the advantages and disadvantages. (See **Converting the Advantages of Illness: Practice 12**). Spelling out the consequences may help you increase your motivation for change and may uncover the factors that undermine change. For example, does smoking give you a chance for time out and reflection? This is a reinforcer that helps maintain the smoking habit. Is there another way you can give yourself this time out?

ARRANGE NEW BEHAVIORAL CUES

Arrange new cues to help create the positive behavior. Once you are aware of the situations and cues that lead to the unwanted behaviors, you can start rearranging them. You can substitute positive self-talk for negative. Ask yourself, "Is my self-talk making my desired behavior more—or less—likely? Is my inner language rewarding or punishing my behavior?" If you're saying, "She won't like me," stop it and say, "I know what to do. Relax, smile, make eye contact, and say hello." This is called self-instruction. Choose situations that will support, not undermine, the new behavior you are cultivating (e.g., a new ex-smoker can choose to be around nonsmokers, and can choose to avoid puffing friends, alcohol and parties, if those were previously identified as important cues or triggers for the desire to smoke.) Use the memory or the triggering of judgmental thoughts to imagine your new preferred behavior (see **Transform Failure into Success: Practice 10**).

You can pause and do a QR (see Quick and Warm in Chapter 2) when you encounter one of your cues. This is especially important if your problem involves anxiety or tension. Think, "What other alternative do I have besides getting into an argument (or taking a drink or reaching for a cigarette)?" Or you might think, "I choose to focus on what I like about this person instead of getting into an argument" or "I choose to drink a glass of sparkling soda water instead of a beer (or chew a piece of gum instead of smoking a cigarette)." Thus, you are interrupting an automatic response to a cue, and substituting another behavior.

If you foresee a problematic situation, for example, if you are going to a party where you will be exposed to temptation, recruit a friend to remind you of your goal (again, tactfully and gently!).

PLAN REINFORCERS

Plan reinforcers for positive behavior change and be specific about what you must do to earn them. Many behavior changes do have intrinsic rewards; however, sometimes these rewards are not immediate. The compliments from others and the healthy feelings you gain from exercise may not come during the first week of your program, when you have the most need for reinforcement. However, you can plan your own reinforcers. As Watson and Tharp (1981) state: "The best reinforcers are potent, accessible, and easily manipulatable by you." However, don't make these reinforcers so indispensable that you won't be willing to give them up if you don't do the required behavior to get them. You can flash on a quick mental image of yourself as you'll be when you've attained your goal. Give yourself lots of inner pats on the back, and self-praise. You can do this immediately upon performing the behavior: "Good for me! I did it!"

Make sure that the total amount of reinforcements will be greater if you follow your behavior change program than if you don't. For example, if you always go out to dinner or a movie each week anyway, don't make those your only rewards; add some new ones. Your rewards should be small, frequent, and inexpensive ones, like a bunch of flowers or a movie. It is self-defeating to reward yourself with the very behavior you are trying to change, so avoid giving yourself an ice cream cone for a treat if you are attempting to follow a healthier diet.

Some people use tokens, or a point system, for reinforcing their positive behavior; this helps you bridge the gap between the behavior and the reward and allows you to give larger, more meaningful rewards to yourself on a less frequent basis while still getting the positive reinforcer. You may decide to "up the ante" as you go, by requiring more advanced steps in your program to earn the reward. For example, during the first week of a weight loss program, reward yourself for keeping baseline records; during the second week reward yourself for cutting down on fats and increasing vegetables; during the third week earn the reward by adding some exercise as you continue the new diet. Always start with small, easy steps. Nothing succeeds like success!

Another important reinforcer for behavior change is social support. Many successful participants report having had support from friends, family, spouse, partner or roommates. People can support you by joining you in exercising, quitting smoking, or eating vegetarian meals. Friends can praise or reward you for the positive steps you are taking. Please note that having people scold or punish you is NOT helpful; nor is it useful to do this to yourself if you slip up or fall back into an old behavior pattern. Finally, plan for some variety in the rewards so you will stay motivated and not get bored. (A man who was using raisins for rewards found that they didn't inspire him anymore by the third week.)

PLAN AHEAD FOR RELAPSES

Plan what you'll do if you relapse into the old behavior. Pronouncing yourself a failure and quitting is counterproductive. A better approach is to expect some relapses and have a plan to start over immediately with appropriate self-talk such as, "One slip doesn't negate all the good progress I've made; I can pick up where I left off; each day is a new beginning." Ask yourself what happened and learn from the experience (e.g., a dieter might find that parties or Thanksgiving dinner are a problem for a diet and require special preparation). Be gentle with yourself. Have mercy! Self-acceptance, not self-control, is the key to positive change and healing.

INSTRUCTIONS

Describe your specific goal, plan of action, and an analysis of the advantages/disadvantages of your problem on **Worksheet: Self-Healing Project Plan: Practice 14**.

Name: _____ Date: _____

Worksheet: Self-Healing Project Plan: Practice 14

Problem or area of concern: _____

List the advantages and disadvantages of the behavior/problem you are planning to change.

Advantages	Disadvantages
_____	_____
_____	_____
_____	_____
_____	_____

STRATEGY AND PLAN OF ACTION:

1. Goal and subgoals; criteria for success:

_____
_____
_____
_____

2. Description of self-healing plan (include what, when, where, how often, with whom, under which situations):

_____
_____
_____
_____
_____
_____

3. Data collection plan:

_____
_____
_____
_____

4. Objective Baseline Measures:

_____
_____
_____
_____

5.   Subjective Baseline Measures:

_____

_____

_____

_____

6.   Social support:

_____

_____

_____

_____

7.   Imagery use:

_____

_____

_____

_____

8.   Rewards and other reinforcers to make this project fun:

_____

_____

_____

_____

9.   Other aspects of your plan:

_____

_____

_____

_____

_____

_____

_____

_____

_____

_____

_____

✌ IMAGERY FOR SELF-HEALING: PRACTICE 15

Imagery is the mechanism by which will becomes effortless.

For some people, daily relaxation and imagery will be their main focus; for others, imagery may be a useful adjunct for affecting the behavior changes they have outlined after the practice of **Imagery Exploration**. In general, a blend of imagery and behavior change is most helpful. If you ignore an imagery message that guides you to make a change in your behavior, you may experience a sense of being stuck and fail to make further progress. The underlying assumption is that mind/body/spirit is an integrated whole. Therefore, imagery can affect the body, promote healing, and enhance performance. Self-healing imagery can be helpful for virtually any illness.

Imagery may be either a primary or a complementary strategy for healing. In this way, with or without other treatments, you become an active participant in your healing process. This approach has been utilized in the treatment of cancer patients (Simonton, Matthews-Simonton, & Creighton, 1978). An effective imagery strategy consists of three components: inspecting the problem, illness, or area of discomfort; creating and experiencing an ongoing healing process that prevents relapses from occurring; and, finally, perceiving yourself whole and integrated. After having practiced this imagery, draw or paint your area of concern in either anatomic or symbolic form, whichever came to you in your imagery experience. Also, draw the healing process and yourself as you will be when completely whole, healed, and integrated. These drawings can be done several times and may change over the weeks. In this way they can provide a *before* and *after* measurement of inner change.

Imagery may also be used as an adjunct to behavior change. In this case the imagery is practiced as a form of mental rehearsal (as described in **Transforming Failure into Success: Practice 10**). For example, a man reported that it was much easier for him to go running in the morning if he first took a few minutes in bed picturing himself jogging briskly, enjoying the crisp morning air, and feeling how smoothly his muscles moved. It worked both as a motivator and as a way to stay mindful of his running style; he could see and feel himself breathing diaphragmatically and letting go of unneeded muscle tension.

Often, imagery is paired with activity. The more easily the healing imagery can be incorporated into little routines in your daily life, the more likely it is that it will always be present in the background of your activities. For example, several people reported that they used imagery while doing various forms of exercise and that they found it enhanced their endurance and enjoyment. One jogger pictured his higher self slightly ahead of him, drawing him onward. A woman who was visualizing the healing of an infection drank a glass of water before each visualization practice and then urinated afterward to dramatize ridding her body of the infection. Another person visualized shaking negative feelings (anger, anxiety) out of her body and into the earth while shaking out her arms and legs.

Imagery is the language by which we talk to ourselves and affect our health (previously experienced with the lemon imagery and the hand warming practice). The following **Concept Exercise: Arm-Head Rotation** illustrates that imagery may also affect flexibility. This exercise begins by practicing actual physical movement and then repeats the same practice through visualization. It is best practiced when someone else reads the script to you.

Concept Exercise: Arm-Head Rotation[A]

Stand erect with feet shoulder width apart. Raise your right arm to a horizontal position with your hand pointing straight ahead. Gently rotate your right hand and arm to the right and, when you have gone as far as you can go without straining, look beyond the tip of your fingers and remember a spot or mark on the wall. Gently rotate your arm back to pointing straight ahead, drop it to your side, and relax.

Bring your right arm and hand to a horizontal position pointing straight ahead. Then rotate your arm and head in opposite directions. As your head rotates to the right, your arm rotates to the left and vice versa. Continue to rotate back and forth about 15 times. Be gentle, do not force. Continue to breathe. If you experience discomfort, do not rotate as far. Then, stop, drop your arm to the side, and relax.

While continuing to stand comfortably and allowing your arms to hang alongside your body, rotate your head and eyes in opposite directions. That is, as your head rotates to the left, your eyes rotate to the right and vice versa. Continue to rotate your head and eyes back and forth about 15 times. Be sure to continue to breathe. Then, stop and relax.

Once again, lift your right arm and hand up so that your point straight ahead. Now, rotate your arm and head in opposite directions with your eyes rotating in the same direction as your arm. As your arm rotates to the right, your head rotates to the left and your eyes rotate to the right and vice versa. Continue to rotate your arm, head, and eyes back and forth about 15 times. Then, stop, drop your arm to your side, and relax.

Observation*: In almost all cases, after actual rotation practice, the arm rotated significantly further.*

Once again, raise your right arm to a horizontal position with your hand pointing straight ahead. Gently rotate your right hand and arm to the right and, when you have gone as far as you can go without straining, look beyond the tip of your

---

A. Adapted from an exercise developed by Moshe Feldenkrais.

fingers and remember a spot or mark on the wall. Gently rotate your arm back so that you are pointing straight ahead, drop it to your side, and relax.

Now, raise your left arm to a horizontal position with your hand pointing straight ahead. Gently rotate your left hand and arm to the left and, when you have gone as far as you can go without straining, look beyond the tip of your fingers and remember a spot or mark on the wall. Gently rotate your arm back so that you are pointing straight ahead, drop it to your side, and relax.

With your eyes closed and without actually lifting your arm, imagine that you are lifting your left arm and hand up so that they point straight ahead. Imagine rotating your left arm and head simultaneously in the opposite direction. That is, as you imagine your head rotating to the right, imagine your arm rotating to the left and vice versa. In your imagination, continue to rotate back and forth about 15 times. Then, stop and imagine dropping your left arm to your side and relaxing.

While continuing to stand comfortably, imagine rotating your head in the opposite direction of your eyes. Imagine that, as your eyes rotate to the left, your head rotates the right and vice versa. Continue for about 15 rotations. Be sure to continue to breathe. Then, stop and imagine relaxing.

Now, imagine that you lift your left arm up and you rotate your left arm and eyes in one direction and that you are rotating your head in the opposite direction and vice versa. That is, as you imagine your left arm rotating to the right, imagine your head rotating to the left and your eyes rotating to the right. Imagine rotating back and forth about 15 times. Then stop; imagine dropping your arm and relaxing.

Finally, actually raise your left arm and hand to a horizontal position pointing straight ahead. Gently rotate your left arm and hand to the left and, when you have rotated as far as you can without straining, look beyond the tip of your fingers and remember a spot or mark on the wall. Gently rotate your arm back so that you are pointing straight ahead, drop it to your side, and relax.

Observations: *In almost all cases, after imagined rotation practice, the arm rotated significantly further. This practice demonstrates that the visualized practice is as effective as the actual practice. Hence be careful what you think about or visualize, since visualization is as powerful as actual practice.*

Note: *In both cases, increased rotation occurred without effort or force. One of the major mechanisms underlying the success was the breaking apart of habitual patterns (e.g., the eye, head, arm, and hand normally going in the same direction, such as when reaching for a cup of tea). When the habitual pattern was inhibited through the non-habitual and contrary rotations, increased freedom and rotation will occur when the eyes, head, arm, and hand are used, again, to do a task.*

Concepts that Underlie Self-Healing Imagery

For 30 years my body has done its best to attract the attention of my conscious self.

STUDENT

1. All areas of distress or illness are the body/mind's attempts to give us some important information, to help us get back on our life's path. As one student reported:

   > I had a dream in which I was riding a beautiful horse that was following a well-marked trail. Suddenly, my legs went into a spasm and squeezed the horse, forcing him to the right. Immediately, I felt embarrassed and got off the horse. He reared up and then looked me very sternly in the eye as though saying, "It's not okay for you to do that! I was on the path!" I take this to represent my mental tension pushing my physical being off the path.

   So our task in imagery is to pay attention and get the message the symptom is trying to convey to us.

2. The person and the illness are separate. Imagery is meant to mobilize the higher self or the more creative aspects of the self. You are not your illness; the core of you is healthy.

3. The simple act of imaging a healing mechanism, which implies activity, will shift the sense of helplessness to a sense of control. Even if the healing mechanism makes no biological sense, simply conceiving of a tool for change is empowering. If you are receiving medical treatments concurrently, you may imagine them working in cooperation with your own healing process.

4. Include an image of wholeness or integration, even if complete physical recovery is not always possible. It is as valuable to mobilize a sense of wholeness/integration in a person who will never be physically healthy as it is to mobilize a sense of wellness in a person who has the biological possibility of becoming well. The image of wholeness/integration creates a sense of hope or possibility. Often a diagnosis implies an internal, stable, and global situation. Patients may perceive the illness as their fault, lasting forever, and affecting all aspects of their life. The situation then feels hopeless, and change appears impossible. By imaging a process for change and a new situation where there is no illness or problem, the internal, global and stable concepts are changed. As you describe your images, note language that implies these attitudes and experiment with reframing the images by changing the descriptive language.

5. Letting go of the initial image that represents the illness or symptoms creates a possibility. Letting go of the image is often challenging, especially when there are significant emotional experiences connected with the symptoms. The tendency is either

to hold on to the image or to throw it away aggressively. Ideally, you want to encourage an attitude of passive attention toward the image; for example: "I notice this image, it is interesting, and I am not invested in it or attached to it." Surprisingly, this attitude of passive acceptance and open exploration allows the image to shift and change.

6. The imagery may change as the problem/illness changes. Always inspect your problem, as it is RIGHT NOW. If you are truly in the present, you will see the problem/ illness somewhat differently each time you inspect it. For example, if you have a broken leg, at first the image may be similar to the X-ray you saw at the doctor's office. The tendency is to keep this same mental picture of the X-ray each time the imagery exercise is done. In reality, the body continuously changes. Hence, you need to be aware of the body's progress and observe changes each time. These changes may be subtle or drastic. In order to mobilize the self-healing potential, the images must be of the current state of affairs. As the inspected image changes, the healing process will also have to change in order to be appropriate and useful with the new image of your problem area.

7. The goal is for the inspection and maintenance of a healing mechanism to become a constant background activity. Like humming a favorite song, imagery can occur in the back of the consciousness at all times. It will take some time and a true understanding of the concepts before this type of integration takes place. The ultimate goal is to feel the healing occurring and to continually reassess and imagine the healing taking place. Many times throughout the day you will be touching with awareness and love that part of you that is ill or in pain.

8. Provide adequate time for relaxation, especially when you are first beginning your imagery practice. Images flow most easily into a relaxed and non-judgmental mind.

9. Whatever image comes up—no matter how bizarre, illogical or biologically incorrect—is the image to work with in the exercise. Our subconscious often accesses very important information for us through our images. These images seem to make no sense; they may, however, be metaphors for some element involved in our condition. They may be very useful, especially as they relate to past events in our lives. Trust these images.

10. The healing mechanism makes sense within the imagery. The healing is not magic. There is a logical transition between the problem area as it is at this moment and as it is when you are well or whole. The transition does not need to be realistic or literally possible, but it needs to make sense. The healing process must be stronger than the disease process. For example, if a person images his or her asthma as a brick wall and the healing process as a magical swirl of light that suddenly creates a clear space, the healing process becomes magical rather than something over which the individual might have some control. A more efficacious image might include a bulldozer breaking the wall down and workers carrying the debris away and permanently disposing of it.

11. Explore associations to the image. It is important to understand what the image represents to *you*. Some images are universal or archetypal while others may have very personal and individual meanings.

12. Create a process by which the illness/problem cannot return. For example, a woman with asthma imaged cleansing all the pollens from her lungs. The final step in the process was putting up a mesh screen so that the pollens could not enter in the future. (This could be a metaphor for the activation of the cilia, whose function is to sweep the particulates from the airways.)

13. Externalize the image; that is, represent it in a physical form. This serves several purposes. In making the image tangible, it becomes changeable. It also separates the image from the person. Young children express their images in three dimensions as they play with their friends. Adults need help accessing their images in a form with which they can work comfortably. The following techniques, among others, can be used to externalize the image. Use one or more of these techniques not just once but several times over the course of your self-healing program; in this way you can gain added insights and, also, see changes in your images over time.

    ◆ Draw or paint three different images: 1) the area of concern as it is at this moment; 2) the healing process; and 3) health, wholeness, or integration. If drawing or painting feels difficult, try a collage of images you select from magazines. It is helpful to do the visual representation before writing or talking about the image. Otherwise, the images will often stay on an intellectual level if they are just thought about.

    ◆ Describe the images verbally to others.

    ◆ Model the three images out of clay. This may be more comfortable than drawing for some people.

    ◆ Imagine spontaneous sounds or select three musical compositions that represent the images. For example, one woman described her back pain like steak sizzling on a grill. Another woman, working with depression, selected depressing music, neutral music, and joyful music; she also began humming and singing the joyful music.

    ◆ Act out the images physically; you may even involve others. For example, one or more people could represent the area of concern and others could play the part of the healing process as you direct the play.

    ◆ Take pictures with a camera that represent the images you saw in your inspection and healing process. This technique is useful for people who find it difficult to express their images using any of the other modalities.

    ◆ Take a walk and find flowers, rocks, clouds, and so on that symbolize the images.

EXAMPLES OF SELF-HEALING IMAGERY

Participants, clients, and students find that imagery aids significantly in healing. Some people have complex and biologically correct images while others see very abstract and/ or simple images. Some incorporate humor in their imagery, which helps them to maintain an objective distance from the problem. Images can be incorporated in self-healing with conditions ranging from stopping smoking to a simple strain to life-threatening diseases. They can be changed as the symptoms change. Following are a few examples of imagery that have been shared with us. In each case, the individual felt they had more control over their healing and reported quick results.

◆ **Carpal tunnel syndrome**: A woman with carpal tunnel syndrome described the self-healing imagery process as follows:

> "My experience with the self-healing image dramatically changed from the first vision of pain to one of healing. At first my hand was gray and cold. I felt aching pain in the wrist and fingers of my right hand. When visualizing health, at first only the fingertips of my hand were changed in color to a reddish hue. Eventually, as the exercise progressed, my entire hand became physically warm with a pleasant feeling of free-flowing blood and nerves transmitting through the wrist to the tips of my fingers. My entire hand took on a reddish glow. This image became the final image of health—one I found I could easily bring into focus. . . I found when I followed my self-healing recommendations—wearing my splint at night, being aware of muscle fatigue and consciously relieving it through muscle relaxation, and exercising the self-healing imagery—my hand became asymptomatic. However, if I deviated from this schedule, as I did a few times, the symptoms returned. My awareness of muscle fatigue has become more automatic in most activities involving my hand."

◆ **Sprained ankle**: A competitive tennis player who had twisted her ankle 2 weeks before a scheduled tournament imaged blood cells and lymph flowing to and from her ankle and calcium being brought for the tendons to grow. Her ankle healed and she played in the tournaments.

◆ **Back pain**: A student with back pain saw "an image of a brick mason trying to patch up a hole in a wall." As she tried to see what was behind the wall, a sentry appeared to guard it. "A big wave of fear came over me. It really scared me that there was something so powerful hidden behind that wall and that it was trying to burst out." As she continued with the imagery, she reported, "I saw the pain as a sharp thorn in my back which was blocking the flow of energy." As she directed the free flow of energy, she saw her chest "opening up in the front so that the pain did not need to push out the back." She tried to visualize the removal of the thorn: "I realized that the thorn was my husband, and I couldn't pull it out. Although we had been separated for almost a year, I had put off getting a divorce. The fear I was feeling was fear of my unknown future. Rather than face an uncertain future, I was keeping that tie to my husband even though it was causing me pain." As she began to let go of the past, she was able to pull the thorn out a little. "I saw the tip of the thorn break off inside me and I felt it bloom into something wonderful. I felt that meant that the good things I had gotten from my marriage would continue to stay with me and I could let the rest go." While she continued using visualization, movement, and sound, she filed for a divorce, and the pain diminished greatly in 4 weeks.

◆ **Warts**: A man began the process of shrinking his wart by imagining a tiny warrior shooting lasers at it. He wrote:

> "Philosophically speaking at least, the last thing anyone needs is more violent imagery. And further, there is no telling what sorts of negative effects such imagery has on the body or mind, even when the intended outcome is achieved. One thing I would like to try instead would be to visualize a negotiated settlement with the virus in question. Maybe I could get the virus to pack up his wart and leave."

He was able to modify his imagery in order to become more comfortable with it.

◆ **Hepatitis and gastrointestinal distress**: One man with chronic hepatitis and gastrointestinal distress, who happened to have a strong background in biology, integrated relaxation and visualization every day: Picturing himself to be very small, he would imagine going inside his liver and watching the hepatitis viruses replicate. He could see the white cells eat the virus particles after they had burst from the liver cells where they had replicated. He also saw some of the viruses enter new liver cells and continue to replicate and burst. What he imaged for 3 months was the perfect model to maintain the status quo, namely, a picture of white cells destroying some of the virus particles while others were free to invade more healthy liver cells. There was no mechanism in his model to prevent the liver cells from being infected by the virus. In his new image, the man saw himself painting his liver cells with a protective chemical that would prevent the virus from attacking the healthy cells. Now his white cells could make progress instead of simply preventing things from getting worse, and within a month his liver functions were normal. It is essential that the healing mechanisms being imaged contain a protective component or create a permanent change in the illness so that it cannot come back.

◆ **Endocarditis**: One woman was hospitalized with a life-threatening bacterial infection of the heart. Once her illness was diagnosed, she immediately began her imagery. She reported:

> "I realized that the bacteria were doing just what they were created to do. It's just that they were in the wrong place. My imagery was of a loving mother entering my heart and seeing a single, large, cartoon-like bacterium in the midst of making the mess—similar to what most mothers encounter at home with children. The bacterium was munching away on my heart. The mother sternly said, "No, no, no. You don't belong here. Now, clean up your mess and leave this room just the way you found it." I could see in my imagery a bacterium stopped in the middle of his munch-

ing and looking very guilty—caught in the act! He removed from his mouth the piece upon which he was munching and began to paste it back to my heart wall. A few days later I felt that the bacteria had left my heart, but there was a hole in it. I then changed my imagery to that of the mother quietly rocking in her chair, knitting my heart back together. I think that these images helped me to heal quickly and avoid open-heart surgery."

The following examples of imagery include copies of the drawings that were made by the individuals:

◆ **Binge Eating:** A 28 year-old woman suffered from binge eating with frequent purging since age 15. She gained greater insight, awareness, and control that positively reduced her binge eating. Through her self-healing process, she reported that she found a relationship between food and comfort, and food and control. "When my mom returned to work, when I was 10, I was suddenly allowed to fix my own snacks, and there was more junk food in the house than before. Suddenly, foods that had been "treats" were available to me all the time and so I "treated" myself. A link between food and loneliness was made." Her strategy during the four weeks of self-healing imagery also included reducing or eliminating consumption of foods while alone (or hidden), avoiding eating during emotional upsets, keeping a food diary, eliminating sweets and treats from the house, and keeping her house filled with fruits and vegetables. She significantly reduced her binge eating. It gave her the confidence and belief that this problem could be overcome. The following three drawings in Figure 4.2 illustrate her imagery process.

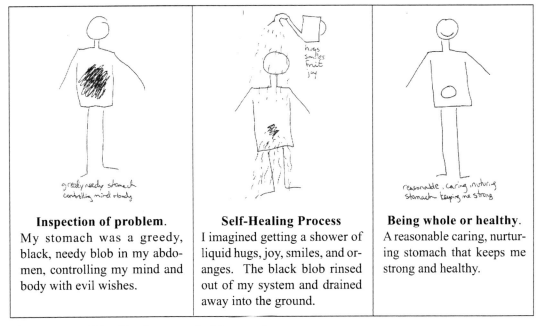

| **Inspection of problem.** My stomach was a greedy, black, needy blob in my abdomen, controlling my mind and body with evil wishes. | **Self-Healing Process** I imagined getting a shower of liquid hugs, joy, smiles, and oranges. The black blob rinsed out of my system and drained away into the ground. | **Being whole or healthy.** A reasonable caring, nurturing stomach that keeps me strong and healthy. |

Figure 4.2. Self-healing imagery for binge eating.

◆ **Depression:** A 28 year-old woman had intermittent bouts of depression for the prior 6 years. Despite returning to school, finding a good part time job, and mending relationships, her depression refused to budge. She did not want to use antidepressant medication because of working in a psychiatric clinic. Her self-healing strategy included accepting depression as part of herself—to be acknowledged rather than despised—, keeping detailed log to monitor lifestyle habits, socializing regularly, decreasing coffee intake to two cups per week, increasing exercise by getting out of the bus a stop earlier to walk to school, limiting alcohol consumption to less than 4 drinks per week and never drinking alone, daily self-rating of moods, and watching TV less (there was no TV time after she began to socialize). Finally, she integrated her positive image of how she could feel into daily activities.

In the course of the four weeks, she realized that in recent years, she had ceased doing activities that made her happy, such as singing, and decided to make them part of herself. The outcome was very successful. She reported, "I know now that I can recover my sense of joy in life... my mood and energy has enabled me to work more effectively and cut down on procrastination... My schedule is still demanding, but is feeling more invigorating than draining as a result of a good balance between work and play...My only wish for the project is that I had started it sooner: Months and months ago." Her self-healing images are shown in Figure 4.3.

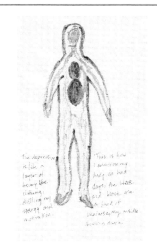 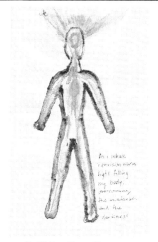 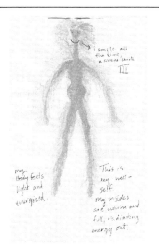

Inspection of problem.	**Self-healing Process**	**Being whole or healthy.**
The depression is like a layer of heavy blue clothing, draining my energy and motivation. This is how I envision my body on bad days; the blue and black are a kind of malaise, my insides feeling dark.	As I inhale I envision warm light filling my body, overcoming the malaise, and the darkness.	This is my well-self. My insides are warm and full, radiating energy out. My body feels light and energized.

Figure 4.3. Self-healing imagery for depression.

◆ **Back pain:** A 25 year-old man injured his back at work 4 months previously. The pain was impossible to ignore. He reported that it felt like a red-hot flare about twice a day with an average pain rating of 6 on a scale from 0 (none) to 10 (extreme). His healing project included listening to his body, relaxing, and practicing his personal imagery exercises. In the course of the project, he became aware that there were no separate parts of his body, only different areas. As he said: "My body is whole and anything that affects one area has affected or will affect another area..." "After 4 weeks my pain had been reduced to 0. This does not mean that I never experience back pain anymore, but when I do it is the exception rather than the rule.... The visualization exercises provided a center of calm in the storms that are part of life, a refuge for sanity, and thankfully relief from back pain." His self-healing visualization included a number of different images as shown in Figures 4.4 and 4.5.

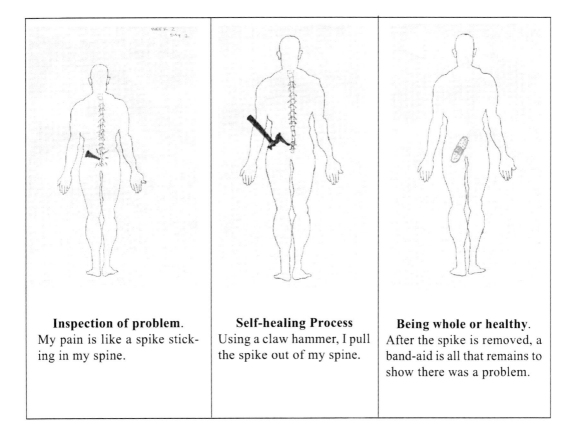

| **Inspection of problem.** My pain is like a spike sticking in my spine. | **Self-healing Process** Using a claw hammer, I pull the spike out of my spine. | **Being whole or healthy.** After the spike is removed, a band-aid is all that remains to show there was a problem. |

Figure 4.4. Self-healing imagery for back pain.

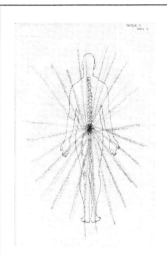  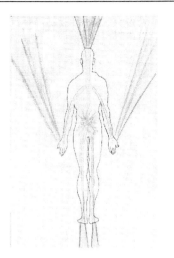

Inspection of problem. An angry red sphere at the junction of my spine and leg, pulsing with pain. The knot prevented positive energy flow through my body.

Self-healing Process I blasted the pain knot with cool, loving energy. Seeing the nerve in front of me, I took a breath and gently blew on it. The painful knot fell apart like dry sand and joy overtook me.

Being whole or healthy. My whole body is powerful. Energy courses though it unimpeded.

I concentrated my blue energy until it pulsed in my abdomen. I beamed the tumorous mass with cool, loving blue light. The analgesic effect of this meditation was immediate and pronounced. My pain went from 6 to 1 or 2.

Figure 4.5. Self-healing imagery for back pain.

There is no right way to experience an image. Respect whatever images you have in whatever forms they come to you, as they will most likely provide you with valuable information. And be willing to allow new images to replace images that are not working for you. The four steps of the self-healing imagery are done with an attitude of openness to other intuitive images that may relate to the healing process. The specific steps are:

1. Relaxation. Becoming quiet and peaceful so that critical and judgmental thoughts are in abeyance.

2. Inspection of the problem. Inspect and explore with an attitude of openness as if this is the first time you have ever explored or seen the area of concern.

3. Self-healing process. Develop a process that transforms the area of concern into wholeness or health. The healing process affects the area of concern so that it becomes whole or healthy.

4. Being whole or healthy. Seeing, sensing, or knowing that the area of concern is now whole or healthy.

5. Keeping a record. Write down your experience and draw the images of inspection, healing process and wholeness or health.

NOTE: When making your own tape, substitute your personal relaxation script (see **Creating Your Own Relaxation: Practice** 7) in place of the indented sample script.

RELAXATION AND SELF-HEALING IMAGERY SCRIPT

Wiggle around and make yourself comfortable... Loosen any constricting clothing; loosen your collar, take off your glasses, take off your watch, remove your wallet and keys from your pocket (if you wear hard contacts, you might want to take them out as it is difficult to relax your eyes while wearing them)... Be sure your belt, upper buttons, and upper 2 inches of your pants zipper are loose. Sit comfortably in a chair or lie comfortably on a sofa or bed (when lying down, make sure you have a pillow beneath your knees and under your head).

*Insert your personal relaxation script (***Creating Your Own Relaxation: Practice** 7*) or use the following sample relaxation script.*

Now, close your eyes and slowly scan your body. If you notice any place that feels uncomfortable, tighten that area and let it go... Scan your whole body from the top of your head to the tips of your toes—face, neck and shoulders; lower back, arms, and hands; chest, stomach, and buttocks; legs, feet, and toes. Now, lift your hands slightly from your lap and make a fist with both hands... Feel the tightness in your arms while you keep breathing... Be sure that the rest of your body stays relaxed. Feel the tension in your arms; let go and relax... Feel the relaxation flowing down your arms and out your hands.

Now, while breathing and keeping your neck and jaw relaxed, raise your shoulders to your ears... Feel the tightness in your upper chest and shoulders. Let go and relax... Feel the relaxation flowing down your shoulders and arms like an ocean wave. Now, curl your toes up as you press your heels down... While feeling the tightness in your legs, be sure that you are breathing and that your jaw, neck, and shoulders are relaxed... Let go and relax... Imagine a wave of relaxation going down your legs and out your feet... Feel your body relaxing and let your breathing become slower... and... slower....

Let the air move easily in and out like an ocean wave... Be sure to exhale by gently pulling your stomach in at the end of the exhalation. When you inhale, allow your abdomen to expand and widen. Let your breath flow easily in and out... in and out... Let it go slower and slower...

As you inhale, imagine that you can feel the air coming through your feet into your ankles, calves, knees, thighs, and buttocks... As you exhale, imagine the air flowing down your arms and legs and out your fingers and toes... Imagine the air going outward forever, flowing down your arms and legs and out your hands and feet.....

As you exhale, imagine the warmth flowing down and outward... Let each breath be slower and longer... Let your breath slow down... If your attention wanders, let the distraction be a reminder to breathe slowly and regularly while feeling the air going down your arms and legs... Become aware of the throbbing of the pulse in your fingers... Feel your hands warming as your breath moves down and through your arms... Continue breathing easily for the next few minutes.

After completing your personal relaxation script, or the sample scrip above, continue with the following script.

The more you practice, the easier it becomes and the easier it is to reach a deeper awareness that allows you to mobilize your self-healing potential and become whole... The more you practice, the more you will know that you are mobilizing your own health potential...

Let your breathing slow down and deepen.... As the breath flows calmly and regularly, continue to repeat your own phrase such as "I am at peace"... For the next few minutes allow your attention to go with your breathing while you continue to repeat your phrase... Let your breathing become slower and deeper... As your breath slows down, know that you are mobilizing your health.

Now, let go of the phrase and allow your breath to continue slowly and evenly... Begin to inspect your area of concern as if you have never looked at it before... Just look and feel inside to see what this area looks like at this moment in time... Allow any image, sensation, or thought to occur. The image may be in black and white or in color or it may be a bodily sensation or an emotion... Whatever occurs, let it be.

Now, let go of that image... Imagine a process by which healing and wholeness will occur, a process that transforms what you saw during the inspection into health and wholeness... See and feel the healing process... For the next few minutes, allow the healing process to continue.

The healing process continues all the time; it is often beneath our awareness, yet it continues. For some, it becomes like a melody that we hear in the back of our minds all day long... Feel the healing being carried through to completion... Let a single image or symbol come to you that you can hold in your mind throughout the day.

Now, shift your imagery and experience yourself whole and integrated... Know that you are part of the universe... Experience a deep, gentle quietness... Allow your breath to move easily in and out... in and out. Imagine that as you inhale, a healing energy comes into you like the rays of the sun, penetrating every cell with a shimmering light, and as you exhale, the healing energy spreads outward like a blue cloud or wave... Allow this process to continue for a few minutes... See yourself joyously moving through your day, doing the things you love to do, enjoying just being yourself, feeling free and content...

After a few minutes, continue with the next section.

Remember, each time you practice you are mobilizing your self-healing potential... Congratulate yourself for enhancing your own wholeness and health and allow the healing process and healing imagery to continue to flow through you during the day.

You can choose to become more aware of the present environment or allow yourself to fall asleep... If you want to get up, take a deep breath, feeling relaxed yet alert, then gently open your eyes while stretching your arms. Whether asleep or awake, be aware that the healing process continues all the time.

Each day after you have gone through the script, describe your experience on the **Log Sheet: Imagery for Self-Healing: Practice 15** and on separate sheets of paper draw the images of the problem area, the healing process and wholeness/integration. When you describe your healing imagery, be sure that the healing process is concrete and not "magical" and that the problem has been permanently changed so that it cannot return. Drawings may range from a simple black blob to a very complex biological rendition or a multicolored abstract picture. These are all equally valid images.

At the end of the week, answer **Questions: Imagery for Self-Healing: Practice 15.** Then review your experience by answering the **Questions for Reflection: Imagery for Self-Healing: Practice 15.** Finally, meet with your group and complete **Discussion and Conclusions: Self-Healing: Practice 15.**

Name: _____ Date: _____

Log Sheet: Imagery for Self-Healing: Practice 15

After each practice, describe (a) the self-healing imagery and (b) your subjective experience as a result of the imagery and how you practiced evoking the self-healing imagery during the day.

Problem to be healed: _____

Day 1   a. _____
Date _____   _____
                  _____
                  _____

               b. _____
                  _____
                  _____
                  _____

Day 2   a. _____
Date _____   _____
                  _____
                  _____

               b. _____
                  _____
                  _____
                  _____

Day 3   a. _____
Date _____   _____
                  _____
                  _____

               b. _____
                  _____
                  _____
                  _____

Day 4   a. _____
Date _____   _____
         _____
         _____

         b. _____
         _____
         _____
         _____

Day 5   a. _____
Date _____   _____
         _____
         _____

         b. _____
         _____
         _____
         _____

Day 6   a. _____
Date _____   _____
         _____
         _____

         b. _____
         _____
         _____
         _____

Day 7   a. _____
Date _____   _____
         _____
         _____

         b. _____
         _____
         _____
         _____

Name: _____ Date: _____

Questions: Imagery for Self-Healing: Practice 15

1. What benefits occurred as a result of your practice?

_____

_____

_____

2. What were your self-healing images?

_____

_____

_____

3. How did you remember to evoke the self-healing imagery during the day?

_____

_____

_____

4. As you looked at your drawings, what insight did you uncover?

_____

_____

_____

5. What problems/challenges, if any, occurred?

_____

_____

_____

6. How did you solve the problems/challenges?

_____

_____

_____

7. If you could do the practice over, how would you do it differently?

_____

_____

_____

Name: _____ Date: _____

Group Discussion and Conclusions: Imagery for Self-Healing: Practice 15

1.   What benefits did the group members notice as a result of the practices?

_____
_____
_____
_____

2.   How did the drawings help or hinder the healing process?

_____
_____
_____
_____

3.   What difficulties were encountered and how did the group members solve them?

_____
_____
_____
_____

4.   How did the experiences that occurred during and following the self-healing imagery vary among group members? Was there any correlation between these differences and age, gender, medical background, previous experience with imagery, meditation, creative art, etc.?

_____
_____
_____
_____

5.   Topics or concerns to discuss with the instructor:

_____
_____
_____
_____

List your group members:

_____   _____
_____   _____
_____   _____
_____   _____

✆ CARRYING OUT AND ADAPTING YOUR STRATEGY: PRACTICE 16

Write up a contract specifying what you plan to do and then sign it. You may also ask a good friend or family member to cosign it. This helps you solidify your commitment. Carry out your strategy, keeping log notes on your self-devised log forms. Evaluate your strategy as you go, making changes when appropriate. Sometimes a strategy that looks perfect on paper will reveal a few flaws as you put it into practice; in fact, it is nearly impossible to construct a perfect strategy for self-healing without having to make modifications somewhere along the line. You may discover new information in your readings that you want to incorporate. You may realize that it is because your data collection system is too cumbersome that you aren't doing it; a simplification of your system may be all you need to get back on track.

Continue to keep progress notes throughout your behavior change project. Making graphs and charts can show very satisfying evidence of changes and can also help you troubleshoot. If you're not progressing as you'd like, find out what's getting in the way, and revise your program. People often set subgoals that are too big. If jogging is your plan, starting with a quarter mile may be too ambitious, especially if you've been sedentary. Perhaps you need to start with walking around the block for the first week. Perhaps you need more enticing rewards—or prompter ones. Do you have the social support you need? Are you using mental rehearsal to practice the new behaviors before you go into them? Adapt the self-healing imagery script so that you see yourself acting in the way you would like to be. For example, if you plan to stop drinking alcohol, imagine yourself going to a party and ordering orange juice. Or when someone asks you, "Do you want some wine?," see yourself saying, "No thank you, but I would like some lemon flavored Calistoga".

Each day after you have gone through the script, complete **Log Sheet: Self-Healing: Practice 16 (Week 1)**. At the end of the week, answer **Questions: Self-Healing: Practice 16 (Week 1)**. Then review your experience by answering the **Questions for Reflection: Self-Healing: Practice 16**. From that analysis, adapt your self-healing strategy and outline any changes you plan to make. Finally, meet with your group and complete **Discussion and Conclusions: Self-Healing: Practice 16**.

Use the information from **Questions for Reflection: Self-Healing: Practice 16** and **Discussions and Conclusions: Self-Healing: Practice 16** to fine-tune your self-healing practice. Continue these practices for the next 3 weeks. Each day, complete the appropriate **Log Sheet: Self-Healing: Practice 16** and then review your experience through **Questions for Reflection: Self-Healing: Practice 16** and meet with your group and complete the **Discussion and Conclusions: Self-Healing: Practice 16** worksheets for the week.

Name: _____ Date: _____

Log Sheet: Self-Healing: Practice 16 (Week 1)

Each day, (a) describe your experience with your self-healing practice and (b) record the objective and/or subjective data. You may need to use your self-devised data sheets here.

Day 1   a. _____

Date _____   _____

_____

_____

b. _____

_____

_____

_____

Day 2   a. _____

Date _____   _____

_____

_____

b. _____

_____

_____

_____

Day 3   a. _____

Date _____   _____

_____

_____

b. _____

_____

_____

_____

Day 4   a. _____
Date _____   _____
               _____
               _____
               _____

             b. _____
               _____
               _____
               _____
               _____

Day 5   a. _____
Date _____   _____
               _____
               _____
               _____

             b. _____
               _____
               _____
               _____
               _____

Day 6   a. _____
Date _____   _____
               _____
               _____
               _____

             b. _____
               _____
               _____
               _____
               _____

Day 7   a. _____
Date _____   _____
               _____
               _____
               _____

             b. _____
               _____
               _____
               _____

Name: _____ Date: _____

Questions: Self-Healing: Practice 16 (Week 1)

1. What benefits occurred as a result of your practice?

_____

_____

_____

_____

_____

2. How did your mood and physical state change before, during, and after the practices?

_____

_____

_____

_____

_____

3. What changes did you observe in your objective/subjective data?

_____

_____

_____

_____

_____

4. How will you change or adapt the practice for next week to enhance your success?

_____

_____

_____

_____

_____

5. What problems/challenges occurred and how did you solve them?

_____

_____

_____

_____

_____

Name: _____ Date: _____

Discussion and Conclusions: Self-Healing: Practice 16 (Week 1)

1. What benefits and successes did the group members notice as a result of the practice?

    _____
    _____
    _____

2. What were some of the common challenges that interfered with the self-practice?

    _____
    _____
    _____

3. What new strategies will group members use to increase success?

    _____
    _____
    _____

4. How do levels of commitment and rewards relate to achieving small successes in this first week?

    _____
    _____
    _____

5. What are some of the creative ways by which group members monitor their behavior?

    _____
    _____
    _____

6. Topics or concerns to discuss with the instructor:

    _____
    _____
    _____

List your group members:

_____   _____
_____   _____
_____   _____
_____   _____

Name: _____ Date: _____

Questions for Reflection: Self-Healing: Practice 16[4]

_____ What is my level of commitment to my self-healing project?

_____ Do I need to explore ways to increase my level of commitment?

_____ Are my goal and subgoals clear?

_____ Do I need to change or modify my subgoals and goal?

_____ Are my subgoals and goals expressed in measurable behavioral terms?

_____ Have I broken down my strategy into small manageable chunks?

_____ Did I establish a clear baseline or do I still need to collect more data?

_____ Do I need to revise my log form for data collection and what improvements can be made?

_____ Am I keeping consistent written records? If not, what do I need to do to change it?

_____ Do I need assistance in monitoring my behavior? How could I get it?

_____ What is getting in my way? What are my excuses, and how can I talk myself out of them?

_____ Have I carefully examined the advantages of changing and compared them with the advantages of not changing?

_____ How helpful is my inner language? Can I improve it?

_____ Have I asked for, and received, social support for carrying out my plans? If not, what do I need to do to include social support?

_____ Have I given myself positive reinforcement, or small rewards, for getting started on my project? If not, what reward system do I need to develop?

_____ How effective were my reinforcers in motivating me?

_____ Am I using mental rehearsal to help me develop new behaviors?

_____ Have I incorporated insights from imagery into my strategy?

_____ Am I keeping my sense of humor about it all?

_____ Is it fun to do? If not, what do I need to do to make the practice enjoyable (If it isn't fun, why bother???)

---

4. Adapted from Watson, D.L. & Tharp, R.G. (1992). *Self-Directed Behavior: Self-Modification for Personal Adjustment* (6th ed). Monterey: Brooks/Cole.

AFTER REFLECTING ON YOUR PROGRESS, OUTLINE ANY CHANGES YOU PLAN
TO MAKE IN YOUR STRATEGY:

_____

_____

_____

_____

_____

_____

_____

_____

_____

_____

_____

_____

_____

_____

_____

_____

_____

_____

_____

_____

_____

_____

_____

_____

_____

_____

_____

_____

_____

_____

_____

Name: _____ Date: _____

Log Sheet: Self-Healing: Practice 16 (Week 2)

Each day, (a) describe your experience with your self-healing practice and (b) record the objective and/or subjective data. You may need to use your self-devised data sheets here.

Day 1   a. _____

Date _____   _____

                 _____

                 _____

           b. _____

                 _____

                 _____

                 _____

Day 2   a. _____

Date _____   _____

                 _____

           b. _____

                 _____

                 _____

                 _____

Day 3   a. _____

Date _____   _____

                 _____

           b. _____

                 _____

                 _____

                 _____

Day 4
Date _____

a. _____
_____
_____
_____

b. _____
_____
_____
_____

Day 5
Date _____

a. _____
_____
_____
_____

b. _____
_____
_____
_____

Day 6
Date _____

a. _____
_____
_____
_____

b. _____
_____
_____
_____

Day 7
Date _____

a. _____
_____
_____
_____

b. _____
_____
_____
_____

Name: _____ Date: _____

Questions: Self-Healing: Practice 16 (Week 2)

1. What benefits occurred as a result of your practice?

_____
_____
_____
_____
_____

2. How did your mood and physical state change before, during, and after the practices?

_____
_____
_____
_____
_____

3. What changes did you observe in your objective/subjective data?

_____
_____
_____
_____
_____

4. How will you change or adapt the practice for next week to enhance your success?

_____
_____
_____
_____
_____

5. What problems/challenges occurred and how did you solve them?

_____
_____
_____
_____
_____

Name: _____ Date: _____

Discussion and Conclusions: Self-Healing: Practice 16 (Week 2)

1. What benefits and successes did the group members notice as a result of the practice?

    _____
    _____
    _____

2. What were some of the common challenges that interfered with the self-practice?

    _____
    _____
    _____

3. What new strategies will group members use to increase success?

    _____
    _____
    _____

4. How do levels of commitment and rewards relate to achieving small successes in this first week?

    _____
    _____
    _____

5. What are some of the creative ways by which group members monitor their behavior?

    _____
    _____
    _____

6. Topics or concerns to discuss with the instructor:

    _____
    _____
    _____

List your group members:

_____   _____

_____   _____

_____   _____

_____   _____

Name: _____ Date: _____

Log Sheet: Self-Healing: Practice 16 (Week 3)

Each day, (a) describe your experience with your self-healing practice and (b) record the objective and/or subjective data. You may need to use your self-devised data sheets here.

Day 1   a. _____
Date _____   _____
    _____
    _____

    b. _____
    _____
    _____
    _____

Day 2   a. _____
Date _____   _____
    _____
    _____

    b. _____
    _____
    _____
    _____

Day 3   a. _____
Date _____   _____
    _____
    _____

    b. _____
    _____
    _____
    _____

Day 4   a. _____
Date _____   _____
               _____
               _____

            b. _____
               _____
               _____
               _____
               _____

Day 5   a. _____
Date _____   _____
               _____
               _____

            b. _____
               _____
               _____
               _____

Day 6   a. _____
Date _____   _____
               _____
               _____

            b. _____
               _____
               _____
               _____

Day 7   a. _____
Date _____   _____
               _____
               _____

            b. _____
               _____
               _____
               _____

Name: _____ Date: _____

Questions: Self-Healing: Practice 16 (Week 3)

1. What benefits occurred as a result of your practice?

_____

_____

_____

_____

2. How did your mood and physical state change before, during, and after the practices?

_____

_____

_____

_____

3. What changes did you observe in your objective/subjective data?

_____

_____

_____

_____

4. How will you change or adapt the practice for next week to enhance your success?

_____

_____

_____

_____

5. What problems/challenges occurred and how did you solve them?

_____

_____

_____

_____

Name: _____ Date: _____

Discussion and Conclusions: Self-Healing: Practice 16 (Week 3)

1. What benefits and successes did the group members notice as a result of the practice?

    _____

    _____

    _____

2. What were some of the common challenges that interfered with the self-practice?

    _____

    _____

    _____

3. What new strategies will group members use to increase success?

    _____

    _____

    _____

4. How do levels of commitment and rewards relate to achieving small successes in this first week?

    _____

    _____

    _____

5. What are some of the creative ways by which group members monitor their behavior?

    _____

    _____

    _____

6. Topics or concerns to discuss with the instructor:

    _____

    _____

    _____

List your group members:

_____   _____

_____   _____

_____   _____

_____   _____

Name: _____ Date: _____

Log Sheet: Self-Healing: Practice 16 (Week 4)

Each day, (a) describe your experience with your self-healing practice and (b) record the objective and/or subjective data. You may need to use your self-devised data sheets here.

Day 1   a. _____

Date _____   _____

                         _____

                         _____

               b. _____

                         _____

                         _____

                         _____

Day 2   a. _____

Date _____   _____

                         _____

                         _____

               b. _____

                         _____

                         _____

                         _____

Day 3   a. _____

Date _____   _____

                         _____

                         _____

               b. _____

                         _____

                         _____

                         _____

Day 4
Date _____

a. _____
_____
_____
_____

b. _____
_____
_____
_____

Day 5
Date _____

a. _____
_____
_____
_____

b. _____
_____
_____
_____

Day 6
Date _____

a. _____
_____
_____
_____

b. _____
_____
_____
_____

Day 7
Date _____

a. _____
_____
_____
_____

b. _____
_____
_____
_____

Name: _____ Date: _____

Questions: Self-Healing: Practice 16 (Week 4)

1. What benefits occurred as a result of your practice?

_____
_____
_____
_____
_____

2. How did your mood and physical state change before, during, and after the practices?

_____
_____
_____
_____
_____

3. What changes did you observe in your objective/subjective data?

_____
_____
_____
_____
_____

4. How will you change or adapt the practice for next week to enhance your success?

_____
_____
_____
_____
_____

5. What problems/challenges occurred and how did you solve them?

_____
_____
_____
_____
_____

Name: _____   Date: _____

Discussion and Conclusions: Self-Healing: Practice 16 (Week 4)

1. What benefits and successes did the group members notice as a result of the practice?

    _____
    _____
    _____

2. What were some of the common challenges that interfered with the self-practice?

    _____
    _____
    _____

3. What new strategies will group members use to increase success?

    _____
    _____
    _____

4. How do levels of commitment and rewards relate to achieving small successes in this first week?

    _____
    _____
    _____

5. What are some of the creative ways by which group members monitor their behavior?

    _____
    _____
    _____

6. Topics or concerns to discuss with the instructor:

    _____
    _____
    _____

List your group members:

_____   _____
_____   _____
_____   _____
_____   _____

⑨ INTEGRATING YOUR EXPERIENCE

Integrating what you experienced by summarizing what you learned and writing up your results can enhance the self-healing process. Write about your experience as suggested in the section **Reflection and Integration: Summarizing Your Experience** at the end of Chapter 1. Reflect over the last weeks, reread your logs, and gently ask yourself the following questions: How did this self-healing process change me? What did I learn from this? How did I grow? Respect both setbacks (or challenges) and successes. Your self-report is a testament to change, as some of the following reports indicate.

REPORT 1: WEIGHT AND SELF-IMAGE

My body did change during my practice. I lost a total of 3 pounds and 7.5 inches from my body. My inner sense of my body also changed. As the weeks continued, my blimp became smaller and smaller. The blimp is still there, but it has decreased from being about the size of a whale to about the size of a very small fish (see Figure 4.6). My feelings that were buried beneath my obsession with my weight also became uncovered. My sensuality is related to my obsession. I

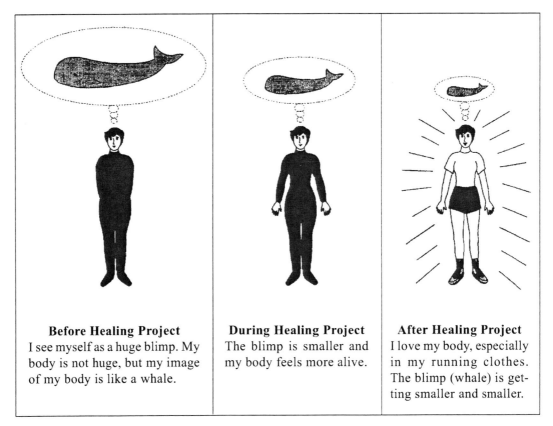

Before Healing Project
I see myself as a huge blimp. My body is not huge, but my image of my body is like a whale.

During Healing Project
The blimp is smaller and my body feels more alive.

After Healing Project
I love my body, especially in my running clothes. The blimp (whale) is getting smaller and smaller.

Figure 4.6. Self-image change during healing process

am afraid to become close with any man, and yet I long for the intimacy. I have been in a committed relationship for 5 years, yet I feel extreme ambivalence about the relationship. During the past few weeks, as I have confronted my own fears of intimacy, the ambivalence has lessened. Not only have I become a little lighter in body weight but my emotional weight has decreased.

REPORT 2: PHYSICAL EXERCISE

When I began this project, my focus was on physical exercise and creating a mental image of the body that I would like to have. My project carried me to places deep inside myself that I didn't know existed. I realized that body weight was an obsession. Beneath this obsessiveness was a layer of fear and rage. I feared being sensual and felt rage that I really wanted to be desirable. I have not gotten through this yet, but this was the beginning of uncovering the layers of feelings that have run my life for 20 years. In addition, I felt the power of using visualization while running. My running distance doubled and I enjoyed my running more than ever before. Something inside me opened to feel the energy of life flow through me. I felt connected with my body. I began to get a glimpse of grace.

REPORT 3: MOOD SWINGS

In my imagery, at first I saw myself on top of a beautiful green hill. There was a swing set at the apex and I got on it. As I swung out I saw a beautiful valley with three different roads all leading off into the horizon… but when the swing came down, it was as if I had lost sight of this beautiful valley and it was too much to bear. I decided to get off the swing…. This allowed me to see that possibilities stretched on forever. Getting off the swing in this visualization made me feel that I had made a conscious decision to do so in my life as well. Once I had a clear view of this valley, I realized that there weren't three roads after all. There was really only one, on which it was possible to go off on a confusing side road—or go too fast and get out of control if one was not careful. I worked with this visualization as a 20-minute meditation every morning for about two weeks. I realized that there was a car on this road and that the driver of the car was not I (I was only the passenger). I changed this arrangement...

I was surprised to find that I didn't need the full 20 minutes every morning to have this imagery work for me. I was also using this imagery for quick adjustments throughout the day. If I was feeling harried or down, I would close my eyes and look at the car on the road. Was I going too fast? I would take my foot off the accelerator a bit. What was causing me to be disagreeable? If I was tired, I would rest; if hungry, I would eat...

This self-healing strategy feels very successful... I had a couple of occasions in which I was more out of control than I wanted to be... By summoning up my imagery I was able to see what was happening to me. I then quickly apologized and tried to explain the situation to whomever I had offended. In this way then, a mood wasn't able to further get out of control. Most of my ups and downs were stabilized within minutes...Another measure of success for me is that I was able to go through my PMS with only slight irritation and disorientation...what I thought was a completely chemical reaction going on in my body that I had no control over was something different. I could see that at least part of my symptoms were caused by my thoughts.

Observations of changes in a person that are made by others provide an even more dramatic testimonial to progress. The roommate of the woman just quoted reported as follows:

J. has always been an emotional person.... her angry outbursts....have been venomous... Her bouts of depression have been sad to witness, and at its worst [the depression] usually manifested itself by her staunch refusal to get out of bed. So there she would lie, all day, under the covers, feeling very pathetic... These fluctuations...always seemed to be part of her nature. Something to be endured...

[This self-healing program] has certainly had a profound effect on J. If mood swings were once sudden, unpredictable, and extremely wide-ranging, now—if they occur at all—they are controlled and very short lived. The sense I get is that J. has become more centered. Rather than learning to simply control her mood swings, it seems J. has become a better person, a more peaceful and a stronger person, and so has become more stable and less inclined to exhibit the types of uncontrolled behavior usually associated with an unstable personality. She has become easier to deal with, and has also been able to deal with me in a more diplomatic way (and I am no Mother Theresa). The best part of all this is that J. has shared her wisdom gained in the last few weeks with me; so perhaps I have become a better person too.

REFERENCES

Chapter 1

Cannon, W.B. (1939). *The Wisdom of the Body* (2nd ed.). New York: Norton.

Easwaran, E. (1990). *Words to Live by: Inspiration for Every Day*. Petaluma, CA: Nilgiri Press.

Egoscue, P. (1998). *Pain Free: A Revolutionary Method for Stopping Chronic Pain*. New York: Bantam Books.

Frank, A.W. (1991). *At the Will of the Body*. Boston: Houghton Mifflin.

Green, E.E. and Green, A.M. (1977). *Beyond Biofeedback*. New York: Delacorte. 33-34.

Justice, B. (2000). *Who Gets Sick: How Beliefs, Moods and Thoughts Affect Your Health*. Houston, TX: Dimensions.

Kiecolt-Glaser, J.K., McGuire, L., Robles, T.F. & Glaser, R.(2002). Psychoneuroimmunology and psychosomatic medicine: back to the future. *Psychosom Med*, 64(1),15-28.

Kunz, D. (1985). *Spiritual Aspects of the Healing Arts*. Wheaton, IL: The Theosophical Publishing House, 295-296.

Levy, S.M. (1985). *Behavior and Cancer*. San Francisco: Jossey-Bass.

McEwen, B.W. (1990). Hormones and the nervous system. *Advances*, 7(1), 50-54.

Nixon, P.G.F. (1989). Human functions and the heart. In Seedhouse, D. and Cribb, A. (eds). *Changing Ideas in Health Care*. New York: John Wiley & Sons.

Nixon, P. & King, J. (1997). Ischemic heart disease: Homeostasis and the heart. In: Watkins, A. (ed.). *Mind-body Medicine*. New York: Livingstone.

Ornish, D. (1998). *Love & Survival*. New York: HarperCollins Publisher

Pelletier, K.R. (1994). *Sound Mind, Sound Body*. New York: Simon & Schuster.

Peper, E. & Holt, C.F. (1993). *Creating Wholeness: A Self-Healing Workbook Using Dynamic Relaxation, Images and Thoughts*. New York: Plenum.

Peper, E. and Williams, E.A. (1981). *From the Inside Out: A Self-Teaching and Laboratory Manual for Biofeedback*. New York: Plenum, 187-188.

Rossman, M.L. (2000). *Guided Imagery for Self-Healing*. New York: New World Library.

Selye, H. (1956). *The Stress of Life*. New York: McGraw-Hill Book Co.

Selye, H. (1974). *Stress Without Distress*. New York: J.B. Lippincott.

Simonton, O.C., Matthews-Simonton, S., and Creighton, J.L. (1992). *Getting Well Again*. New York: Bantam Books.

Thayer, R.E. (1996). *The Origin of Everyday Moods—Managing Energy, Tension, and Stress*. New York: Oxford University Press.

Thorenson, C.E. and Mahoney, M.J. (1974). *Behavioral Self-Control*. New York: Holt, Rinehart & Winston.

Vaillant, G. (2002). *Aging Well: Surprising Guideposts to a Happier Life from the Landmark Harvard Study of Adult Development*. New York: Little, Brown & Co.

Watson, D.L. & Tharp, R.G. (1992). *Self-Directed Behavior: Self-Modification for Personal Adjustment (6the ed)*. Monterey: Brooks/Cole.

Whatmore, G.B. and Kholi, D.R. (1974). *The Physiopathology and Treatment of Functional Disorders*. New York: Grune & Stratton.

Chapter 2

Ader, R. Cohen, N., Felten, D. (1995). Psychoneuroimmunology: Interactions between the nervous system and the immune system. *Lancet,* 345 (8942), 99-103.

Bernstein, D. A., Borkovec, T. D. & Hazlett-Stevens, H. (2000). *New Directions in Progressive Relaxation Training: A Manual for the Helping Professions*. New York: Praeger Pub.

Bloch, S., Lemeignan, M. & Aguilera, N. (1991). Specific respiratory patterns distinguish among human basic emotions. *International Journal of Psychophysiology*, 11 (2), 141-154.

Cousins, N. (1989). *Head First, The Biology of Hope*. New York: E.P. Dutton, 89-90.

Fahrion, S., Norris, P., Green, A., Green, E., & Snarr. C. (1986) Biobehavioral treatment of essential hypertension: A group outcome study. *Biofeedback and Self-Regulation*, 11, 257-278.

Freedman, R. (1987). Long-term effectiveness of behavioral treatments for Raynaud's disease. *Behavior Therapy*, 18, 387-399.

Freedman, R.R. & Woodward, S. (1992). Behavioral treatment of menopausal hot flushes: evaluation by ambulatory monitoring. *American Journal of Obstetrics and Gynecology*, 167 (2), 436-439.

Ghanta, V., Hiramoto, R., Solvason, H. and Spector, H. (1985). Neural and environmental influence on neoplasia and conditioning of natural killer cell activity. *Journal of Immunology*, 135, 848s-852s.

Green, E.E. and Green, A.M. (1977). *Beyond Biofeedback*. New York: Delacorte.

Hanh, T.N. (1976). *The Miracle of Mindfulness! A Manual on Meditation*. Boston: Beacon Press.

Jacobson, E. (1970). *Modern Treatment of Tense Patients*. Springfield, ILL: Charles C. Thomas.

Jacobson, E. (1976). *You Must Relax*. New York: Whittlesey House.

Jacobson, E. (1974). *Progressive Relaxation* (3rd ed.). Chicago: University of Chicago Press.

LeShan, L. (1994). *Cancer As A Turning Point*. New York: Dutton.

Levey, J. and Levey, M. (1987). *The Fine Arts of Relaxation, Concentration and Meditation*. Boston: Wisdom Publications.

Lum, L.C. (1976). The syndrome of habitual chronic hyperventilation. In: Hill, V. (ed.). *Modern Trends in Psychosomatic Medicine*. London: Butterworth. 196-230.

Mackenzie, J.H. (1886). The production of the so-called 'rose cold' by means of an artificial rose. *American Journal of Medical Science*, 91, 45-57.

Middaugh, S. J., Haythornthwaite, J.A., Thompson, B., Hill, R., Brown, K.M., Freedman, R.R., Attanasio, V., Jacob, R.G., Scheier, M. and Smith, E. A. (2001). The Raynaud's treatment study: Biofeedback protocols and acquisition of temperature biofeedback skills. *Applied Psychophysiology and Biofeedback,* 26 (4), 251-278.

Norris, P. and Porter, G. (1987). *I Choose Life.* Walpole, NH: Stillpoint Publishing.

Palmer, S., Tibbetts, V., & Peper, E. (1991). The effects of self-willed unilateral vasodilation on the healing rates of bilateral wounds. *Proceedings of the Twenty-second Annual Meeting of the Association for Applied Psychophysiology and Biofeedback.* Wheat Ridge, CO: AAPB, 124-127.

Peper, E. (1990). *Breathing for Health.* Montreal: Thought Technology, Ltd.

Peper, E. and Gibney, K.H. (2000). *Healthy Computing with Muscle Biofeedback: A Practical Manual for Preventing Repetitive Motion Injury.* Woerden: Biofeedback Foundation of Europe. Available from: Work Solutions USA, 2236 Derby Street, Berkeley, CA 94705.

Peper, E. and Grossman, E. (1979). Thermal biofeedback training in children with headache. In: Peper, E., Ancoli, S., and Quinn, M. *Mind/Body Integration: Essential Readings in Biofeedback.* New York: Plenum, 489-492.

Peper, E. & MacHose, M. (1993). Symptom prescription: Inducing anxiety by 70% exhalation. *Biofeedback and Self-Regulation*, 18 (3), 133-139.

Schwartz, M.S. and Andrasik, F. (1995). *Biofeedback: A Practitioner's Guide, 2nd Ed.* New York: Guilford Press.

Stroebel, C.F. (1982). *QR: The Quieting Reflex.* New York: G.P. Putnam's Sons.

Van Dixhoorn, J., Duivenvorden, H.J., Staal, J.A., Pool, J. and Verhage, F. (1987). Cardiac events after myocardial infarction: Possible effect of relaxation therapy. *European Heart Journal*, 8, 1210-1214.

Wittrock, D., Blanchard, E. & McCoy, G. (1988). Three studies on the relation of process to outcome in the treatment of essential hypertension with relaxation and thermal biofeedback. *Behavior Research and Therapy*, 26, 53-66.

Chapter 3

Ellis, A. (1988). *Rational-Emotive Therapy.* Boston: Allyn & Bacon, Inc.

Kobasa, S.C., Maddi, S.R., and Kahn, S. (1982). Hardiness and health: a prospective study. Journal of Personality and Social Psychology, 42(1), 168-177.

LeShan, L. (1994). *Cancer As A Turning Point.* New York: Dutton.

Meichenbaum, D.H. (1977). *Cognitive Behavior Modification.* New York: Plenum.

Pennebaker, J.W. (1991). *Opening Up: The Healing Power of Confiding in Others.* New York: William Morrow & Co.

Seligman, M.E.P. (1998). *Learned Optimism.* New York: Pocket Books.

Solomon, G.F., Temoshok, L., O'Leary, A. & Zich, J. (1987). An intensive psychoimmunologic study of long-surviving persons with AIDS. Pilot work, background studies, hypotheses, and methods. *Ann N Y Acad Sci*, 496, 647-55.

Visintainer, M., Volpicelli, J. and Seligman, M. (1982). Tumor rejection in rats after inescapable or escapable shock. *Science*, 216, 191-199.

Chapter 4

Capacchione, L. (1991). *Recovery of Your Inner Child.* New York: Simon & Schuster.

Capacchione, L. (1988). *The Power of Your Other Hand.* North Hollywood, CA: New Castle.

Rossman, M.L. (2000). *Guided Imagery for Self-Healing.* New York: New World Library.

Watson, D.L. & Tharp, R.G. (1992). *Self-Directed Behavior: Self-Modification for Personal Adjustment* (6the ed). Monterey: Brooks/Cole.

Appendix A

Audiotapes and Temperature Monitoring Devices

Audiotapes of the practices can be ordered from:

Work Solutions USA
2236 Derby Street
Berkeley, CA 94705
Tel: 510-841-7227
Fax: 510-658-9801
Email: worksolusa@aol.com

Temperature cards (about $1.00 and similar to the card enclosed in this workbook) and hand-held alcohol thermometers (about $1.00) can be ordered from:

Conscious Living Foundation
P. O. Box 9
Drain, OR 97435-0009
USA
Tel: 800-578-7377
        541-836-2358
Fax: 541-836-2358
Email: info@cliving.org   www.cliving.org

American Biotechnology Corp
24 Browning Drive
Ossining, NY 10562
USA
Tel: 800-424-6832
        914-762-4646
Fax: 914-762-2281
Email: whatis@mindfitness.com   www.mindfitness.com

Stens Corporation
3020 Kerner Boulevard, Suite D
San Rafael, CA 94901-5444
USA
TEL: 800 257 8367
        415 455 8222
Fax: 415 455 0333
Email: sales@stens-biofeedback.com   www.stens-biofeedback.com

Portable temperature or electromyography biofeedback devices can be ordered from:

Thought Technology Ltd
180 Belgrave Avenue
Montreal, Quebec, H4A 2L8
CANADA
Tel: 800-361-3651
        514-489-8251
Fax: 514-489-8255
Email: mail@thoughttechnology.com   www.thoughttechnology.com

Conscious Living Foundation
P. O. Box 9
Drain, OR 97435-0009
USA
Tel: 800-578-7377
        541-836-2358
Fax: 541-836-2358
Email: info@cliving.org   www.cliving.org

American Biotechnology Corp
24 Browning Drive
Ossining, NY 10562
USA
Tel: 800-424-6832
        914-762-4646
Fax: 914-762-2281
Email: whatis@mindfitness.com   www.mindfitness.com

Stens Corporation
3020 Kerner Boulevard, Suite D
San Rafael, CA 94901-5444
USA
Tel: 800 257 8367
         415 455 8222
Fax: 415 455 0333
Email: sales@stens-biofeedback.com   www.stens-biofeedback.com

Bio_Medical Instruments, Inc.
2387 East Eight Mile Road
Warren, MI 48091-2486
USA
Tel: 810-756 5070
Fax: 810-756-9891
Email: sales@bio-medical.com   www.bio-medical.com

Appendix B

Suggested Readings on Holistic Health

Achterberg, J., Dossey, B. & Kolkmeier, L. (1994). *Rituals of Healing*. New York: Bantam Books.

Achterberg, J. and Lawlis, G. F. (1978). *Imagery of Cancer*. Champaign: Institute for Personality and Ability Testing.

Backhouse, K.M. and Hutchings, R.T. (1986). *Color Atlas of Surface Anatomy*. Baltimore: Williams & Wilkins.

Bernstein, D. A. Borkovec, T. D. & Hazlett-Stevens, H. (2000). *New Directions in Progressive Relaxation Training: A Manual for the Helping Professions*. New York: Praeger Pub.

Borysenko, J. (1993). *Minding the Body, Mending the Mind*. Reading, MA: Addison-Wesley

Bresler, D. (1979). *Free Yourself from Pain*. New York: Simon and Schuster.

Broyard, A. (1992). *Intoxicated by my Illness*. New York: Fawcett Columbine.

Capacchione, L. (1991). *Recovery of Your Inner Child*. New York: Simon & Schuster.

Chopra, D. (1989). *Quantum Healing*. New York: Bantam.

Cousins, N. (1983). *The Healing Heart*. New York: W. W. Norton & Co.

Cousins, N. (1989). *Head First: The Biology of Hope*. New York: E.P. Dutton.

Davis, M... McKay, M. & Eshelman, E.R. (2000). *The Relaxation & Stress Reduction Workbook*. Oakland: New Harbinger Publications.

Dossey, L. (1993). *Healing Words*. New York: HarperCollins.

Easwaran, E. (1981). *Dialogue with Death*. Tomales, CA: Nilgiri Press.

Easwaran, E. (1994). *Take Your Time*. Tomales, CA: Nilgiri Press.

Ellis, A. (1988). *Rational-Emotive Therapy*. Boston, MA: Allyn & Bacon, Inc.

Farhi, D. (1996). *The Breathing Book*. New York: Henry Holt and company.

Fiore, N. A. (1984). *The Road Back to Health*. New York: Bantam.

Fish, R., Weakland, J. H. and Segal, L. (1982). *The Tactics of Change*. San Francisco: Jossey-Bass.

Frank, A.W. (1991). *At the Will of the Body*. Boston: Houghton Mifflin Co.

Frank, J. D. (1977). *Persuasion and Healing*. New York: Schocken.

Fried, R. (1999*). Breathe Well, Be Well : A Program to Relieve Stress, Anxiety, Asthma, Hypertension, Migraine, and Other Disorders for Better Health*. New York: John Wiley & Sons.

Gendlin, E. T. (1981). *Focusing*. New York: Bantam Books.

Goleman, D. (1995). *Emotional Intelligence*. New York: Bantam Books.

Goleman, D. & Gurin, J. (1993). *Mind/Body Medicine: How to Use Your Mind for Better Health*. Yonkers, NY: Consumer Reports Books.

Gordon, J.S. (1996). *Manifesto for a New Medicine*. Reading, MA: Addison-Wesley Pub.

Green, E.E. and Green, A.M. (1977). *Beyond Biofeedback*. New York: Delacorte.

Hanh, T.N. (1976). *The Miracle of Mindfulness! A Manual on Meditation*. Boston: Beacon Press.

Hanna, T. (1988). *Somatics*. Reading, MA: Addison-Wesley.

Holt, C. (2000). *The Circle Of Healing: Deepening Our Connections With Self, Others And Nature*. Berkeley: Talking Birds Press.

Hrdy, S. B. (1999). Mother Nature: *A History of Mothers, Infants. and Natural Selection*. New York: Pantheon Books.

Kabat-Zinn, J. (1990). *Full Catastrophe Living*. New York: Delacorte Press.

Klauser, H.A. (2000). *Write It Down, Make It Happen*. New York: Simon & Schuster.

Krieger, D. (1992). *The Therapeutic Touch*: New York: Simon & Schuster.

Kunz, D. (1991). *The Personal Aura*. Wheaton: Quest Books.

Kunz, D. (1985). *Spiritual Aspects of the Healing Arts*. Wheaton: Quest Books.

Lehrer, P.M. & Woolfolk, R.L. (1993). *Principles and Practice of Stress Management* 2nd ed. New York: The Guilford Press.

Lerner, M. (1994). *Choices in Healing*. Cambridge: MIT Press.

LeShan, L. (1994). *Cancer As A Turning Point*. New York: Dutton.

LeShan, L. (1974). *How To Meditate*. Boston: Little, Brown and Co.

Levey, J. and Levey, M. (1987). *The Fine Arts of Relaxation, Concentration and Meditation*. Boston: Wisdom Publications.

Lichstein, K.L. (1988). *Clinical Relaxation Strategies*. New York: John Wiley & Sons.

Matthews Simonton, S. (1984). *The Healing Family.* New York: Bantam Books.

McKay, M., Davis, M. and Fanning, P. (1998). *Thoughts & Feelings. The Art of Cognitive Stress Intervention*. Oakland: New Habinger.

Nilsson, L. (1985). *The Body Victorious*. New York: Delacorte Press.

Norris, P. and Porter. G. (1985). *I Choose Life*. Walpole, NH: Stillpoint Publishing.

Nuernberger, P. (1981). *Freedom From Stress*. Honesdale, PA: Himalayan International Institute of Yoga Science and Philosophy Publishers.

Ornish, D. (1992). *Dr. Dean Ornish's Program for Reversing Heart Disease*. New York: Ballantine Books.

Ornish, D. (1998). *Love & Survival.* New York: Harper Collins.

Pelletier, K.R. (1994). *Sound Mind, Sound Body*. New York: Simon & Schuster.

Pelletier, K.R. (1979). *Holistic Medicine: From Stress to Optimum Health*. New York: Delta.

Pennebaker, J.W. (1991). *Opening Up: The Healing Power of Confiding in Others*. New York: William Morrow & Co.

Peper, E. (1990). *Breathing for Health with Biofeedback*. Montreal: Thought Technology Ltd.

Peper, E. , Ancoli, S. and Quinn, M. (Eds). (1979). *Mind/Body Integration*. New York: Plenum.

Rama, S., Ballentine, R. & Hymes, A. (1979). *Science of Breath*. Honesdale, PA: Himalayan International Institute of Yoga Science and Philosophy Publishers.

Rossman, M.L. (2000). *Guided Imagery for Self-Healing*. New York: New World Library.

Sapolsky, R. 1994). *Why Zebras Don't Get Ulcers*. San Francisco: W.H. Freeman.

Samuels, M. & Lane, M.R. (2000). *Spirit Body Healing*. New York: John Wiley & Sons, Inc.

Samuels, M. and Samuels, N. (1975). *Seeing with the Mind's Eye*. New York: Random House.

Sarno, J.E. (1991). *Healing Back Pain*. New York: Warner Books, Inc.

Schlosser, E. (2002). *Fast Food Nation*. New York: HarperCollins.

Seligman, M.E.P. (1998). *Learned Optimism*. New York: Pocket Books.

Siegel, B.S. (1986). *Love, Medicine & Miracles*. New York: Harper & Row.

Simonton, O. C., Matthews-Simonton, S. and Creighton, J. L. (1992). *Getting Well Again*. New York: Bantam Books.

Smith, M. (1975). *When I Say No, I Feel Guilty*. New York: Bantam Books.

Snowdon, D. (2001). *Aging with Grace*. New York: Bantam Books

Stroebel, C. F. (1982). *QR The Quieting Reflex*. New York: G. P. Putnam's Sons.

Tannen, D. (2001). *You Just Don't Understand*. New York: Quill.

Thayer, R.E. (1996). *The Origin of Everyday Moods—Managing Energy, Tension, and Stress*. New York: Oxford University Press.

Thayer, R.E. (2001). *Calm Energy*. New York: Oxford University Press.

Tulku, T. (1979). *Kum Nye RelaxationPart 1: Theory Preparation, Massage*. Berkeley: Dharma Publishing.

Vaillant, G. (2002). *Aging Well: Surprising Guideposts to a Happier Life from the Landmark Harvard Study of Adult Development*. New York: Little, Brown & Co.

Vaughan, F. (1979). *Awakening Intuition*. New York: Doubleday.

Watson, D.L. & Tharp, R.G. (1992). *Self-Directed Behavior: Self-Modification for Personal Adjustment* (6the ed). Monterey: Brooks/Cole.

Watzlawick, P., Weakland, J. and Fisch, R. (1988). *Change*. New York: W. W. Norton & Co.

Weil, A. (2000). *Spontaneous Healing*. New York: Ballantine Books.

Yogananda, P. (1998). *The Law of Success: Using the Power of Spirit to Create Health, Prosperity, and Happiness*. Los Angeles: Self-Realization Fellowship.

Yogananda, P. (1987). *Scientific Healing Affirmations*. Los Angeles: Self-Realization Fellowship.

INDEX

serenity, 114
Serenity Prayer, 26
sexual abuse, 175
sexual processes, 17
sexuality, 5
shoulder tension. *See* muscle tension
Siegel, B., 137
Simonton, O. C., 27
Sisyphus, 147
skill development model, 17
skin problems, 6, 28, 197
sleep, 4, 47, 66
    chronic worry and, 15
    insomnia and, 6, 16
    solutions, 50
sleeping pills, 12
smile, 95, 106
smoking, 4, 9, 197. *See also* nicotine
    strategies to quit, 211
Snarr, C., 97
SNS. *See* nervous system, sympathetic
social support system, 1, 5
Solomon, G.F., 147
soma, 50, 129
    definition of, 2
    intrinsic drive of, 2
specificity, 169
spirituality, 2, 5
startle response, 111
stimuli, conditioned, 78
stomach problems. *See* gastrointestinal
    disorders
stress. *See also* fight/flight or freeze response;
    hand warming; tension
    anxiety and, 94
    chronic, 14
    coping with, 29
    energy levels and, 26
    hormones, 14
    human function curve and, 14
    illnesses and, 6
    management, 7, 24, 26
    organ systems and, 97
    reduction of, 2, 98, 197
    response, 7, 21, 29, 93
    skill development model for, 17
stressors, 6, 14, 21, 93–94, 112

striving, 100
Stroebel, C., 93
subgoals, 208, 232
sugar, 3, 198–199
summary paper, 40
sympathomimetic medications. *See*
    medications
Syrus, P., 43
systematic desensitization, 134
systems perspective of health, 132

T

T-cell levels, 24
tachycardia. *See* heart rate
tai chi, 4
tapes
    making your own, 38–39
    ordering, 38
Temoshok, L., 147
temperature, 105–106. *See also* handwarming
    observation, 101
    training
tension, 114
    chronic, 48, 121
    muscular
    residual, 44
Tharp, R.G., 38, 207, 212
Thayer, R., 22–23
thermometer, 102, 104
Thorensen, C.E, 38
thoughts. *See* cognitions
threats. *See* reframing
throat, 101–102
thyroid supplement, 12
Tibbetts, V., 97
tranquilizers, 12
trapezius, upper, 49
traumas, 12
    writing about, 175–176
trust, 137, 195

U

ulcers, 6
unconscious, 194–195